John Reynolds

# Thames Ship Towage
# 1933–1992

# Thames Ship Towage
# 1933–1992

## John E. Reynolds

The Pentland Press Ltd.
Edinburgh·Cambridge·Durham

First published in 1993 by
The Pentland Press Ltd.
1 Hutton Close
South Church
Durham

ISBN  1  85821  028  3

Typeset By Spire Origination Ltd., Norwich
Printed and bound in England by Bookcraft (Bath) Ltd

To my father,
George E. Reynolds,
who first gave me the
enthusiasm

# FOREWORD

In January 1975, the Alexandra Towing Co. Ltd. of Liverpool arrived in the River Thames on gaining control of London Tugs Ltd. This latter company was the result of a series of takeovers and amalgamations of all the old established Thames ship towing companies which had commenced in 1938 when the Gravesend United Steam Tug Company, or 'Ring Tugs', as they were known locally, was absorbed into the fleet of William Watkins Ltd. In 1950, William Watkins Ltd. and the Elliott Steam Tug Co. (1949) Ltd., merged and at the same time took control of Gamecock Tugs Ltd. They thereafter traded as Ship Towage (London) Ltd. In 1965 Ship Towage (London) Ltd., took over four tugs of Gaselee & Son Ltd, and all the ship towage contracts of that company. This left just one more amalgamation before all the river ship towage was under one banner and that came about on 27 January 1969 when Ship Towage (London) Ltd. and W. H. J. Alexander Ltd. joined forces under the name of London Tugs Ltd.

On the centenary of William Watkins Ltd. in 1933 they published the book *One Hundred Years of Towing* which had been written by Frank C. Bowen to mark the occasion. This book is an attempt to fill the sixty years gap from 1933 to 1992 in relation not only to William Watkins Ltd., but to all the Thames ship towage companies and their tugs.

In 1933 seven companies, including the Port of London Authority, operated ship towing tugs. The oldest of these companies was William Watkins Ltd., founded in the summer of 1833 by John Rogers Watkins, a London waterman and sailing ship owner, together with his son William. The firm had gone from strength to strength to become one of the principal ocean, coastal and river towage companies of the last century. In 1933 they were the owners of seventeen tugs, these beings: *Canada* (built 1880), *Hibernia* (1884), *Nubia* (1890), *Scotia* (1894), *Arcadia* (1895), *Simla* (1898), *Java* (1905), *Doria* (1909), *Vincia* (1909), *Badia* (1909), *Palencia* (1916), *Rumania* (1919), *Muria* (1914), *Fabia* (1919), *Gondia* (1927), *Kenia* (1927) and *Tanga* (1931).

In 1860 Captain T. W. Elliott entered the tug owning business. In 1881 his company came under the management of Messrs Matthew Dick & John Page, shipbrokers of Cornhill in the City of London and in 1897 the company name was changed to the Elliott Steam Tug Company Ltd. In 1933 they owned the following seven tugs: *Revenger* (1880), *Crusade* (1881), *Champion* (1892), *Vanquisher* (1899), *Security* (1904), *Venturous* (1904) and *Challenge* (1931).

Gaselee & Son Ltd. was founded in 1897 by Charles Gaselee as a craft towage company, expanding into ship towage towards the end of the century. At that time their operations were largely based on the Pool of London. Apart from two large tugs, *Result* and *Revenge*, acquired in 1890 and used for 'seeking' down Channel, the ships owned by the company were of the craft tug type. In 1933 the larger units of the fleet which undertook the bulk of the ship towing were: *Vespa* (1921), *Musca* (1922), *Culex* (1924), *Naja* (1924), *Tayra* (1926), *Fossa* (1929), *Betty* (1907) and *Gnat* (1898).

1880 saw the formation of the Gamecock Towing Company Ltd. by a consortium of London River Pilots. In 1928 the company was acquired by the Ocean Salvage & Towage Company Ltd., which company had Turkish origins. In 1933 Gamecock owned eight tugs plus a salvage ship: *Falcon* (1892), *Spreadeagle* (1911), *New Stormcock* (1921), *Watercock* (1923), *New Gamecock* (1930), *Crested Cock* (1930), *Ocean Cock* (1932), *Atlantic Cock* (1932), and the salvage ship *King Lear* (1906).

In 1883 W. H. J. Alexander entered the tug business when the tug *Little England* was built for him by the Castle Iron & Steam Works at Milford Haven. Initially a Lighterage firm it soon expanded into ship towage. In 1899 the *Sunrise* and *Sunshine* were built and from that date the prefix 'SUN' was used on all subsequent tugs. In 1933 the company owned twenty-three tugs: *Sunfly* (1883), *Sunlit* (1890), *Sunclad* (1893), *Sunny* (1898), *Sundial* (1899), *Sunrise* (1899), *Sunshine* (1899), *Sunbeam* (1901), *Sun* (1906), *Sunbird* (1907), *Sunfish* (1907), *Sun II* (1909), *Sun III* (1909), *Sun IV* (1915), *Sun V* (1915), *Sun VI* (1915), *Sun VII* (1918), *Sun VIII* (1919), *Sun IX* (1920), *Sun X* (1920), *Sun XI* (1925), *Sun XII* (1925) and *Sun XV* (1925).

The Gravesend United Steam Tug Company, known locally as 'Ring Tugs' on account of their funnel markings of two white bands, was founded in the 1890s by a loose syndicate of Gravesend business men and local pilots. In 1933 they operated five tugs: *Doralia* (1914), *Tamesa* (1925), *Dilwara* (1930), *Dongara* (1932) and *Florida* (1902).

The Port of London Authority established in 1908 has always operated a large range of service craft associated with the running of a major port, such as dredgers, heavy lift vessels, wreck lighters, tugs and survey craft. In this book we shall be concerned only with ship towing tugs operated by the P.L.A. in the enclosed docks. In 1933 they operated seven tugs in this capacity: *Sirdar* (1899), *Deanbrook* (1908), *Darent* (1908), *Walbrook* (1910), *Beam* (1910), *Beverly* (1910) and *Lea* (1912).

Dhulia, Sun XXI, *and* Sauria.

# 1933

In 1933 over sixty tugs were in the ownership of the ship towing companies. With the recession biting hard many of these tugs were laid up, some on a semi-permanent basis, others on a day-to-day basis, the crews being taken on when needed and laid off when not required.

Three tugs were sold and two were built. The *Contest* was completed at Aberdeen by Alexander Hall & Co. Ltd. for the Elliott Steam Tug Company. This fine tug measured 213 tons gross and was powered by a 1,150 i.h.p. triple expansion steam engine. A near sister to the *Challenge*, she was built to replace her namesake the *Contest* built in 1931 by the same builders but sold soon afterwards to Italian interests at Naples and renamed *Vesuvio*. Gaselee & Son had the *Aboma* built by Cochrane & Sons Ltd. of Selby. She measured 66 tons gross and was powered by a 500 i.h.p. British Polar diesel engine. This tug was principally a craft tug but was used on the company's shipping contracts as required. Although diesel driven she was built with a large drop funnel which gave the impression that she was steam propelled. It then became company policy for their tugs to have large funnels and the practice continued right up to the completion of the *Fossa* in 1961.

Gravesend United Steam Tug Co. (Ring Tugs) sold their *Florida* during January to Lamey's of Liverpool without change of name. She had been built at South Shields in 1902 and measured 114 tons gross. The other two tugs sold were both owned by the Gamecock Towing Co. the *Falcon* built in 1902, going to S.C. Roberts of Bristol without change of name and the *New Gamecock* of 1930 going to Palestine in the warmer waters of the Mediterranean under the name *Steady*.

At this time the Elliott Steam Tug Co. was engaged in towing brick barges from Boom just above Antwerp on the River Scheldt to London. This trade had started in the mid 1920s and continued until 1939. A series of these barges, named *Thames I* to *V*, loaded 2,500 tons of bricks and carried a crew of three. A couple of these barges would be towed at a time and *Revenger, Crusade, Vanquisher* and *Venturous* were the mainstays of the run as they were not so heavy on coal as *Challenge* and *Contest*. Of the three *Venturous* was not as powerful as *Vanquisher* or *Security*. She had been acquired in 1927 from the Dublin Port and Docks Board and was considerably altered to cope with her new work. The after cabin was stripped, pig iron ballast was put in and then filled with water. The extra weight forced her stern down and she handled the barges as well as the more powerful tugs. As she only bunkered 45 tons of coal, a further 20/30 tons was carried on deck enabling her to complete the round voyage without having to coal again.

Dongara *being launched 1932.*

# 1934

In 1934 *Revenger* of Elliott's which had been built in Belgium in 1880 and acquired by them in 1922 with the name *John Bull* was broken up at Grays by Ward's to whom she was delivered on the 10 May. Elliott's had won a large contract from the Navy after the First World War towing obsolete warships to the breakers. The *Revenger* and *Crusade* were acquired to enable them to fulfil this and the brick run from Antwerp. William Watkins laid up a further tug during the year, the *Scotia* joining other members of the fleet which were already laid up in Ramsgate Harbour.

The *Crested Cock* of Gamecock Towing was sold to Russia, sailing to Murmansk under the name *Shuga*. She had been built in 1930 at Aberdeen by Alexander Hall & Co. Ltd. There were two reasons for selling the *Crested Cock* and her sister *New Gamecock* which had been sold the year previously. The first of these reasons was that vessels of over 1,000 h.p. (these two craft were each of 1,150 h.p.) were required to carry certificated engineers. The owners did not like this requirement preferring their own 'shovel' engineers, men who had started as a boy and worked up learning the trade to become highly experienced tug engineers. The 'Cock' tugs built after these two, *Ocean Cock*, *Atlantic Cock* and later *Crested Cock*, were all built with slightly less power, not exceeding the 1,000 h.p. limit, so as not to require certificated engineers. The regulations regarding certificated engineers remained in force until the Second World War when they ceased being applied. The second reason for the sale of the two tugs was that they were heavier on coal consumption than the smaller tugs.

The *Gnat*, of Gaselee & Son Ltd., sank off Tilbury Dock new entrance just after 05.00 on 25th January. She was inward bound with five craft when she was run down in hazy conditions by the outward bound German ship *August*

*Cords*, 1273/10. The Master and Fireman were both drowned, the Mate and Engineer being picked up from the water, although the Engineer spent twenty minutes in the river before a barge rescued him.

The P.L.A. salvage department raised her the same evening and beached her at Little Thurrock, half a mile above Tilbury Dock new entrance at a place known locally at that time as Botany Bay. She was scrapped and replaced by a new *Gnat* of 66 tons gross which was built by Cochrane & Son of Selby and powered by a British Polar diesel of 500 i.h.p.

The various tug owners got together in the latter half of the year and the British Tug Owners Association came into being.

# 1935

1935 started with Elliott's selling the *Crusade* for scrap, on 4 January, to Wards for demolition at Grays, Essex. She had been built in 1881 in Belgium and acquired by Elliott's in the twenties as the *Washington*.

During May, Watkins' disposed of four tugs. One, the *Rumania* was sold on 14 May to Nash Dredging Co. of Southampton for £4,500. She had been built in 1919 for the Royal Navy as H.S.79 and acquired by I.C. Guy of Cardiff and renamed *Welsh Rose*, and came into Watkins, ownership in June 1928. The other three tugs were all scrapped. They were the *Scotia*, built in 1894, *Nubia* of 1890, and *Canada* of 1880, all going to G. Cohen & Son for £160, £140 and £110 respectively.

Prior to being sold all three had been laid up in Ramsgate Harbour, the *Scotia* from the year previously and the *Canada* since she had finished dredging work on the new Tilbury Dock extension in 1930.

There were two new buildings. Gamecock Tugs had the *Crested Cock* completed by Alexander Hall & Co. Ltd. of Aberdeen. A near sister to *Ocean Cock* and *Atlantic Cock* and with a gross tonnage of 177, she was a coal fired with a 1,000 i.h.p. triple expansion engine. Soon at work on the coast, together with the *New Storm Cock*, she assisted the *City of Lancaster*, 3,040/24, which was suffering from steerage problems. They towed her from London to Liverpool and then returned to the Thames. Gaselee had the *Mamba* built by Cochrane & Son of Selby. Of 67 gross tons, she was powered by a British Polar diesel of 500 i.h.p.

The only other change was Ring Tugs' *Dilwara*, built in 1930 which had her name changed to *Denderra* in order to leave the old name clear for the new British India liner *Dilwara* which was building on the Clyde.

On 3rd January the *Contest*, assisted by two Dover Harbour tugs, refloated the *Appledore*, 5,218/29 from the Goodwin Sands. *Contest* made fast alongside and the *Lady Brassey* and *Lady Duncannon* foreward. After she had been refloated *Appledore*, which was carrying a cargo of timber, was escorted to Surrey Commercial Docks, London, by the *Contest*.

# 1936

Two tugs were disposed of in 1936, the *Sunny* a small tug of 25 gross tons belonging to W.H.J. Alexander Ltd. was an interesting little tug built in 1898 as the *Clive* for S. Pearson & Co. Ltd., the contractors engaged in the construction of Dover Harbour. Alexander's acquired her during the First World War and renamed her *Sunny*. The second being Elliott's *Champion*, built at London in 1892, she arrived at Ward's yard at Grays on 21st February for scrapping.

Elliott's also laid up three tugs during the year owing to an industrial dispute regarding wages. *Security, Vanquisher* and *Venturous* were put on the buoy and the crews laid off. *Security* was underway again after a short period, but *Vanquisher* and *Venturous* stayed on the buoy until the outbreak of War in 1939.

During the early hours of 29th February *Boden*, 4,265/14 of Stockholm, dragged her anchor in the Upper Gravesend Read and grounded near the Southern Railway Pier. After grounding she developed a 15 degree list before the *Tanga* (Watkins') and *Sun X* (Alexander's) were able to pull her clear. She was laden with iron ore for Ford's car factory at Dagenham.

Another incident with similarities to the previous one occurred on 19th November when *Belpareil*, 7,302/26 of Oslo, laden with timber, dragged her anchor on the ebb tide in Northfleet Hope during a strong gale. She struck a wharf at Gravesend and grounded, developing a dangerous list and 13 of the crew of 16 were taken off as a precaution. She was pulled clear and refloated by 8 Gravesend tugs on the following tide.

On 18th December, a collision occurred between the *Sun X* and *Turquoise*, 810/33 of Antwerp, which was outward bound from Tilbury for Ostend. The *Sun X* was holed on the port side and was beached off the World's End (a licenced house a quarter of a mile seaward of Tilbury Landing Stage). She soon slipped into deeper water and sank, fortunately without loss of life, the nine members of her crew being taken off by *Sun XI*. She was raised on 19th December by the P.L.A. Salvage Department, handed over to *Sun V* and *Sunbeam* and then towed to Alexander's yard at Wapping. From these she was taken on 30th December to Mills and Knight's repair yard at Rotherhithe for drydocking. Repairs completed, she returned to work on 27 January 1937.

# 1937

In 1937 there were two new additions, both built for Gaselee & Son Ltd. They were the *Sauria* of 66 tons gross built by Cochrane & Sons Ltd. of Selby and the *Agama* 84 tons gross built at Aberdeen by Alexander Hall and Co. Ltd. Both were powered by British Polar diesels the *Sauria* developing 500 b.h.p. and the *Agama* 700 b.h.p. In 1938 the *Agama* was reputed to be the first diesel powered tug on the Thames to be engaged in ship towage. With these two additions the *Hornet* became surplus to requirements and was delivered on 17th December to Ward's at Grays for demolition.

The Gravesend United Steam Tug Co. (Ring Tugs) was taken over during June by William Watkins. The company had been founded in the 1890s by local people on a share basis, pilots being the principal shareholders. The four tugs *Tamesa, Doralia, Dongara* and *Denderra* kept their own names and funnel colours for a further twelve months before being brought into line with the rest of the Watkins' fleet.

On the salvage side a collision occurred in fog on 20th March between the Dutch tanker *Sunetta* 7,987/35 of the Hague and the Furness Withy ship *Pacific Ranger*, 6,866/29 of London. *Pacific Ranger* had been lying at anchor off Gravesend Promenade and her cable was broken. Tugs went to her aid and she was safely moored to Gravesend Swing Buoy.

The English Trader grounded on castle ledge rock, Kingswear on 23rd January while attempting to enter the River Dart. Rocks penetrated the hull and all attempts at refloating failed, necessitating cutting off the bow before the ship could be refloated. The English Trader minus her bow was towed into Dartmouth on 23rd February, where her cargo of grain was unloaded and temporary repairs carried out. Gamecock's *Crested Cock* and *Atlantic Cock*

9

went down to Dartmouth to tow her stern first to Southampton for repair, sailing on 4th April from Dartmouth. They were assisted by the salvage vessel *Recovery of Leith*, which had a wire made fast to the bow, to help stop the ship shearing. This was successful until *Recovery of Leith* broke adrift, the ship sheared and the swell that was running up Channel caused her to roll quite heavily. This rolling washed out grain that was lodged in small holes in her bottom plating, with the result the ship started making more water than the pumps could hold. It was decided to make a dash for Portland for more repairs, being assisted into Portland by the tug *Portwey*, of the Portland & Weymouth Coaling Co. (*Portwey* is now preserved and kept in a steaming condition on the Thames by the Maritime Trust.) *Crested Cock* stood by the ship in Portland while the *Atlantic Cock* was released and towed a barge to London from Southampton. Both tugs completed the tow the following month after emergency repairs had been completed.

# 1938

Gamecock sold the *Spread Eagle* during the year to Newport Screw Towing Co., her name being changed to *Dunson*.

The *Spread Eagle* had been built in 1911. She was powered by a 500 i.h.p. two-cylinder compound engine and had a gross tonnage of 143.

In March Watkins took *Fabia* out of lay-up at Ramsgate and employed her berthing the cruise ships that had started to run to the Upper Pool. Their original idea was to keep her underway during the summer only and return her into lay-up for the winter. With the Second World War looming over the horizon the company changed their mind and she was retained in service.

On 17th June the four tugs of the Gravesend United Steam Tug Co., which had been taken over the year previously, had their names and colours changed, the two narrow white bands on the funnel being replaced by a broad red band. *Doralia* (built 1914) became *Napia*, *Tamesa* (1925) became *Cervia*, *Denderra* (1930) became *Racia* and *Dongarra* (1932) became the *Persia*.

On Thursday 9th June at 22.30 a tragedy occurred in Gravesend Reach. Gamecock's *Ocean Cock* was rounding to put the Pilot and waterman aboard the inward bound vessel *Tairoa* 7983/20, of the Shaw Savill Line, when she collided with the outward bound Port Line vessel *Port Nicholson*, 8402/19. The *Ocean Cock* was struck just abaft the bridge and sank immediately with the loss of four lives: the Chief Engineer, Fireman, Cook and the Waterman. Raised by four wreck lighters of the P.L.A. Salvage Department, she was beached at Globe Wharf, Grays, and, after patching the *New Stormcock* towed her to the River Humber for permanent repairs by Doigs at Grimsby.

Watkins sent the *Muria* to Falmouth in June to tow the *Cutty Sark* on her last sea voyage to the Thames. She had been presented to the Incorporated Thames

11

*1938 — Ocean Cock in dry dock after collission with Port Nicholson.*

Nautical Training College by the widow of Captain Dowman who had bought her from the Portuguese in 1922 and restored her to her original rig. The *Muria* towed her to Greenhithe where she joined H.M.S. *Worcester* as a training ship for Merchant Navy Officer cadets.

On 3rd October Silvertown Services was brought into being by a consortium of W.H.J. Alexander (Sun Tugs), Tilbury Contracting & Dredging and Tate & Lyle, Tilbury Dredging put two tugs into the company and Sun Tugs put in four tugs and over 150 barges. These included the 29 Lunar barges, *Lunar II–XXX* and the six largest barges in use on the Thames at that time, the 500 ton *Phoebus II–VII*. The tugs transferred by W.H.J. Alexander Ltd. were the *Sunbeam*, of 60 gross tons, built in 1901, *Sundial* 54.81 gross built in 1899 as the *Prince,* *Sunclad* 54.48 built in 1892 as *Star of the East* and *Sunlit* built in 1890 as the *Stockwell*.

Following the transfer the prefix SUN was changed to SILVER and the ships became respectively the *Silverbeam, Silverdial, Silverclad* and *Silverlit*. With the disposal of these tugs and barges W.H.J. Alexander ceased trading as

12

a lighterage company and concentrated their energies on ship towage and as Wharfingers at St. John's Wharf, Wapping. The *Sunfly* became surplus to requirements at this time and was sold for scrap. She had been purchased from the Thames Conservancy Board in 1910 as the *Lizard* and was unusual in that her main engine could be declutched from the propeller shaft to drive a 200 ton per hour salvage pump.

On 30th December *Britannia*, 4216/29, of Swedish Lloyd, grounded off Southend and although tugs went to her aid they were unable to refloat her on that tide. They landed her passengers and refloated her on the ensuing tide.

Sunfly *using her large salvage pump to pump out Millwall drydock when the pump house was being built.*

# 1939

Watkins sold the *Palencia* during the year to James Towing of Southampton. She had been built in 1916 as the *Sloyne* for Alexandra Towing of Liverpool. Watkins had purchased her in 1920 and she had been laid up in Ramsgate for a number of years. She was subsequently resold to the Shell Oil Company for service at Gibraltar.

Gaselee had the *Wasp* completed by Cochrane & Sons Ltd. at Selby. She was of 67 gross tons and powered by a 500 b.h.p. British Polar diesel.

Cunard's new liner *Mauretania*, 35739/39, docked in the King George V dock on 6th August assisted by tugs of W.H.J. Alexander Ltd. At the time she was the largest liner to dock in London and was also the largest ship built in England.

On 22nd May Watkins' *Cervia* was escorting the *Valparaiso*, 4979/17 inward bound when she was in collision with the *Dicky*, 507/01. The latter vessel was owned by the Goole & Hull Steam Towing Co. of Goole and was anchored in Erith Reach above Coldharbour Point. She sustained extensive damage in the foreward hold on the starboard side and was beached in a sinking condition by the *Cervia* and *Sun X*. *Cervia* stood by the *Dicky* whilst she was patched and refloated her on the afternoon of 24th May.

Two weeks before the outbreak of War, Elliott's *Security* towed two barges loaded with scrap iron from the Thames to Hamburg. She then proceeded to the River Schelde via the canals to tow a barge from Antwerp to London. Whilst on passage she received a telegram instructing her to return to Gravesend immediately because of the deteriorating situation. On her return she joined the *Kenia, Doria, Sun II, Sun III, New Stormcock* and *Tayra* under the Naval control at Southend Pier in the week prior to the declaration of War. *Tayra* was later transferred to Scotland.

On September 3rd, when War was declared, *Java* was off the Isle of Wight bound for Portsmouth with two barges. She subsequently met up with the *Tanga*, which had left Gravesend on 9th September for Devonport and both were sent on to Brest, arriving there on 12th September. After three days they were sent to Lorient and from there to St Nazaire arriving on 16th September. The two tugs worked at St Nazaire until the 30th October on which day they left for Devonport encountering bad weather *en route* and arriving on 1st November. *Tanga* then returned to Gravesend and *Java* to Ramsgate where she joined the *Kenia, Fabia, Vincia* and *Sun VII* on the Downs Patrol, examining ships and routing them as they passed through the Dover Straits. *Java* and *Vincia* had been on the same patrol twenty-five years previously during World War One serving under the White Ensign as H.M.S. *Carcass* and H.M.S. *Chub* respectively.

The Ellerman liner *City of Paris* 10,902/22 sustained mine damage off Lowestoft on 16th September and was subsequently towed to London by *Contest* and *Atlantic Cock* with *Hibernia* assisting from the Estuary.

During November *Security* was part of the first convoy that sailed from Southend departing at 06.30 on the 24th. The normal practice was for the tug allocated to the convoy to escort it north as far as Great Yarmouth and then return with a south bound convoy to Southend. On 17th December Watkins' *Napia* was mined in the Ramsgate Channel and sank with the loss of all hands. Built in 1914 as the *Doralia* for Gravesend United Steam Tug Co. she had joined the Watkins' fleet in 1938 as *Napia*. She had been hired by the Navy as an examination vessel on 6th December.

Elliott's *Venturous* and *Vanquisher* were returned to service due to the shortage of tugs on the river but the hull of *Vanquisher* proved to be in a bad condition and she was scrapped at Ward's yard at Grays.

Gamecock's salvage ship *King Lear* was placed under the control of the P.L.A. Salvage Department for the duration of the War.

# 1940

During January 1940, Watkins' *Persia* towed a barge from Falmouth to Glasgow and on the return trip to London assisted in refloating *Permuda* loaded with coal and ashore on the Goodwin Sands. She then towed her to Cory's Wharf at Purfleet for discharging.

*Tanga* left Gravesend on 31st January to tow a disabled ship from anchorage in the Downs to Blyth. The ship hove up at 06.00 on the 2nd February and all went well until 22.00 on the 4th when the tow rope parted in a severe easterly

Tanga.

17

gale. *Tanga* was unable to pass a new tow rope in the prevailing weather conditions and stood by.

The ship anchored and *Tanga* put into Grimsby. On leaving Grimsby again, *Tanga* ran into dense fog and was forced to anchor for 24 hours. On arrival at the ship again she found that she had been in the tow of a trawler for the previous 29 hours owing to the ship having lost both anchors in the storm. The *Tanga* took over from the trawler and towed the ship to Grimsby for new ones to be fitted. The *Arcadia* was in the Tyne at the time and was sent to assist the *Tanga* from Grimsby, the ship finally arriving at Blyth on 16th February.

On the run south *Tanga* was diverted to Lowestoft meeting up with *Muria* which had been sent up from Harwich. Both were to assist in the refloating of *Royal Crown* 4,364/27 which was ashore there.

Five tugs towed on her unsuccessfully during the morning tide by the *Tanga* and *Muria* refloated her on the evening tide at 21.00 hours on 24th February and she was berthed at Lowestoft at midnight.

*Royal Crown* had been bombed and machine-gunned by enemy aircraft off Lowestoft on 30th January causing her damage and resulting in her being beached. *Tanga* then returned to Gravesend, arriving on the 26th.

*Sun VI* was hired by the Navy as a dockyard tug at Sheerness and *Sunfish* and *Sunbird* were sent to Chatham. All three remained with the Admiralty for the duration of the War.

The *Sun, Sunrise* and *Sunshine* stayed on the Thames for the duration of the War as did the *Hibernia* and *Badia*. Others came and went as required.

During May when the German Army was advancing through Holland *Security* and *Sun III* were despatched from Southend to Rotterdam to assist in the evacuation of the Port but when on passage in the North Sea, a destroyer stopped them and they were re-routed to Harwich as Rotterdam had already fallen to the Germans. *Security* returned to Southend and then proceeded to London for a refit by Mills and Knight at Rotherhithe. *Security* and *New Stormcock* were replaced at Southend by *Sun VIII* and *Sun IX*.

Watkins' *Simla* and *Gondia* were stationed at Dover, *Simla* staying for four years, returning to the Thames prior to the invasion of Normandy. *Gondia*, however, only remained there until the evacuation of Dunkirk. Atlantic Cock was sent to Milford Haven for approximately three weeks.

As the German Army swept relentlessly across Europe the British Expeditionary Force became besieged within the area of Dunkirk. Operation Dynamo was set in motion to rescue the B.E.F. from the beaches there and all manor of small craft were requisitioned by the Navy for this purpose. They included private pleasure craft and sailing barges, many loaded food, water and ammunition to keep the troops supplied, and all types of commercial vessels. Ships in the docks were stripped of their lifeboats and these were towed across the Channel by many of the local tugs.

*Java* took the first of the small boats across to Dunkirk on 28th May. She sailed from Ramsgate towing an R.N.L.I. lifeboat and leading a flotilla of drifters and 4 M.L.'s. A naval officer was on board and at that time the crew had no idea where they were bound. Mr H. Griffiths the deckhand (later master of *Rumania* was awarded the D.S.M. and Mr V. Smith, the mate, was mentioned in dispatches for their work transferring troops from the beach in the tug's lifeboat to the *Java*. When returning to Ramsgate loaded with troops she rescued two British airmen from the sea 5 miles off Dunkirk and troops from the paddle minesweeper *Waverly* that had been sunk, landing 140 men at Ramsgate.

During the evening of 31st May the following Thames tugs reached Dunkirk with a varied assortment of small craft and barges in tow. The *Racia* with 12 lifeboats, *Vincia* with 3 lifeboats, *Tanga* 6 boats, *Ocean Cock* 6 motorboats, *Crested Cock* a barge, *Sun IV* 6 motorboats, *Sun VII* R.A.F. seaplane tenders 243, 254, 276, 291 and A.M.C.3, *Sun VIII* 12 lifeboats, *Sun XI*, a barge, *Sun XII* sailing barges *Tollsbury & Ethel Everard*, *Fairplay I* (managed by Watkins) a sailing barge, *Foremost 87* (managed by Watkins) 2 sailing barges. *Cervia* under the command of Captain W. Simmons, sailed from Dover towing the sailing barge *Royalty* loaded with food, cans of water and cigarettes. She was accompanied by *Persia* (Captain Aldrich) towing the sailing barges *Lark* and *Glenway*.

*Persia* had orders to take her barges inside Dunkirk harbour whilst the *Cervia* was ordered to beach the *Royalty* at Port Malo, one mile east of Dunkirk pier head. This she did at 08.20 on 1st June and at 08.30 fifteen aircraft appeared and attacked the rescue craft, *Cervia* defending herself with her Lewis gun. *Vincia, Cervia* and *Persia* were all attacked when off the beaches, fortunately without damage.

Following the attack *Cervia* proceeded to the sailing barge *Tollesbury* which was at anchor and loaded with troops. As there were many badly wounded in the hold it was impossible to transfer them to the tug and *Cervia* therefore passed her towing spring and the barge started to heave her anchor. However, the wash from a passing sloop caused the tow wire to snatch, with the result that the wooden windlass was pulled from its bed. This made it impossible to heave the anchor so *Cervia* towed her to Ramsgate with 15 fathoms of chain still out.

On arrival in the Downs at 16.00 1st June 270 men were landed from the tug and barge.

The *Persia* went to the assistance of the destroyer *Ivanhoe* which had been disabled by dive bombers, 26 men were killed and 30 wounded, the remaining troops being transferred to the destroyer *Havant*, the minesweeper *Speedwell* and steam schooner *Grive*. The *Persia* towed the *Ivanhoe* to Sheerness for repair, escorted by the m.l. *Haig*.

The *Vincia* went to the assistance of the destroyer H.M.S. *Keith* which had been bombed and had her stern blown off when the depth charges aft had exploded. *Vincia* picked up some survivors from the sea assisted by the naval tug *St Abbs* but unfortunately *St Abbs* was soon to be sunk as a result of a direct hit.

The *Tanga* made three trips to the beaches taking lifeboats on one of them. On the return from her third trip she towed the sailing barge *Pudge* loaded with French troops to Ramsgate.

Vincia.

On 2nd June Gaselee's *Fossa* was stranded on the beach and had to be abandoned, her crew returning in other vessels.

The *Racia* under Captain Addison made two trips to the beaches and was credited with bringing 423 troops back to England including 80 French. She was one of the last vessels to leave Dunkirk before it was abandoned. The hospital ship *Paris*, 1790/13 was bombed and sank north of Dunkirk on 2nd June. The *Sun XV* went to her assistance and made fast, but had to abandon any attempt to tow her to port. The *Fabia* and *Sun IV* were among the vessels sent to seek survivors, but when the *Sun IV* arrived she found the *Paris* abandoned and in a sinking condition, so returned to Ramsgate. *Gondia, Contest, Crested Cock, Watercock, Sun, Sun III, Sun V, Sun VIII, Sun X, Sun XI, Sun XII* and *Duke* were the other London tugs that took part in the evacuation. The eight Sun tugs rescued 1,421 men in all. Altogether 338,226 troops were brought back to England, London tugs playing no small part in this achievement not only in rescuing troops but in keeping them supplied with food and ammunition while the evacuation took place. A total of 41 tugs took part in the evacuation, 3 being lost. A further 6 tugs were on harbour duties in the Kent ports.

After the evacuation *Persia* assisted by *Foremost 87*, towed a Polish destroyer stern first from Dover to Portsmouth. This proved to be a difficult tow as the destroyer, which had sustained extensive bow damage, sheered badly.

Following arrival at Portsmouth *Persia*, joined by *Contest* and *Crested Cock*, was sent to Newhaven to assist in the evacuation of St Valery-en-Caux. The *Persia* was sent across to France and was warned by the tug *Fairplay I*, which was returning from St Valery, to be careful when entering as the Germans were closing in. On arrival at the port the master decided to back his tug into the harbour and this proved to be a wise decision as she was attacked by gunfire on entry but as she was facing seaward was able to make a dash for the open sea and escaped. The defenders of St Valery-en-Caux surrendered to the German army on 12th June. After St Valery was overrun the *Crested Cock* returned to Gravesend and river work. The *Persia*, in company with *Tanga* was sent to Brest to assist British ships that were trapped in port. She then patrolled outside Brest turning ships away. One of those diverted was the Cunard liner *Lancastria*, 16243/22 which was subsequently bombed and sunk off St Nazaire on 17th June with great loss of life amongst the troops whom she had evacuated.

After Dunkirk, *Gondia* and *Java* were sent to Milford Haven on harbour duties, the *Gondia* relieving the *Atlantic Cock*. At the same time *Kenia* was sent to Devonport for orders and from there she was sent in company of the

*Atlantic Cock* to St Nazaire. *Kenia* with *Atlantic Cock*, had orders to tow a partly finished destroyer to England but permission to do so was refused by the French who wanted it to be towed south. *Atlantic Cock* was then requested to tow a tanker from St Nazaire to England but owing to the conditions prevailing at the time this proved impossible and *Kenia* and *Atlantic Cock* both returned to Falmouth. *Kenia* remained at Falmouth whilst *Atlantic Cock* returned to Gravesend in company with *Watercock* and *Persia*.

Following their escape from France, a considerable number of ships were anchored at Falmouth, and *Kenia*, which had a large water tank fitted under her fore cabin floor, was used to supply fresh water to them. She carried out these duties for about three weeks and then returned to the Thames for a refit. On completion of this refit she was sent to Harwich as a rescue tug and given the pennant number W47 joining *Muria* which was already on station there. Gaselee's *Musca* and *Vespa* were also hired by the navy and armed and stationed for about a year at Cliffe on patrol duties in the Sea Reach area. When *Security* had finished her refit in June she towed two barges to Southampton and from there she was sent to Portland Naval Base. She remained on station at Portland in Company with the navy tug *St Martin*.

On the 13th June the tanker *British Inventor*, 7101/26 struck a mine five miles from St Albans Head. Well down by the head, she was taken in tow by *Security* and *St Martin* and was towed into Weymouth Bay where she grounded. The bow eventually broke off but a new false bow was built on enabling her to be towed to Southampton for permanent repairs.

After Dunkirk *Cervia* was employed returning ships' lifeboats and sailing barges to London from Ramsgate and on 9th June she was towing the sailing barges *Basildon* and *Ashington* when she was ordered to the assistance of the *Empire Commerce*, 3857/28, which had struck a mine near the northeast spit buoy off Margate and had been severely damaged in her stokehold. The naval trawler *Edwardian* which had her in two was having difficulties controlling her as she was sheering badly and this caused the *Edwardian* to be girted. *Cervia* took hold of *Empire Commerce* and beached her on the Margate sands. *Kenia* then stood by *Empire Commerce* and dismissed *Cervia* who recovered her barges and completed the tow to London. Subsequently the *Empire Commerce* was towed to the Thames and beached on the Mucking Flats in the Lower Hope and her cargo of timber was salved.

The *Fabia* was stationed at Sheerness during June under the control of the Royal Air Force and flew the R.A.F. ensign. She spent about a year victualling and attending on the various barrage balloon vessels that were moored in the estuary.

On July 31st *Cervia* left London in convoy for Methil, the convoy being subjected to air attacks whilst on passage. On arrival at Methil on 2nd August she was placed under naval control, her work including general towage around the port and also supplying water and attending to the needs of the large volume of ships that were anchored in the Firth of Forth awaiting convoys. Whilst stationed at Methil she successfully berthed larger ships in the dock than had ever been attempted there before.

*Atlantic Cock* and *Fairplay I* left London on 19th October towing the Port of London Authority heavy lift crane *Atlas* for Scapa Flow. At this period of the War tugs only towed in daylight on the east coast when not escorted and anchored at night. After delivering *Atlas*, the *Atlantic Cock* then towed a trawler to Buckie via Wick and from there ran to Inverness and on through the Caledonian Canal to Oban, taking up station there on arrival on 17th November.

Towards the end of 1940, *Sun IV, Sun XV, Ocean Cock, Contest*, and the *New Stormcock* were all transferred to the Clyde where more tugs were required to cope with the increased volume of shipping which was now using the River. Whilst on the Clyde, the *New Stormcock* had a fire pump fitted on her after deck enabling her to maintain a fire watch.

The *Watercock* also left the London river going to Southampton during the same period and being placed under the control of Risdon Beazley Ltd. In October *Tanga* was sent to the stormy waters of Iceland being stationed at Reykjavik for the next three years. She subsequently attended to the needs of the large number of convoys that sailed from Iceland for the northern Russian ports of Murmansk and Archangel.

On the first night of the Blitz on London in September, *Persia* and *Atlantic Cock* assisted the tanker *Amsterdam* that had been attacked on its berth at Purfleet. Three crew members from the tugs and two local watermen went on board the ship letting go of the mooring ropes because the crew had abandoned her. *Persia* and *Atlantic Cock* towed the *Amsterdam* to a safe mooring in St Clements Reach. Then on 22/23rd September *Persia* assisted the tanker *Barendrecht* which was moored on Long Reach buoys. The tanker had suffered bomb damage to her bridge which had resulted in a fire in her midship superstructure. The *Persia* successfully fought the fire and extinguished the blaze.

The closing months of 1940 proved disastrous for Thames tugs, four, together with their crews, being lost. At around noon on Saturday 2nd November the P.L.A. tugs *Deanbrook* and *Lea* were laying on the inner knuckle at the lower side of Tilbury Lock awaiting a crew change. Both crews were below when a parachute mine exploded sinking both tugs. It was thought that the tugs' wash had disturbed the mine from its previous location where it had gone undetected by Royal Navy Minesweepers. Of the twelve crew members on board the two tugs eleven were killed instantly and the twelfth died of his injuries the following March. My uncle Mr J. Rathbone, deckhand of the *Lea*, died in this unfortunate incident.

*Deanbrook* had been built by J.P. Rennoldson & Son of South Shields in 1908 for the London & India Docks Company. She was to have been named *Edward VII* but this was refused by the Board of Trade and the second choice of name, *Cromer* was also refused. She was accordingly completed as *Power*, her name being changed to *Deanbrook* in 1926. The *Lea* was the last of a quartet of twin-screw dock tugs ordered by the P.L.A. on their formation. She had been built by Ferguson Brothers of Port Glasgow in 1912.

On 8th November Watkins' *Muria* was next to fall victim of the magnetic mine. She was struck off North Foreland in position 51°26.5′N. 001°27′E. and sank with the loss of all hands. At the time of her loss she was stationed at Harwich as a rescue tug, and had been relieved by the *Kenia*. *Muria* put into Sheerness to land a crew member and was proceeding to Ramsgate for a refit when she was lost. Royal Navy standing orders for the rescue tugs was on normal passage only swept channels to be used, but if proceeding to a casualty, the shortest route to be used. The *Muria* was lost using the swept channel. With her loss the *Kenia* remained at Harwich as rescue tug until August 1945.

*Muria* had been built by Scott & Sons at Bowling in 1914 as the *Wrestler* for Steele and Bennie Ltd., the navy purchasing her during the First World War and renaming her *Hotspur*. She was acquired by Watkins in 1920 as a replacement for tugs lost during the First World War.

W.H.J. Alexander's *Sun IX* became the next casualty, also to a mine. She was stationed at Southend under naval control and struck a mine between

Nos 1 and 2 Sea Reach on 21st December and sank with the loss of all hands. She was later raised but was found to be beyond repair and was scrapped. She had been built in 1920 by Cochrane & Sons Ltd. of Selby.

# 1941

During December 1940 Watkins' *Arcadia* had been hired by the Ministry of War Transport and was engaged towing barges from London to Great Yarmouth. These barges were bound for Glasgow, via the Caledonian Canal, and were towed on from Great Yarmouth by other tugs. On 12th April 1941 whilst towing two of the barges to Great Yarmouth *Arcadia* was attacked by a German J.U. 88 aircraft near the Rough Buoy 10 miles east of Harwich. She was machine-gunned and bombed, one bomb passing through the funnel and out the other side fortunately without exploding. The holes in the funnel however resulted in a loss of draught to her fires and a reduction in steam pressure. She was therefore assisted by *Kenia* into Harwich where emergency repairs were effected.

On 7th September 1940 three hundred German bombers had attacked London's East End in the first big air raid on the city and Silvertown and the docklands area were badly hit. Two days later during another raid the *Minnie de Larrinaga* of 5,049 gross tons was bombed and sunk. Salved, she was taken to Silvertown and loaded with rubble from the bombed warehouses and factories and when the work was complete she was towed away by the *Arcadia Watercock* and the Dover tug *Lady Brassey* and sunk on 5th February 1941 as a blockship in Dover harbour.

During February *Atlantic Cock* grounded in Oban Harbour and sustained some bottom damage. She was sent to the Clyde for repair and when the work was completed she remained there on station, joining a number of other Thames tugs.

On 6th March another tug struck a mine and sank in the estuary close to the North Knob Buoy. *Sun VII* was the victim together with five of her crew. She had been built in 1917 at Wivenhoe on the River Colne in Essex and was the largest of her class. At the time of her loss she was under naval control from Southend.

On the 22nd of that month the *Kenia* went to the assistance of the *Dashwood*, 2,154 tons, which had grounded on the Long Sand after missing 51 Buoy. This buoy marked the peacetime position of the Sunk Light Vessel which had been withdrawn for the duration of hostilities. When the *Kenia* was in the process of passing her towing gear, the *Dashwood* was attacked by a German aircraft. A bomb came to rest in a watertank of the *Dashwood* but fortunately failed to explode. The aircraft opened fire on the two vessels and the Master of the *Kenia*, Captain H. Russel had a narrow escape when a bullet cut the side of his face. It was three days later before *Kenia* succeeded in refloating the *Dashwood* which she then towed to London handing her over to *Racia* at the gateway of the boom that stretched across the estuary from Shoeburyness to the Isle of Sheppey. *Kenia* then returned to her station at Harwich.

During March the Watkins' tugs that had taken part in the evacuation of Dunkirk received on board a brass plaque to commemorate the event. Most of the tugs mounted them on the foreside of the bridge.

On 9th April Elliott's *Venturous* and Watkins' *Persia* were shifting the Shell tanker *Lunula*, 6,363 gross, from the anchorage to No 4 Jetty Thames Haven (now C Jetty Shell Haven). The *Lunula*'s degaussing coils were inoperative as she had no steam and, as she approached the berth, a mine exploded covering the *Persia*, the watermen and the Jetty in blazing oil. Over 60 lives were lost in this incident including the entirety of the *Persia*'s crew, the Berthing Master, watermen, jetty hands and members of the *Lunula*'s crew. The *Persia* was taken in tow by the Esso tug *Royal Daylight* and anchored on the Blyth Sands. The *Hibernia* which was passing with another ship in tow extinguished the fire. The *Persia* was then towed to Clifton slipway at Gravesend for assessment of the damage which was so severe that she was subsequently condemned as a constructive total loss. However, she was later towed by *Kenia* to the yard at Ramsgate and was rebuilt there.

The *Fabia* finished her spell with the R.A.F. and then towed the coalhoist *Biddenden* from Sheerness to Lowestoft. At Lowestoft she handed over her tow to the Tilbury Contracting and Dredging Company's tug *Danube VII* which was to take it onward to Inverness. She then ran light to Inverness and for two weeks was engaged in towing through the Caledonian Canal the barges which had been towed up previously from London. After that she reconnected with her original tow, *Biddenden*, at Inverness and took her through the canal and across to Londonderry in Northern Ireland. *Fabia* remained in that port as a harbour tug and was later joined by *Java* which had been at Milford Haven since June 1940.

On 15th September, the tug *Flying Kite*, 260 tons, belonging to the Clyde Shipping Company was sunk by a mine off Dalmuir Basin on the River Clyde. *Atlantic Cock* suffered damage in the same incident.

After service at Cliffe on patrol duties, Gaselee & Son's *Musca* and *Vespa* left the Thames for the River Mersey and both spent the rest of the war at Liverpool under the management of the Alexandra Towing Company. *Racia* also left the Thames, towing a barge to the Clyde and remained there, joining the growing number of Thames tugs already in the area.

During the winter of 1941 the *Arcadia* was towing a collier from Harwich to Sunderland and being unescorted anchored at night, the first night in Yarmouth Roads and the second night off Cromer. On the third day, whilst going through the Race (an inshore channel that runs across the outside of the Wash) both the *Arcadia* and the collier which she was towing went aground, the *Arcadia* damaging her rudder badly. Both vessels anchored but *Arcadia*'s anchor chain parted in bad weather after which she drifted around the Wash for four days. After two days, a tug of the United Towing Company of Hull hailed the crew saying that she would return for them after she had towed the collier to port. They were, however, adrift for another two days, by which time they were completely out of food, before a trawler found them and towed them to the River Humber. She then had a refit and her rudder repaired and a set of sails were also made for her, one fitted from her forestay to the side of the bridge and the second from the mizzen mast to aft. I do not believe that she ever had reason to use these sails in earnest.

In 1940 the decision was taken to build forts and position them in the Thames estuary to plug the gap in the anti-aircraft defences and also to serve as a deterrent against E-boat sorties. These forts were constructed on the foreshore at Northfleet on the site where the power station now stands. Of the two types built, the naval manned forts had a boat-shaped base of 168′ by 88′. Built onto this base were two hollow legs 24′ wide and 60′ high. These legs were used for storage and accommodation and led to the large deck area built on top where the guns were mounted. On completion at Northfleet they were towed to Tilbury for fitting out and two 4.5″, two Bofors and two Lewis guns, were mounted. Four tugs were usually used to tow them in their assigned positions; three towing abreast and the fourth towing ahead of the centre tug. These naval forts were positioned at the Knock John, the Sunk, the Rough and the Tongue.

The other design of fort were manned by Army personnel and were smaller. These forts stood on four legs with the accommodation on top and the guns mounted on top of the accommodation. They were sunk in groups of seven with gantries joining them together and were positioned at the Shivering Sands, the Red Sands and at the Nore. *Challenge* and *Crested Cock* were used extensively in towing the forts into position with assistance from *Arcadia, Badia* or whatever tugs were available. When the Army forts were positioned, the tug *Ich Dien* belonging to R.G. Odell, followed with a barge loaded with the gantries for positioning between them.

# 1942

After *Arcadia* had completed her repairs on the Humber she set out with a water barge in tow for London. Bad weather forced her to seek shelter in Great Yarmouth and unfortunately, on entering the harbour, the barge grounded on the beach outside the pierheads. Great Yarmouth, with its narrow entrance, is not the easiest of ports to enter with a tow in adverse conditions. On her return to Gravesend *Arcadia* was engaged in normal river towage with the occasional coastal tow.

*Cervia* had an unusual job in July. An aircraft on a training flight had crashed into the Firth of Forth west of the Isle of May. It was recovered from the sea by H.M.S. *Victoria* and was laid across the after deck of the *Cervia* with the wings overhanging. H.M.S. *Victoria* had a target painted on the funnel and the planes made mock attacks on the ship, cameras being fitted to the gun sights. The plane crashing while making such an attack, the *Cervia* with this significant increase in her beam took it into Methil Dock where it was landed safely. Also in July the first all-welded tank landing craft had trials in the Forth and *Cervia* provided the motive power, towing the L.S.T. head to and beam on to the sea in bad weather conditions to test the strength of the welds.

In August, *Kenia* was sent to Newhaven to take part in Operation Jubilee, the ill-fated raid on Dieppe on the 18–19th. In Dieppe harbour were about 40 German invasion barges and the plan was for *Kenia* and a Navy tug to tow as many barges as could be captured back to England as prizes. The use of tugs was abandoned before the raid was mounted and *Kenia* returned to Harwich. The task of capturing the invasion barges was then allocated to the Navy gunboat H.M.S. *Locust* and seven Free French vessels. The attempt, however, was unsuccessful as the harbour area was too well defended.

Two Sun tugs left the river in August *Sun XII* going to Oban and *Sun X* to the Clyde.

Mr J.R. Watkins, director of William Watkins Ltd. was mentioned in the King's Honours List, receiving the Order of the British Empire. He was adviser to the Government on tugs, first with the Ministry of Shipping and then with its successor, the Ministry of War Transport.

*Gondia* was sent to Iceland arriving at Reykjavik on 23rd April after a stormy passage from Scotland. She was sent to the naval base to relieve a Royal Naval tug which had returned to the United Kingdom. *Tanga* was still working hard at Reykjavik and the amount of work that she was doing can be judged from the fact that 13th June was the first day off that she had had since Christmas Day 1941. On 14th August the tug *Empire Wold* arrived at Reykjavik. Newly completed for the Ministry of War Transport, her management had been allocated to William Watkins Ltd. *Empire Piper* and *Empire Betsy* also served to Iceland under Watkins' management. *Tanga* which was relieved by the *Empire Wold*, left Iceland in convoy on 17th August bound for the U.K. and a refit. Soon after leaving, the convoy ran into bad weather and *Tanga* was instructed by an escorting warship to stand by the *Shell Brilt* while the weather was bad as she was making heavy weather of it. On 19th August the weather deteriorated further and the *Tanga* hove to for 24 hours eventually arriving at Stornaway on the morning of the 22nd. Two days later she sailed for Port Dinorwic via Holyhead, arriving on the 26th. Port Dinorwic is a small harbour on the southeast side of the Menai Strait and was used mainly for the export of slate. *Tanga* was refitted there, leaving on 13th October for Greenock to take bunkers. From there she went on to Oban for a couple of days and then to Stornaway to await a convoy to Iceland. Leaving Stornaway on 4th November she joined a north bound convoy and arrived back in Reykjavik on 8th November to resume work. She was soon employed on salvage work, on 2nd December towing a disabled trawler from sea into Reykjavik. On the 5th she went to the assistance of two corvettes ashore 55 miles from Reykjavik refloating one, the other getting herself off and on the 18th she refloated the steamer *Lyra* which had gone ashore 20 miles from Reykjavik. This salvage work was undertaken in addition to her usual towage duties.

# 1943

On the 1st June *Cervia* was relieved from her base at Methil by the Grangemouth and Forth Towing Company's tug *Grangeburn* and was ordered to proceed to Londonderry in Northern Ireland. She arrived there on 16th June and started work the following day joining the two Watkins' tugs *Fabia* and *Java* which were already stationed there. Londonderry was a base for convoy escorts and one of the jobs undertaken by the tugs there was known as winding. This involved swinging round on the berth between two and five corvettes. Two tugs carried out this manoeuvre between them without any orders from the ships. The objective was to move the inside vessel, which had been fuelled and stored to the outside where she was then ready for sea.

*Persia* returned to work after being rebuilt at Ramsgate following the *Lunula* disaster of April 1941 and her first job was to tow the barge *Monarch* from Ramsgate to London. *Monarch* was then moored in Woolwich Reach, off Sankeys Causeway downstream of North Woolwich pier and used as an up-river mooring for Watkins' tugs.

*Doria* was sent to Southampton and joined the *Watercock* under the management of Risdon Beasley Ltd.

*Security* was renamed *Stoke* by the Admiralty during 1943 and retained this name until returned to Elliott's after the war. *Empire Wold* left Iceland on 10th August for drydocking in the U.K. and on her return she relieved *Tanga* which now left Iceland for the last time. She sailed on 20th October for Loch Ewe but soon lost contact with the convoy in heavy weather. Meeting up again two days later she was re-routed to Greenock arriving there on the 25th. From Greenock she sailed to Port Dinorwic for her refit and returned to the Clyde on completion joining the many other Thames tugs already on station there.

# 1944

When the invasion of Europe was being planned it was realised that it would probably take some time to capture and clear one of the existing French ports and it was therefore decided in 1943 that an artificial harbour would need to be built to keep the invasion forces supplied. The Mulberry harbour was conceived and given the go-ahead and the concrete Phoenix caissons that would form the harbour were built at various places around the coast. The largest weighed 6,000 tons and was the height of a five-storey house. A number of these Phoenix caissons were built on the Thames marshes, a large hole being dug out of the marsh and a block built in it. When ready for launching the sea wall would be cut away and the partly finished block towed to one of the docks to be completed. During January *Vincia* assisted two blocks, one from the marshes at Barking to the South West India Dock and the other from Erith Rands to the Royal Albert Dock. During April a large number of blocks were towed from the docks to Tilbury landing stage and others to Sea Reach where they were handed over to the big tugs for towage round the coast. On 5th April *Vincia, Arcadia* and *Badia* towed one from the Royal Albert Dock to Tilbury Landing Stage and on 16th April *Persia, Vincia* and *Sunshine* towed another from the Greenland Dock to Gravesend. On 21st April *Crested Cock, Persia* and *Vincia* towed A1–59 from King George V Dock to Tilbury and *Simla, Persia* and *Vincia* brought A2–68 from South West India Dock to Tilbury on 25th April. These were but a few of the tows in which the tugs were involved during this period. The work was not accomplished without loss as the Dutch tug *Roode Zee* was sunk by an E-boat off Dungeness on 24th April whilst towing a Mulberry section down Channel.

During May *Atlantic Cock* and *Contest* left the river Clyde, the former towing two barges for Plymouth. She put into Holyhead and was diverted to the River Conway to tow a Mulberry harbour section that was too big for the *Contest* to handle. This was not a wise decision because *Atlantic Cock* was less powerful than the *Contest*. *Atlantic Cock* was later assisted in the tow by the Trinity House vessel *Patricia* and the two vessels finally got the Phoenix caisson safely into Holyhead. After delivering the caisson *Atlantic Cock* carried on with her tow of two barges for Plymouth and then returned to Gravesend in convoy. The caisson was subsequently towed south by a French Abeille tug and *Contest* towed another Mulberry caisson from the river Conway to Southampton.

During 1944 a number of large ocean towing steam tugs were being delivered to the Ministry of War Transport and placed under the management of commercial towage firms. *Empire Winnie* was allocated to the management of William Watkins Ltd. and crewed by them also. *Empire Humphrey, Empire Susan* and *Assiduous* were also allocated to Watkins and took part in the Normandy landings along with *Empire Winnie*. The latter tug had escorted from Scotland a convoy of old ships which were to form part of the Gooseberry harbour off Arromanches where the vessels were scuttled to form a rudimentary harbour to protect the ships supplying the beach head from the weather until the Mulberry harbour could be towed into position. *Empire Winnie* assisted these ships to their allocated positions and held them there while they were scuttled. She then joined the large fleet of tugs engaged in towing the Phoenix caissons across the Channel to make the Mulberry harbour.

On 3rd July *Vincia* and *Challenge* were assisting the American ship *Fort Gibraltar* from the locks to her berth in the Victoria Dock, *Vincia* was forward and the *Challenge* dragging aft. An air raid warning sounded when they were at the top of the Royal Albert Dock waiting for the Connaught bridge to swing open and at 19.15 a doodlebug flying bomb (a V-1) crashed into the dock and exploded just off the *Challenge*'s port side, causing considerable damage to her although fortunately without any loss of life. A Gaselee tug towed her the next day to Mills and Knight's yard at Rotherhithe where repairs lasted three months. On 12th July Gaselee's *Naja* sustained a direct hit from a V-1 while on duty as the Tower Bridge tug in the Upper Pool and became a total loss. The timing of her casualty could not have been worse as two crews were on board at the time. (When Tower Bridge was built it was a condition that a steam tug would always be kept on station at the bridge to keep it clear of any obstructions. Gaselee and Son had secured the contract for supply of that tug.)

In September the American ammunition ship *Richard Montgomery* loaded with 7,000 tons of high explosives grounded on the Sheerness Middle Sand and after all attempts to refloat her had failed she broke her back. *Atlantic Cock* was used to supply steam to the *Richard Montgomery*'s winches in an attempt to salve her dangerous cargo and approximately 3,500 tons were discharged from the two after holds into the collier *Flathouse* and the *Empire Nutfield*. After three weeks, *Atlantic Cock* was relieved by *Gondia*, and *Kenia* also worked on the ship before she was finally abandoned. *Richard Montgomery*, with her cargo of bombs, still lies to this day on the northern edge of the Medway channel 1½ miles from the beach at Sheerness.

Nine members of the crew of *Empire Wold* were lost when she was torpedoed and sunk off the coast of Iceland by the German submarine U300 on 10th November.

*Fairplay One* under Watkins' management was working in Ostend harbour on 12th November 1944 when she set off a mine while shifting a ship from a foul berth and sustained considerable damage aft. Her propeller was blown off, her after cabin set on fire and her steering damaged. She was towed to Grimsby for repairs by *Empire Jester* which was managed at the time by United Towing Company of Hull and became Watkins' *Napia* after the war. While the *Fairplay One* was being dragged up the slipway at Grimsby she fell off the blocks and had to be lowered gently back into the water listing heavily. Her Master was heard to comment: 'This tug seems determined to kill us all one way or another.'

Apart from the dangers associated with the war, ships still got into difficulties on the final stages of their voyage. One such incident involved *Armathia* on the evening of 23rd December. When swinging in Limehouse Reach to dock in the Greenland Dock entrance of the Surrey Commercial Docks she fouled one of the barge roads and laid athwart it. *Vincia* went to her assistance taking a rope off the port bow and Gaselee's *Aboma* took one off the port quarter. The two tugs pulled her clear but she then grounded on the south shore. A further tug, *Agama*, was then taken on and after about thirty minutes the three tugs refloated *Armathia* and docked her safely in the Greenland Dock.

On 8th November the *Abraham Baldwin* grounded on the Goodwin Sands. The *Empire Susan* was at Southend and was sent to assist in refloating by the Senior Naval Officer, Southend. The ship was successfully refloated on 11th November by *Empire Susan* and the Dover tugs *Lady Brassey* and *Lady Duncannon*.

# 1945

*Java* finished her spell in Londonderry and after being relieved on 1st August went to Coleraine to tow a Royal Air Force pumping unit from there to Rye in Sussex. She then had a boiler clean in London before going to Harwich to attend on the troopships running between Harwich and Cuxhaven carrying the British Leave Army (B.L.A.). She undertook this work until January 1946 when she was relieved. The two remaining Watkins' tugs in Londonderry *Cervia* and *Fabia* also ended their duties in the Northern Ireland port; both were relieved on 5th December by the Admiralty tugs *Sparkler* and *Exploiter,* *Cervia* sailing the same day bound for Belfast arriving there on 9th December for refit.

In September Gaselee's *Musca* and *Vespa* returned to London after serving in Liverpool under the management of the Alexandra Towing Company. Gaselee also sold the *Betty* at this time to Holland and she left the Thames for the continent in tow of Watkins' *Kenia.*

Elliott's *Venturous* became surplus to requirements and was scrapped at T. Ward's yard at Grays. She had been built in Dublin in 1904 as the *Anna Liffey*, coming under Elliott's ownership in 1927.

During the war years many of the large number of tugs built for the Ministry were placed under the management of the Commercial tug companies. The following fifteen tugs were placed under the management of William Watkins Ltd. Three served in Iceland, the *Empire Piper, Empire Betsy* and the *Empire Wold*. Coastal tugs were *Empire Humphrey, Empire Martha, Empire Stella, Empire Spruce, Lynch, Foremost 22* and *Fairplay I*. Ocean tugs were *Empire John, Empire Winnie, Empire Susan* and *Empire Jean*. The *Assidious* on Atlantic convoy tug, she was also at the D-Day landings along with the *Empire Humphrey, Empire Winnie* and the *Empire Susan*.

Kenia.

# 1946

With the return of peace, the tug companies commenced a programme of replacement for the losses sustained during the six years of conflict. W.H.J. Alexander Ltd. purchased two standard design Empire tugs on the stocks at Alexander Hall & Co.'s yard at Aberdeen and these were completed as *Sun XVI* and *Sun XVII*. Prior to purchase, the former had been allocated the name

Sun XVII.

*Empire Leonard* and the latter *Empire Margaret*. These two tugs were the largest in the Sun fleet, being of 233 tons gross with a length of 105.2 feet B.P. and they had a triple expansion engine of 1000 i.h.p. taking its steam from an oil-fired boiler.

   William Watkins sold two tugs during the year, the first being *Cervia* which was still under refit at Belfast and was sold on 24th May to Ridley Tugs of

Newcastle and renamed *Monty*. The second was *Fabia* which had a tow from Birkenhead to Southampton and upon arrival was sold to Hemsley Bell & Co. of Southampton without change of name. She was then employed towing bunker barges in and around the port of Southampton until the following year when she was sold to the Liverpool Screw Towing Co. who renamed her *Moor Cock*. During 1946 the name of *Persia* was changed by Watkins to *Muria*.

Watkins received two tugs as war loss replacements these being *Empire Raymond* and *Empire Jester*. The former, built by Alexander Hall & Co. at Aberdeen in 1946, was identical to the *Sun XVI* and *Sun XVII*. She was renamed *Cervia* in December. The other acquisition, *Empire Jester*, and been built by Goole Shipbuilding and Repairing Co. Ltd. at Goole in 1943. She was slightly larger than *Cervia* and was fitted with a coal-fired boiler feeding a triple expansion engine of 1200 i.h.p. Watkins renamed her *Napia*.

The company returned to ocean towing in December 1946 when they purchased *Empire Winnie* and *Empire Susan* from the Ministry of (War) Transport and took *Empire John* on a long-term charter. All three tugs had previously been managed by Watkins during the war. *Empire Winnie* and *Empire John* were of identical design, built by Clelands (Successors) Ltd., Willington Quay-on-Tyne and were flush decked with a gross tonnage of 479. *Empire John* had been completed in 1943 and *Empire Winnie* in 1944, the latter becoming *Zealandia* under Watkins's ownership. *Empire Susan* had also been completed at Clelands yard in 1944 but she had a raised forecastle giving her a gross tonnage of 592. On her sale to Watkins she was renamed *Rumania*. All three tugs had triple expansion engines and were oil-fired.

Gaselee & Sons Ltd. acquired three tugs during the year. The new building *Fossa* was completed by Cochrane & Sons Ltd. at Selby, had a gross tonnage of 66 and was powered by a six-cylinder British Polar engine developing 450 b.h.p. The other two tugs were acquired secondhand, the first of them being *Evelyn Broadstone* which was purchased from Blackfriars Lighterage and renamed *Vespa*. She had been completed in 1934 by Alexander Hall & Co. at Aberdeen and was powered by a six-cylinder British Polar diesel engine of 500 b.h.p. The other tug purchased during the year was the *Servis* which was bought from Phillip Mills and was renamed *Naja*. With these three additional diesel tugs in the fleet the steam powered *Vespa* became surplus to requirements and was sold to Harrison (London) Ltd. and renamed *Markrock*. *Tayra* was sent to Lowestoft where she was converted to diesel power, her steam engine being replaced with a five-cylinder British Polar engine developing 750 b.h.p.

On 1st January *Empire Stella*, which was owned by the Ministry of Transport and managed by William Watkins Ltd., was inward bound from Weymouth to Gravesend with two barges in tow. When off the Knock John Buoy she suffered a serious boiler explosion with the result that four crew members were killed, two reported missing and others including her master, Captain Woolnough, were injured. She was towed into Sheerness by a naval vessel and her barges which had broken adrift at the time of the explosion were rounded up. The *Empire Susan* left Gravesend with her in tow on 17th February for the River Humber, later being sold to The United Towing Co., Hull and renamed *Serviceman*.

Also during January the training ship *Worcester* was towed by tugs of William Watkins Ltd. from the East India Dock to her permanent mooring at Greenhithe where she joined the *Cutty Sark*, which had been there since 1938. *Worcester* had been built by Vickers at Barrow in 1905 as the *Exmouth* for the London County Council and during World War II had been towed to Scapa Flow and used as a base by a minesweeping flotilla.

On 28th January with trade beginning to return to normal *Sun XII* docked the *Jamaica Producer* in the Royal Docks. The arrival was significant because *Jamaica Producer* was loaded with the first shipment of bananas to arrive in the capital after the war.

On the 14th July *Racia* went to the assistance of *Samuel Very* which was disabled in the vicinity of the Rough Tower, 8 miles east of Harwich, with a broken cylinder cover. The *Samuel Very* was successfully towed to London and berthed on West Woolwich Ship Tier.

During 1946 Watkins' *Gondia*, *Kenia* and *Java* were engaged in coastal towage of some of the large quantity of vessels that had become surplus to requirements at the end of hostilities. Various ships and landing craft were towed from south coast ports to the continent and on occasion vessels were towed from the builders yard straight to the scrap yard.

*Java* carried out various tows between Kings Lynn, Southampton and the Continent during the year and on 11th September she received orders to proceed from Gravesend to Southampton via Ramsgate and then to Flushing. The crew refused to sail, saying that they considered the forty-one-year- old ship to be unseaworthy in her present condition. She was sailed by her master to Ramsgate for survey, with shore staff serving as a crew and on 1st October she was passed by Lloyds as being seaworthy and a new crew joined, the old crew being sacked. This brought an unpleasant incident to a close. After leaving Ramsgate on 2nd October *Java* towed on the *Fort Vermillion* which was ashore on the Goodwin Sands. Salvage operations lasted until 5th October when five tugs succeeded in refloating her; *Java* was waiting her turn to make fast to the ship when she refloated. Two days later *Java* made an unsuccessful attempt in company with the tugs *Dapper* and *Lady Duncannon* to refloat the fore half of the *Helena Modjeska* which had also grounded on the Goodwin Sands but broke her back before she could be refloated. *Java* rounded off the year by refloating Harrison's tug *Markrock* (ex *Vespa*) on 27th December from a position two miles up Holeshaven Creek behind the Mobil oil refinery. I should think that not many of the ship towing tugs had every been that far up the creek before. London's rubbish was taken up there in barges by tugs of Flower & Everett and later by William Cory & Son to be dumped on the Pitsea marshes until 1985 when the service was containerised. *Java* towed on the *Markrock* for two hours, refloating her on the high water and then towed her to Tilbury Dock Basin.

*Empire Susan*, which as mentioned previously William Watkins were in the process of buying, sailed from Southampton in March bound for Port of Spain, Trinidad, under the command of Captain Harry Griffiths, D.S.C., D.S.M. Bunkering in Las Palmas, she arrived after 22 days in Port of Spain from where she was to tow a liberty ship belonging to the South American Saint Line to London. Her crew believed the ship to be light but on inspection found it to be fully laden with sugar. She had been lying in Port of Spain for some months and consequently her hull was covered in marine growth. *Empire Susan* eventually sailed from Trinidad with the ship in tow and for the next 10 days averaged 100 miles a day. She then encountered severe gales and progress was reduced to 78 miles in the ensuing 5 days. On the 26th day out from Trinidad, when about 150 miles from Las Palmas, she again encountered gales and was hove to for 3 days, eventually arriving at Las Palmas after 31 days at sea with only ten tons of fuel left in her bunkers. After taking on bunkers and stores, the crew spent the next 3 days scraping the marine growth off to reduce the drag. On leaving Las Palmas *Empire Susan* encountered bad weather again all the way to the Thames, taking 29 days to Southend. Assisted by river tugs she then berthed the ship on Charlton Buoys.

*Empire Susan* was to have had modifications and a major refit at this time but Watkins secured a contract for her to tow two L.S.T.'s from Appledore in North Devon to Rio de Janeiro in Brazil. After storing, she left Gravesend and ran to Appledore, on arrival finding the Smit tug *Witte Zee* already there preparing an identical tow.

Whereas *Empire Susan* would have to refuel *en route*, *Witte Zee*, being diesel driven, was able to make the voyage non-stop to Rio.

Both tugs left Appledore together on 21st September and *Empire Susan* gradually pulled away from *Witte Zee* losing sight of her off Ushant. However, she then ran into bad weather in the Bay of Biscay and one of her L.S.T.'s broke adrift. It was soon reconnected and the tug arrived in Las Palmas after 18 days for bunkers and stores. After sailing from Las Palmas the tows streamed and the master was concerned that they were shearing as they had towed straight on the first leg of the voyage. A boat was lowered and on inspection it was found that the propellers had been removed by cutting through the shafts whilst they had been lying at Las Palmas. *Witte Zee* had by now overtaken the *Empire Susan* but after a week of towing in excellent conditions *Empire Susan* caught up with her and after passing her proceeded to the Cape Verde Islands for bunkers. Three days out from the islands, she once again came upon the *Witte Zee* and lowered her boat and passed over fresh fruit and beer to the Dutchmen. She eventually delivered her tows at Rio de Janeiro on 3rd November, 22 days after leaving the Cape Verde Islands. *Witte Zee* arrived non-stop from England 24 hours later.

From Rio de Janeiro *Empire Susan* was sent to Freetown in West Africa to tow home the tanker *British Mariner* 6,996 gross tons which had been lying there since being torpedoed on 20th October 1941 in position 07°43′N 14°20′W. The master of the tug insisted on certain repairs being carried out as the tanker was in a poor condition. The crew rigged steam hoses to enable the steering gear and ballast pump to be put into working order so that the rudder could be centred and the tanker trimmed by the stern. They worked 12 to 14 hours a day for a week in temperatures approaching 100 degrees fahrenheit to get the tow seaworthy. The patch over the torpedo hole foreward was strengthened with timber and anything else suitable that came to hand.

*Empire Susan* left Freetown on 21st November towing the tanker stern first and averaged about 4 knots but the tanker sheared very badly from side to side and after approximately 7 days the master of the tug decided to put into Lagos for further repairs. When entering the port, however, the tow struck the Palm Line ship *Matadian* and started to make water. The *Empire Susan* beached the tow on the nearest sandbank and on arrival at Lagos was detained by the Port Authorities until the insurance claims had been cleared. From Lagos the tug was ordered to proceed to the Azores and whilst *en route* went to the assistance of the French tug *Abeille 10* which was experiencing boiler trouble during a voyage to Marseilles with a dredger in tow. The *Empire Susan* towed both ships safely to Funchal, Madeira and then ran light to St Michael Island in the Azores. From the Azores she towed a lifting lighter to Birkenhead, a voyage of 14 days in very bad weather arriving 12th January 1947.

Tragedy struck the Gravesend tug community during December when the *Security, Contest* and *Watercock* were engaged in towing the Anglo-Saxon tanker *Kelletia* 7,434/29 from Falmouth to the River Tyne. Heavy weather was encountered in the Channel and when in position 12 miles from Anvil Point off the Dorset coast the *Security* foundered without warning late on Sunday 8th December. The *Contest* and *Watercock* slipped their tow-ropes to search for survivors and the *Watercock* under the command of Captain A. Couves, rescued five survivors from the water under very difficult conditions, landing them at Portland. A destroyer and a lifeboat joined the search but the remaining four crew members were lost including her master Captain A. Pattison and his son who was the deckhand. *Security* had been built in 1904 as the *Kingfisher* and acquired by the Royal Navy 22nd March 1906 and renamed *Diligence*. The Admiralty fitted her with a raised forecastle and renamed her *Security* in 1914 when she was stationed at Sheerness in order to avoid confusion with the naval paddle tug *Diligent*. Elliott's acquired her in February 1927 and was used extensively on their brick run from Antwerp to London before the war. The *Kelletia* was towed into Southampton and from there was towed to the Tyne by United Towing's *Merchantman* and *Tradesman*.

The Port of London Authority acquired the *Empire Percy* from the Ministry of Shipping and renamed her *Thorny* the following year, built by Richard Dunston on the Humber in 1943 and powered by a 525 i.h.p. triple expansion engine. On completion she was placed under the management of Steel & Bennie Ltd., Glasgow. When purchased by the P.L.A. she was placed in the dredging department, but on rare occasions she was used ship towing.

Muria.

# 1947

Rumania.

The *Empire Susan*'s next tow was L.C.T. 7047 from Birkenhead to Flushing Roads, going on to Grimsby to be refitted, her name being changed to *Rumania* at this time. During her refit *Rumania* ex *Empire Susan*, was fitted with a mizzen mast and a new funnel and also given a new motor lifeboat. On completion of the refit she ran to Gravesend and stored for a long trip, for her next job was to tow two former naval sloops the *Tuck shing* (ex H.M.S. *Kittiwake*) and the *Tuck Loong* (ex H.M.S. *Sheldrake*) from Southampton to Shanghai. Both ships, which had been purchased by the San Peh Steam Navigation Co. Ltd., Shanghai, had been lying at Harwich and were towed from there (*Tuck Loong* by *Gondia* and *Tuck Shing* by *Kenia*) to Southampton where they were handed over to the ocean tugs.

As it was the winter season in the Bay of Biscay *Zealandia*, which was bound light to the Mediterranean, towed *Tuck Shing* to Algiers handing her over there to *Rumania*. *Rumania* herself sailed on 29th January and averaged 9 knots with tow before running into gales in the Bay of Biscay which lasted until she was abeam of Lisbon. She arrived in Algiers 12 days after leaving Southampton. After taking on bunkers and rigging both tows the *Rumania* was assisted out of Algiers by the *Zealandia* and then set course for Port Said. Her average towing speed was 5.3 knots on 10 tons of fuel per day. *Rumania* entered the Suez Canal on 4th March at 05.00 towing the sloops through one at a time leaving the first at Port Tewfik and returning to Port Said for the second one. She reconnected the two sloops at Port Tewfik and then set course for Aden in extremely hot calm weather arriving in Aden after 12 days steaming.

Whilst bunkering at Aden *Rumania* received a Mayday call from a French ship that had lost its propeller about 200 miles west of Aden. *Rumania* was the only tug in the area since the salvage tug normally stationed at Aden was in drydock and the nearest other tug was a thousand miles away. The French ship agreed a Lloyd's Open Form over the radio with the *Rumania* but on arrival the ship's master stated that he was waiting for a ship of his own company to take him in tow and that he would only accept assistance from *Rumania* at normal towing rates. With the tidal currents prevailing at the time it was estimated that the casualty would ground on Socotra Island in 30 hours but this other ship was over 60 hours away. *Rumania* then departed after first asking the master if he was happy with his position. After a couple of hours he recalled the *Rumania*, signed Lloyd's Open Form and was towed into Aden.

The tug with her two former naval craft in tow then left for Colombo in excellent weather arriving there after 23 days. From Colombo she proceeded to Singapore, taking 21 days and remained in the port for a week rectifying an engine defect. *Rumania* then left Singapore on the last leg of her voyage to Shanghai and when approximately 60 miles from the Yellow River received a typhoon warning from the Blue Funnel Liner *Eurymedon*, 7314/43. *Rumania* was struck by the typhoon as she shortened her tow and steamed head to wind in the very fierce conditions for about twelve hours. The typhoon abated the following day and the *Rumania* steamed up river to Shanghai at the beginning of May and handed the two former sloops over to their new owners. She sailed from Shanghai on 8th May and ran to Formosa (Taiwan) and from there towed a Blue Funnel Liner to Hong Kong taking approximately 10 days. From there she ran to Singapore for a boiler clean and repairs and then received orders to run to Sydney, Australia, 4,700 miles away. When off Java she developed engine trouble and put into Surabaya, carrying out repairs that lasted 3 days. Then, 4 days out from Surabaya *Rumania* sighted Cape York the northern tip of Australia and sailed down inside the Great Barrier Reef for about 1,000 miles. She left the reef around Brisbane and encountered bad weather on the run from there to Sydney from where she was to tow the interstate liner *Canberra* 7710/13, to Genoa, Italy following the latter's sale to Greek buyers for service as an emigrant ship.

Whilst in Sydney 200 tons of fuel was put into 40 gallon drums and loaded aboard the *Canberra*. A special trough was made to hang over the ship's side with four hoses from it to reach the *Rumania*'s bunkers enabling her to refuel *en route*. After three weeks in Sydney the tow was ready and *Rumania* sailed at 09.00 on 8th September. The *Canberra* was manned by an Australian run-crew of 28 men who were to provide steam for winches, steering and lights. They would stay with the ship until it reached Singapore where the Greek owners would take over. A banner reading 'FAREWELL CANBERRA' was hanging on Sydney Harbour Bridge when she passed under it. An average speed of $6^1/2$ knots on 10 tons of fuel a day was obtained on the run up the Australian coast. *Rumania* steered a course back up through the Great Barrier reef and when off Cape York, 20 days out from Sydney, she shortened tow and lashed alongside the *Canberra* to refuel. The trough was rigged over the ship's side, the drums being lifted from the hold three at a time for tipping. At midday with the sun at its hottest and the temperature around the 100 degrees mark the Australians refused to carry on without a four hour break until it was cooler. The *Rumania*'s crew were ordered aboard by the master and they carried on bunkering, the master operating the winch himself. At sundown the Australians took over again. On the second morning a joint on the *Rumania*'s main steam pipe started to blow and a complete shutdown was necessary to repair it. It was decided to make for Thursday Island to anchor, conditions being very unpleasant down below during the tow. Repairs were carried out, fresh water and the remains of the bunkers taken from the *Canberra*, and the *Rumania* then set a course for Singapore arriving 22 October 47 days after leaving Sydney. The Australian run-crew left the ship there and were replaced by seven Greek runners. *Rumania* then sailed for Colombo, taking 28 days and then on to Aden where she arrived after a further 21 days. The Port Authorities would not allow *Canberra* to enter Aden without steam so the Danish salvage tug stationed there was engaged to hold the ship outside the port while the *Rumania* bunkered and stored. From Aden she encountered bad weather all the way up the Red Sea with the tow broad off on the port side most of the time. Since leaving Singapore there had not been any steam for steering on the ship and she had been sheering ever since then. It took 18 days to cover the 1300 miles to Suez where they arrived on 23rd December. Passage was made through the Canal on Christmas Eve and the next 3 days were spent at Port Said. *Rumania* arrived in Genoa 12 days later to complete the final leg of the four month tow and met up with the *Empire John* which was already in port.

After *Zealandia* had passed over the former H.M.S. *Sheldrake* to the *Rumania* in Algiers in February, she ran light to Ceuta in Morocco and then towed a Liberty ship to Naples. On completion she returned to Gibraltar and towed a further Liberty ship to Genoa. The *Zealandia* then ran to Lisbon and towed a vessel referred to as 'HITLER'S YACHT' to Genoa. She then returned to the U.K. and had a refit at Falmouth after which she was engaged in coastal towing for a time.

Early in the year *Empire John* had taken a dredger in a tow from Plymouth bound for Piraeus but when off Vigo the dredger capsized and sank. The *Empire John* then returned to Gravesend.

During May the tanker *Newhall Hills* 10441/44 broke in two at the foreside of the bridge following a collision off the South Goodwin Sands in the English Channel. The bow section sank but the *Gondia* and *Kenia* took the stern section in tow and brought it into Sheerness during 24–25th May. It was later towed to Tilbury dock and on 30th September it left Gravesend swing buoy in tow of the *Empire John, Kenia* and *Cervia* for Southampton where it was laid up pending sale.

On 7th August *Ferriby* 5573/28, loaded with pulp, caught fire while moored at Swanscombe Tier. The fire was successfully extinguished by the *Racia, Vincia, New Stormcock, Sun V, Sun XI* and Esso's tug *Crown Diamond*.

Also in August the *Kenia* towed from the River Fal to Antwerp half of a tanker that had broken in two in the Bay of Biscay.

The stern half of the *Helena Modjeska* was refloated from the Goodwin Sands and the *Sun X* and *Sun XVI* brought her to the Thames.

Four tugs were sold during the year. Watkins sold the three 'Teddy Bears' the *Doria, Vincia* and *Badia* for further trading. (The reason why these three tugs had the nickname 'Teddy Bears' I have never been able to establish.) All three had been built in 1909 by Philip and Son Ltd., Dartmouth, were each of 150 tons gross and had an indicated horsepower of 500. The first to go was the *Badia* sold on 2nd October to the Fowey Tug Co. Ltd. and renamed the *Penleath*. As an experiment she had been fitted with a Kort nozzle a few years previously but the experiment had not been very successful. The *Doria* and *Vincia* were both sold to Societa Rimorchiatoria Riunity and were renamed *Eolo* and *Euro*. Both ships left Ramsgate on 29th November in the tow of the *Empire John* bound for Genoa. When crossing the Gulf of Lions the *Empire John* had problems with her fuel oil and hurricane force winds forced her to seek shelter in Puerto Selva on the French/Spanish border. The *Empire John* spent Christmas 1947 in Selva and was the first foreign ship to enter the port for 40 years. She arrived in Genoa on New Year's Day in 1948 and delivered the two tugs to their new owners.

*1947* — Doria & Vincent *leaving Ramsgate as* Euro & Eolo *bound Genoa in tow of* Empire John.

The fourth tug to be sold was W.H.J. Alexander's *Sunrise* which had developed boiler troubles and was sold to T.W. Ward for scrapping at Grays. Of 103 tons gross, she had been built at Southampton in 1899 by J.F. Fay & Co. Ltd. and was powered by a 450 i.h.p. engine. When *Sunrise* and her sister *Sunshine* were built they were the first to be given names incorporating the prefix SUN, a style followed by all succeeding tugs in this owner's fleet.

During November Alexander's *Sunbird*, of 64 tons gross, was sunk by the Ellerman Wilson Line's *Angelo* 2199/40 at the top of Limehouse Reach, rounding Cuckolds Point. The *Sunbird* was under the bow of *Angelo* taking her towrope when she came into contact with the bow which rolled her over. The Chief Engineer and Fireman were both drowned in this unfortunate accident. *Sunbird* was raised, refurbished and returned to work.

The ill-fated four masted barque *Pamir* 2,796/05 arrived in London during December under the Finnish flag and owned by Captain Gustauf Erikson. On the 23rd the *Kenia* towed her to her berth in the Victoria Dock from Gravesend lower swing buoy. Nobody could foresee on that December day she would be lost ten years later. She became a training ship back under the German flag in 1951 and while homeward bound from the Argentine loaded with 4,000 tons of grain she encountered a hurricane on 21st September 1957 and sank.

Ocean Towage & Salvage Ltd (Cock Tugs) salvage ship *King Lear* was engaged in the Mediterranean early in the year on salvage operations of the numerous wrecks that had littered Tobruk Harbour since the end of the war.

# 1948

The *Rumania* and *Empire John* had both completed their tows at Genoa in January and were then chartered by the British Government to tow barges to ports in East Africa from Suez, for use in conjunction with the groundnut scheme that was being implemented at the time. Both tugs left Genoa together for Port Said and on arrival the *Rumania* first towed a naval pontoon to Haifa. The *Empire John* was to tow four large barges from Port Said to Lindi in Tanganyika (now Tanzania) and she left with two in tow. The *Rumania* sailed from Suez on 1st February towing L.C.T. 1199 and L.C.T.556 for Dar-es-Salaam a distance of 3,500 miles, arriving in Aden after 10 days for bunkers and stores, but was unable to get all that was required owing to riots and strikes taking place in the port. Food and water had to be rationed for the next 14 days until reaching Dar-es-Salaam. After sailing, *Rumania* ran to Aden taking 10 days and while bunkering received a Mayday call from the T.2. tanker *Gladys Moller* 10,712 gross tons with a complete engine failure in position 16°00′N. 52°36′E. and drifting 16 miles daily. The *Rumania* left Aden on 8th March, for the ship a run of about 500 miles, but with the amount of growth on her hull could only make 11 knots. The other nearest tug was 1,000 miles away and making 14 knots for the ship. The *Rumania* arrived at the ship first two days later, the ship having now grounded on the coast of Yemen in position 14°48′N. 52°50′E. The towing gear was run away in the life-boat and started towing at midnight. The *Gladys Moller* refloated at 04.00 on 11th March and was towed to Aden at an average speed of 4 knots, arriving on 15th March.

After the *Empire John* had delivered her barges at Lindi and was returning to the Suez Canal she went to the assistance of the Italian tanker *Olterra* 4,995 gross tons anchored at Port Taufiq on 14th March. The *Olterra* loaded with

8,000 tons of crude oil had been in collision with another Italian ship, holed amidships, set on fire and abandoned by her crew. The *Empire John*'s crew successfully fought the blaze and when extinguished shifted the ships anchorage to Green Island, four miles away. All shipping had been stopped in the canal, but with the danger of an explosion now over, was able to resume normally. The *Empire John* then set sail with *L.C.T. 7021* and *L.C.T. 536* on 16th March for Lindi passing the *Rumania* in the Red Sea.

On arrival at Suez the *Rumania* was informed that this would be her last trip as the *Zealandia* was leaving the Thames with two barges and would tow the remaining two L.C.T.'s to Mombasa. The *Rumania* sailed in record time on 26th March with *L.C.T. 7027* and *L.C.T. 601* and the 60' tug *Witch* in tow for Mombasa. While towing down the East African coast it was observed that the *Witch* was making water. A boat was launched and it was found that the water was entering fast via her tail-end, but with all the entrances welded up it was impossible to save her, and she sank. On arrival at Mombasa she towed one L.C.T. on to Dar-es-Salaam. She then escorted a coaster south towards Durban. After three days the coaster released her and she returned to Aden. On arrival the *Rumania* was informed that the *Gladys Moller* was having trouble with her repairs and might require towing to the U.K. After a few days the ship left on trials and stated if all O.K. would carry on to Suez. After 36 hours the ship was out of sight over the horizon. The *Rumania* carried on to Suez, encountering a dust storm while in the Red Sea forcing her to batten right down; the temperature in the stokehold rose to 132°F. during this period. The *Rumania* had taken maximum bunkers in Aden and on arrival at Suez only water was needed to be taken and two Greek firemen paid off. She then passed through the canal not stopping at Port Said and on leaving the harbour passed the *Zealandia* arriving from the Thames. The growth on the *Rumania*'s hull was so bad that she only averaged 8 knots on the run to Grimsby. She arrived on 19 July, 19 months after leaving and had steamed 47,000 miles of which 38,000 was towing. One of her tow-ropes, 120 fathom of 16" manila, which had been used on all the tows, was taken away by British Ropes for their exhibition room.

The *Empire John*'s next job was to run to Genoa, pick up a run crew and return to Port Said to tow a liberty ship to Venice. This ship had broken its back and was strapped together in the middle. While on passage a storm blew up and the ship broke in half again. The *Empire John* slipped her tow-rope and rescued the run crew from a lifeboat. She then reconnected to her towing wire foreward and towed the bow section to Taranto. The stern section of the ship grounded later on the North African coast. After leaving Taranto the *Empire John* returned to Grimsby via Algiers light tug.

The *Rumania* had a refit at Grimsby and sailed on 19th August for Gravesend. She then ran to Portsmouth to tow the oil survey research ship *Jesoura*, 508 gross tons belonging to Petroleum Development (Qatar) Ltd. She had been built as a L.C.T. in 1943 and converted in 1948 into a survey ship. She sailed in September taking 28 days to Port Said, 2 days through the canal, spending the night at Ismalia. From Suez 11 days to Aden and a further 9 days to Bahrain and delivered her tow. She then ran to Muscat and anchored for 16 days awaiting orders.

The *Rumania* then ran to Karachi and towed a British India Line ship to Bombay in 9 days. She then ran light to Suez through the canal to Port Said and while awaiting orders went to the assistance of a Greek ship sinking off Sicily in a gale. The *Rumania* lost her starboard lifeboat and vents off the foredeck while making for the ship in the heavy seas. The *Rumania* connected with the ship and delivered her safely to Naples. She then ran to Samos Island in the Aegean Sea and towed a Norwegian ship to Carthagena, Spain taking 21 days. She then ran to Malta and when passing Panterleria Island in the Sicilian Channel went to the assistance of the *Fort Patreux* ashore there, but was not required. It was now February 1949 and her next tow, was the crane barge *Italico* from Malta to Genoa. The tug parted from the barge during a SW gale in the Sicilian Channel on 2nd March and the *Italico* suffered contact damage by the tug while attempting to reconnect. *Rumania* then returned to Malta and was chartered by the Port Admiral as a rescue tug, the naval tugs being in fleet manoeuvres. She then towed a L.S.T. to Famagusta, Cyprus and then ran to Aden and took over the tow of the L.S.T. *Searcher* on 24th April from the naval tug *Assiduous*. The *Searcher* had been towed from Ceylon (Sri Lanka) and the *Rumania* was to tow her on to Milford Haven. When in the Red Sea one of the crew fell ill with peritonitis; fortunately the *Clan Cummings* was in the vicinity with a doctor on board. The man was transferred to the ship, treated by the doctor prior to being landed and operated on in hospital. The *Rumania* left Port Said for Algiers for bunkers and spent two days adrift with an engine defect. From Algiers she delivered her tow at Milford Haven and then ran light to Grimsby and paid off, it being June 1949 by this time.

In January 1948 the *Pioneer Cove* 8,266 tons belonging to United States Lines, struck a mine off the Dutch coast and suffered damage. Tugs from Gravesend ran to the outer estuary to meet the ship and escorted her safely to London.

*Elder Dempster*, Freetown 5,853 gross tons, grounded in Northfleet Hope on 31st January and was successfully refloated by the *Cervia*, *Napia*, *Kenia*, *Tanga*, *Contest* and the *Sun XVII*. On 1st February while proceeding up river to berth in the Royal Albert Dock she collided with the *Corcrest* 2,373 gross tons at Erith. The *Kenia* assisted in pumping out the *Corcrest* and holding her on shore with the *Arcadia* and *Sun V*.

The four masted barque *Pamir* sailed from London on 30th April. The *Kenia* towed her from the Shadwell Basin, London Dock and handed her over to the *Zealandia* at the Chapman buoy, Sea Reach for towage out of the estuary.

Work on removing the wreck of the Shell tanker *Lunula* from No 4 Jetty Thames Haven, went on during the year. She had struck a mine while berthing in April 1941 causing the loss of the *Persia* by fire. The fore-end of the ship was cut off during July and towed to Ward's for scrap. During November the *Kenia* was working on the stern of the wreck, and on 3rd December towed the remains to the Mucking Flats where it was beached and broken up.

In November, Gamecock Towing Company sold the *Newstorm Cock* to William Croswaite of Middlesbrough going to the River Tees under the name *Kings Cross*. She had been built in 1921 by Danziger Werft at Danzig Germany having a gross tonnage of 197 and powered by a 600 i.h.p. triple expansion engine. Gamecock bought her in April 1922 after having been laid up on Rainham Buoys for a time. In the ownership of William Crosthwaite she was first employed towing new barges to the Thames for about two years.

# 1949

Gamecock sold their salvage vessel *King Lear* in 1949 to Locus Matsas & Sons of Pireaus, Greece, being renamed *Marigo Matsas*. The *King Lear* had been built in 1906 by Earles Company Ltd., at Hull; she had a gross tonnage of 290 and a length of 148.4 feet.

The other change was the acquisition by W.H.J. Alexander Ltd., of the *William Ryan* from W.R.Cunis and renamed *Sunrise*. She was a tug of 102 gross tons, 83′6″ in length built by Alexander Hall & Co. Ltd., Aberdeen in 1928. She had a coal-fired boiler driving a triple expansion engine developing 550 i.h.p. This small class of tugs was used extensively on Alexander's work in the Upper Pool and the up river docks. When Sun Tugs acquired her she had just been towed back to the Thames after a spell on charter to the Tees Towing Co. Ltd., Middlesbrough.

The *Rumania* signed on at Grimsby on 15th July, and then ran to Gravesend. She then towed the four masted barque *Viking* 2,670 tons to Antwerp, then light tug to Amsterdam and took in tow two hoppers bound for Piraeus, Greece, taking 19 days. *Rumania* then ran to Port Said and developed serious boiler trouble *en route*. She ran through the Suez Canal to Port Taufig, to wait for sixty boiler tubes to be sent out from the United Kingdom. It was 9 weeks before repairs were completed and she was ready for sea. *Rumania* then ran down the Red Sea to meet three naval tugs towing a floating dry dock and to assist in towing it to Malta taking 14 days. On completion the *Rumania* left Malta to return light tug to England, but was diverted to Gibraltar to await orders. After 10 days she returned to Malta to tow a L.S.T. to Milford Haven.

It took the *Rumania* 9 days to reach Algiers and a further 21 to Milford Haven. She was hove to abreast of Oporto for 4 days in extremely foul weather.

On delivery of the tow, the *Rumania* ran to Gravesend and from there towed the *Lady Enchantress* 1,474 tons to Dartmouth. The vessel was delivered at Dartmouth 6 days later after the *Rumania* had sheltered behind the Isle of Wight owing to the tow making water. She then ran to Falmouth on salvage station, answering two distress calls, but was outclassed by the *Turmoil* and *Zwarte Zee*. After 12 days in Falmouth she ran light to Gravesend. Another small tow for her in November was the tug *Tid 110* from Dover to Liverpool.

The *Zealandia* sailed from Dover with an ex-German E-boat in tow, delivering her at Genoa, Italy. While in the Mediterranean she received orders to proceed to the assistance of the American ship *Beaver Victory* ashore on Jabal Island in the southern end of the Red Sea. After 12 days steaming she arrived at the vessel but her services were refused by the ship. The *Beaver Victory* was later refloated during August by the Danish salvage tug *Protector* 1,050 h.p. belonging to Svitzers and towed to Aden. The *Zealandia* then went on to Aden for a boiler clean before returning to the Mediterranean.

The P.L.A. sold the *Darent* to J.H. Lamey Ltd., Liverpool, who renamed her *Alfred Lamey*. *Darent* had been built by Ferguson Bros., Port Glasgow in 1908. Although part of the dredging fleet, *Darent* had been used on occasions for ship towage in the docks.

# 1950

On 1st February Ship Towage (London) Ltd. came into being by the amalgamation of William Watkins Ltd., and the Elliott Steam Tug Co. At the same time the two companies took control of the Gamecock Towing Co. Of the three companies William Watkins Ltd. was the oldest dating back to 1833. The Elliott Steam Tug Co. was founded in 1860 by Capt. T.W. Elliott who later became associated with Mr Matthew J. Dick and Mr John Page who were shipbrokers in Cornhill; they later took over management of the Company. Gamecock Towing Co. was founded in 1880 by river pilots on a shares basis. At the time of the merger Watkins owned thirteen tugs and one on charter, Elliott's owned two and Gamecocks four, bringing a total fleet of twenty tugs under one management. All the tugs kept the three companies individual funnel colours until 1965 when the Ship Towage funnel colours were introduced.

Only one change took place in the fleets in 1950: the *Sirdar* belonging to the Port of London Authority was sold for scrap at Thomas Ward's yard at Grays on 1st February. She was a 1,000 i.h.p. twin crew tug of 143 gross tons and employed in the various enclosed docks. The *Sirdar* was completed in 1899 by R.H.Green Ltd. at Blackwall on the Thames for the London & India Docks Joint Committee being transferred to the P.L.A. on its formation in 1908.

Back on the sea towage front the *Rumania* and *Empire John* left Gravesend and ran to Arromanches on the Normandy coast. Watkins had secured a contract to tow sections of the dismantled Mulberry Harbour to Iceland. The *Rumania* took 28 days to deliver one section to Skagerstrond, the concrete block being covered in sea growth and was making water, making it a bad tow. The *Empire John* also had problems with her tow and was forced to return to Arromanches. Owing to the problems involved the two tugs were unable to keep up the schedule and the contract went to the Dutch tugs, Watkins' part being to tow the sections to Amsterdam where they were prepared for on towage to Iceland. The *Rumania* delivered seven safely taking 4 to 5 days to complete each tow. When towing up channel with the eight she ran into very bad weather off Boulogne and the Mulberry began to take water. When abreast of Cap Griz Nez the tow rope was chopped as the block sunk. The *Rumania* then ran to Dover and her master Capt. H. Griffiths informed the crew that Dover was to be their salvage station when not on normal towing work. While at Dover the *Rumania* answered many calls for assistance, the fully laden tanker *Francine Clore* 10,634 tons being one of them. She had suffered a complete engine failure abeam of Beachy Head in March and the *Rumania* towed the ship to Purfleet assisted by river tugs from North Foreland. When discharged *Rumania* and *Cervia* towed the *Francine Clore* to Rotterdam for repairs. Other salvage work included refloating the *Goldenia*, ashore on the Goodwin Sands; she also towed a French dredger to Calais after it broke adrift from its towing tug in heavy seas.

On the normal towing side, *Rumania* next ran to a position southwest of Brest in May and towed the Norwegian vessel *Songa* to Antwerp. From there she ran to Ghent and towed a tug to Liverpool, then light to Milford Haven and towed two corvettes to Hamburg. *Rumania* then proceeded to Antwerp and towed a ship to Hamburg, encountering bad weather and thick ice off the River Elbe, picking up eight survivors from a German coaster that had foundered. A salvage tug from Cuxhaven assisted her into the Elbe. On her return to the Thames the *Rumania*'s next job was to tow the *Black Swan* from the Royal docks to Newcastle. On her return down the east coast she put into the Humber and towed two trawlers from Hull to Ward's yard at Grays for scrap. *Rumania* returned to her Dover station for a while before running to Milford Haven to Tow four Corvettes to Hamburg. She was only allowed to tow one at a time owing to the time of year, a round trip taking about 10 days to complete. On one trip she sheared a rivet in number four fuel tank in severe ice conditions, forcing her to be dry docked in Hamburg for repairs. On completion she ran to Dover, her next job being to tow the B.I. liner *Kenya* to Falmouth with the *Cervia* in foul weather from the Clyde. *Rumania* then ran to Lisbon, and from there had two round trips to Sunderland with ships in tow. She then towed a vessel from Antwerp to London after which *Rumania* returned to Dover on salvage station, it being September 1950 by this time.

On 2nd June the *Tanga*, *Challenge*, and *Crested Cock* ran to Dunkirk to take part in the Tenth Anniversary of the evacuation of the B.E.F. from the beaches.

A march past was held in the town and members of the three tug crews took part representing the many tugman who were off the beaches in the dark days of 1940.

The *Napia* took in tow the Danish ship *Astoria* 4,454 tons with engine problems at the Varn in the Dover Straits on 30th October. The *Napia* towed the *Astoria* 'round the top' through the Skagerrak and the Kattegat to Copenhagen arriving on 5th November. The *Napia* returned to Gravesend via the Kiel Canal.

A concrete block was built at Red Lion Wharf on the site where the wartime forts were built at Northfleet for the Mobil Oil Company. On being launched it was towed to Tilbury Dock to be fitted out. On sailing in November the *Crested Cock* assisted in towage down the dock, handing over to the *Rumania, Napia, Cervia* and *Contest* for on towage down river to Mobil's refinery at Coryton. On arrival it was positioned to form the base of No. 3 jetty Coryton that was in the process of being built. This base has a water intake capable of supplying the refinery with 45 million gallons of cooling water a day.

The *Generton* 4,801 gross tons belonging to R.Chapman & Son, loaded with iron ore, grounded on the Girdler Sands in November. The *Rumania* was towing on her on the 27th, joined on the following day by the *Kenia, Challenge, Crested Cock* and *Cervia*, some of her cargo of iron ore being jettisoned overboard. On the 29th the *Kenia* ran both of the ship's anchors away and then lashed up alongside the *Generton* washing the sand away with her propeller. The Napia was also towing on her as well at the time. On the 30th the wind increased to gale force and with the combined efforts of the tugs the *Generton* was refloated.

The *Zealandia* ran to Leningrad, Russia in November and sailed with a tug the R4 in tow for Constanza, Rumania. The *Zealandia* put into Harwich for repairs to her condenser which was giving trouble. While crossing the Bay of Biscay the tug broke adrift and the *Zealandia* lost contact with it. She put into Ferrol and learnt that a Spanish fishing boat had towed the tug into Santander. On arrival the *Zealandia* was refused permission by the Spanish authorities to take the tug, a gunboat laying alongside to enforce the ruling. The *Zealandia* then ran to La Coruna and laid there over the New Year period.

*Rumania* signed on at Greenock on 5th December and sailed with a L.S.T. bound for Genoa. When in the Bay of Biscay the two parted company, it being 3 days before she was able to reconnect and put into St Nazaire for the bridle on the tow to be repaired in a shipyard. She left, St Nazaire after Christmas when repairs were completed.

The *Napia* was sent to Ramsgate where her boiler was converted to burn oil. She had a reputation as a hard boat to steam as a coal burner and her conversion to oil was welcomed by her fireman.

# 1951

Four new tugs were added to the fleets during 1951 and one deleted. W.H.J.Alexander Ltd. had the *Sun XVIII* built by Philip & Son Ltd., Dartmouth. She had been launched the previous year on 27th July, and completed in early 1951. The *Sun XVIII*, was the first diesel tug owned by Sun Tugs, having a gross tonnage of 105, her dimensions were 88'2" x 22'1" x 9'11", and powered by a seven-cylinder Ruston & Hornsby diesel engine of 750 i.h.p.

The *Rana* joined the fleet of Gaselee & Sons Ltd., having been built by Cochrane & Sons Ltd., Selby. She was 98 gross tons and powered by a five-cylinder British Polar diesel engine developing 750 b.h.p. She was one of Gaselee's larger tugs, her dimensions being 80'3" x 21'6" x 8'6", built with their shipping contracts in mind but still being small enough to be an ideal craft tug. Gaselee also re-engined the *Naja*, removing her old four-cylinder Bolinder and replacing it with a four-cylinder Crossley diesel of 300 b.h.p.

The *Empire John* was returned to the Ministry of Shipping at the end of her charter to William Watkins Ltd. The Ministry then sold her to the Dominian Coal Company of Montreal, Canada. She served her new owners without change of name or her British registry.

The Port of London Authority had placed an order with Henry Scarr Ltd. for four twin screw diesel powered dock tugs. Two being completed in 1951, the *Plagal* and *Plangent*, were placed in the Royal Group of Docks. They were 92'10" x 24'2" of 159 gross tons and powered by two four-cylinder Crossley diesel engines developing 1,200 b.h.p.

The *Rumania* had sailed from St Nazaire with the bridle of her tow repaired at the end of December 1950. All went well until 10th January, 1951 when off Cape St Vincent the tow parted again, the crew reconnecting the following day.

The *Rumania* then received orders to proceed to Lisbon, where she would hand over the L.S.T. to the *Zealandia* who had run down from La Coruna to complete the tow to Genoa. The tow broke adrift once more on the 13th, but was re-connected in two hours, the *Rumania* arriving in Lisbon the following day. Six new ferries were being built in New Orleans, U.S.A. and the *Rumania* was to proceed there and tow them, two at a time, to Rio De Janeiro, Brazil. She sailed from Lisbon on 17th January, for Las Palmas, from there averaging 10.8 knots on the run to Trinidad where she bunkered, then on to New Orleans arriving on 13th February. The *Rumania* sailed on 16th February on the first of the three 5,200 mile tows, her fasted run being seven weeks and one day. She averaged 6.5 knots with the ferries, arriving at Trinidad on 7th March for bunkers. She put into Recife (Pernambuco) on the 29th after running short of food and water. *Rumania* had boiler trouble for 2 days on the final leg of the tow, delivering the first two ferries at Rio on 8th April. She sailed on the 10th taking 13 days to Trinidad where she had a boiler clean. She left Trinidad on 30th April with a stowaway being found aboard the next day and arrived at New Orleans on 9th May. *Rumania* sailed with the next two ferries on 16th May, via Trinidad, all going well until one ferry broke adrift on 26th June, being re-connected in four hours.

She then called at Recife from 1st-4th July, then on to Rio-de-Janeiro, arriving on 13th July, delivering the third and fourth ferries. She sailed the next day going via Trinidad arriving in New Orleans on 7th August. *Rumania* left with the final two ferries the *Maracanan* and *Lacoa* each 136′ x 32′6″ x 10′8″ on the 11th and while towing across the Gulf of Mexico a hurricane warning was received on the 15th. By towing hard the *Rumania* was able to get out of the path of the hurricane with its 130 m.p.h. winds, passing her by a few miles distant on 18th August. She was disabled with boiler problems in the Caribbean Sea on 28th August, it being 3 days before she was under way again and making for Trinidad arriving on 2nd September. The *Rumania* spent the next 11 days having her boiler cleaned, before setting off down the South American coast. Once more she was plagued with boiler trouble and made for Fortaleza arriving on 29th September. From there she went on to Recife spending 10 days in the port, sailing on 17th October for Rio. One of the ferries broke adrift on this stretch but was rounded up again in 6 hours. The *Rumania* arrived in Rio de Janeiro on 25th October and completed the safe delivery of all six ferries to their owners. Her next job was to tow an old hopper from Rio to Recife, sailing on 2nd November. The tow had been laid up for 15 years and proved to be in poor condition, as she took water and sank on 8th November. The *Rumania* then proceeded to Recife arriving on the 10th sailing again on 14th November, bound for the Cape Verde Islands to stand by a Portuguese ship that was to be towed to Lisbon.

The *Zealandia* delivered the L.S.T. she had taken over from the *Rumania* in Lisbon in January at Genoa. She then remained in the Mediterranean for most of the year and the following were some of the tows she undertook: a Schooner from near Algiers to Malta, the hulk of a Naval Cruiser from La Spezia, Italy to Cartagena, Spain and another hulk from Piraeus.

Back on the Thames the *Napia* towed two redundant coal hulks belonging to William Cory from Erith to the Continent, the first going to Terneuzen in the spring handing over to two small Dutch tugs who took it on to Ghent. During the summer she took the second hulk, this one going to Bolougne.

The *Sun XVIII*, towed the *Cutty Sark* to Millwall dry dock in March. She was no longer required at Greenhithe as a training ship since the acquisition of the new larger *Worcester*, and plans were under way to have her put on permanent display. The London County Council provided the capital for her to be dry docked and surveyed and generally smartened up, so she could be moored off Greenwich for the Festival of Britain.

On 18th November, the *Kenia* ran around to Ridham dock on the River Swale. From there she assisted the *Carl Gorthon* from the dock to Thames Haven going via the Swatch Way. She was believed to be the first Watkins' tug to work at Ridham, this work normally being carried out by tugs of Gaselee & Son Ltd.

On the salvage side the *Tangistan* belonging to Strick Line grounded off Canvey Island on 14th March. The *Contest*, *Sun V*, *Sun XI*, and *Sun XVI* successfully refloated her.

Another grounding occurred on 10th July, and it took the combined efforts of the *Sun II*, *Sun V*, *Sun X*, and *Sun XI* to refloat the *Baron Beddes* after she grounded at Greenwich.

The *Sun XVII* went to the assistance of the Finnish Ship *Ulea*, inward bound for Rochester with a cargo of timber. She had grounded by Barrow No. 5 buoy on 14th November. The Ulea jettisoned some of her timber cargo and was then refloated by the *Sun XVII* which towed her to Sheerness.

Sun XVI.

# 1952

The Port of London Authority took delivery of the second pair of tugs of the quartet ordered from Henry Scarr Ltd., Hull. The *Platina*, and *Plateau* joining the *Plangent* and *Plagal* in the Royal Group of Docks. They were the same dimensions and power as the previous two 92'10" x 24'2" their twin screws powered by two four-cylinder Crossley diesel engines developing 1,200 b.h.p. The only difference between the four, was the *Plateau* was fitted with Kort nozzles.

William Watkins Ltd., sold the *Zealandia* in February to the Adelaide Steam Ship Co. Ltd. and renamed *Yuna*. She was a large ocean going tug of 479 gross tons built in 1944 on the Tyne as the *Empire Winnie* and placed under Watkins' management. In December 1946 Watkins bought her outright and she was renamed. With her sale this left just the *Rumania* as the only ocean going tug in the fleet.

William Watkins veteran tug *Arcadia* built in 1895 had her name changed to *Badia* in June. This change was at the request of the P & O Line who wished to name their new 29,500 ton luxury liner being built by John Brown & Co. Ltd., on the Clyde, *Arcadia*.

The tanker *Sovac Radiant* grounded on the South Foreland in January, the *Cervia*, *Tanga*, *Sun XVI*, *Sun XVII*, and the two Dover tugs *Lady Brassey* and *Lady Duncannon* being needed to pull her into deep water refloating on 14th January. The *Sovat Radiant* was later escorted to Ymuiden by the *Sun XVI*.

The *Rumania* left the Cape Verde Islands in January to return home; she had waited there for two months to tow a ship to Lisbon but this had been cancelled. While on passage she received a message from the Swiss Ship *Baden* laden with timber ashore on the Salvage Islands, 100 miles north of Las Palmas. The

67

*Baden* had been refloated by another ship when the *Rumania* arrived on 4th February. She took her in tow, the *Baden* being all awash aft on arrival at Las Palmas on 9th February. The *Rumania* carried on to the Thames after being released and paid off at Tilbury on 23rd February fifteen months after leaving Greenock.

A collision occurred in the Channel in June between the *Baron Douglas* 3,899 tons and the Yugoslav ship *Korenica* 5,180 tons. The Baron Douglas suffered extensive damage to her side and was beached on 14th June at Fairlight near Hastings on the Sussex Coast by the *Rumania* and *Sun XVI*. The ship was awash on the high water, but was patched and pumped out with the assistance of the Naval salvage craft *Kimbrace* and *Uplifter*; these two were engaged in the removal of the block ship at Dover at the time. She was refloated by the *Rumania*, *Sun XVI* and *Sun XVII* and towed to London, with the salvage craft lashed along side and the *Sun XVII* aft as steering tug. On arrival of the ship in the Lower Hope the *Rumania* was relieved by the *Sun X* and the three Sun tugs then berthed the *Baron Douglas* in Tilbury Dock.

Some of the coastal towage carried out during the year was in April. The *Napia* ran down to Le Harve from where she escorted the *Gowa* to Hamburg.

On 1st August the *Sun XVI* towed the *Waterland* from Erith to Grimsby, and in November the *Napia* and *Rumania* towed Ben Lines' *Benvorlock* from London to the Tyne.

Also in November Cunard Lines' *Asia* 8,723 tons grounded, rounding Blackwall Point off Brunswick Wharf Power Station. Seven Sun tugs were engaged to get her afloat on 7th November, these being the *Sun III*, *Sun IV*, *Sun V*, *Sun XI*, *Sun XII*, *Sun XVIII*, and the *Sunrise*.

# 1953

One tug was added in 1953, the Port of London Authority having *Plastron* built by Richard Dunston at Thorne on Humberside. She was a fairly small tug of 80 gross tons, measured 75'10" x 20'10" and powered by a six-cylinder Crossley diesel of 440 b.h.p. She was placed in the Surrey Commercial Docks and the mainstay of her work being craft clearance and towing barges by the lock full, in and out of the Greenland Dock Lock. Timber was the principle cargo handled in the Surrey Docks and large numbers of barges were always in the Dock to tranship it to the various timber wharfs in the River, creeks and canals. Tugs belonging to Ship Towage, Sun Tugs and Gaselee did most of the ship towage in the docks, but the *Plastron* was used on the movement of ships as and when required to do so.

Gaselee's *Vespa* inward bound with six barges in tow was in collision in Galleion's Reach and holed, on her port quarter, she sank. After being raised her old Mirrless engine was replaced by a seven-cylinder British Polar engine of 525 b.h.p., whose previous owner had been the coaster *Petrel*, of the General Steam Navigation Company.

The *Baalbek* 2,160 tons, belonging to Fred Olson Lines collided in fog with the wartime anti-aircraft fort at the Great Nore, Sea Reach during March. Four of the six men on the towers being drowned, the *Baalbek* was left with a ten ton section of the steel catwalk in a gaping hole in her bows and damage down the port side. The *Baalbek* was brought to Gravesend under her own power assisted by the *Sun XVI*, *Sun XVII* and *Sun XI* and moored on the swing buoy.

A collision occurred on 6th May, between the American steamer *Haiti Victory* 7,607 gross tons and the Harwich to the Hook of Holland ferry *Duke of York* 3,759 gross tons owned by the Transport Commission, one and a half miles east of the Galloper light vessel. The impact of the collision being so great that the fore-end of the Duke of York was cut completely off, foreside of her bridge. The *Sun XVII* and the Harwich based tug *Empire Race*, managed for the Ministry of Shipping by C. Rowbotham, took the stricken ferry in tow and bought her stern first into Harwich.

Another collision occurred a week later on 13th May in Gravesend Reach. The Eagle Oil Company tanker *San Florentino* came in contact with the Norwegian ship *Hoegh Bell* 1,656 gross tons loaded with pulp anchored off Gravesend. She received extensive damage to her starboard side aft, with the result the ship was making water and her engine room flooded. Five tugs including the *Gondia*, *Muria*, and *Sun XVI* beached the *Hoegh Bell* off Gravesend Canal entrance where she was later patched and pumped out.

The *Rumania* and *Gondia* were sent down to Spithead to represent William Watkins Ltd., on the occasion of the Coronation Spithead revue, Her Majesty the Queen reviewing the fleet of Merchant as well as Naval vessels from the dispatch vessel H.M.S. *Surprise* on 15th June. The *Gondia* under the command of Captain W. Simmons gave thirty-three handicapped children from the Puckle Hill College a Coronation treat on 24th June. They were taken on a river trip from Gravesend to Greenwich and back to Gravesend. Members of the Rotary Club, local pilots and boys from the National Sea Training School were aboard the *Gondia*, seeing the children's needs and ensuring they had a memorable day.

On Saturday 22nd July, a Royal River Pageant was held on the Thames from Greenwich to Westminster. The *Rana*, *Sauria*, *Mamba* and *Wasp* of Gaselee & Sons and the *Sunrise*, *Sunshine* and the *Sun XVIII* of W.H.J. Alexander Ltd. were among a procession of lighterage tugs, towing barges decorated in various themes of riverside and historic events. The large ship towage tugs were not able to take part, being unable to go above London Bridge having fixed funnels and masts.

The *Rumania* had a tow to northern Spain in November; she left Southampton with the *Verginia* in tow for Aviles.

Also in November Sun Tugs had the *Sun XVI* and *Sun VII* fitted with radar; they were the first Thames tugs so fitted.

Kenia *200/27 761 i.h.p. anchored at the Chapman Explosive Anchorage. Attending on the ''Powder Men'' loading munitions into ships.*

# 1954

The Spanish, *Monte Urquola* 7,723 tons was a regular runner to New Fresh Wharf by London Bridge in the Upper Pool with passengers and fresh fruit and vegetables from the Canary Islands. She was one of the largest ships to berth above Tower Bridge at that time. At 16.15 on 27th January, when leaving the berth she touched the ground aft and swung round on the flood tide and laid athwart of London Bridge. The full force of the tide held her firm against the Bridge, completely blocking the river and causing quite an attraction to the homeward bound city workers who were streaming across the Bridge by the hundreds. It was 19.00 before the efforts of the *Tanga, Java, Kenia, Crested Cock, Sunbird, Sunfish* and *Sun V* were able to pull her clear.

The *Rumania* and *Napia* towed the Eagle Oil Tanker *San Eliseo* 8,042 tons from Southampton to the oil berths at Thames Haven during February. On completion of cargo work the two tugs then towed her on to Newcastle-on-Tyne, arriving on 1st March.

Tragedy struck again on Monday 25th October when the *Cervia* capsized and sank while undocking the P & O Liner *Arcadia* at Tilbury New Entrance with the loss of five of her crew. The accident happened between 23.00 and midnight when the *Arcadia* was being undocked stern first prior to berthing on Tilbury landing stage to embark her passengers. The *Cervia* was positioned on the starboard quarter, the *Challenge* on the port quarter. When the *Arcadia* had backed into the River she went ahead and the *Cervia* getting caught by the wash from her powerful turbine engines and with the ship going away from her, was girted and capsized in seconds, before being able to slip her tow lines.

The Orient Liner *Orcades* was waiting in Northfleet Hope to dock when the *Arcadia* was clear; the *Atlantic Cock* was on forhead and threw life belts to the survivors in the water. The three survivors were all rescued by the *Challenge*; they were the two deckhands and the fireman. The five who lost their lives were her Master, Captain W.Russell, M.B.E., Mate, Second Engineer, Fireman and Cook. She was raised on the following Thursday by P.L.A. lifting craft and the *Sun X*, which was attending on the wreck lighters, beached her at Grays after being lifted clear of the water where she was pumped out. She was shifted to Gravesend and left in tow of the *Gondia* on 2nd November for Ramsgate to be repaired.

On 27th November, the B.P. tanker *British Builder;* under tow of *Masterman* and *Tradesman* belonging to the United Towing Company of Hull, took a shear and grounded at the South East Girdler. The *British Builder* had been towed from Australia by another B.P. tanker and handed over to the Hull tugs off the Isle of Wight for on towage to the Isle of Grain Oil Refinery. It was decided to tow up the Princes Channel having more room than towing through the North Edinburgh Channel. One of the United Tugs also grounded and the seas were breaking right over her, the other Hull tug standing by her to assist if possible. The *Rumania, Napia, Contest* and B.P.'s own tug *Zurmand* from the Medway went to the tanker's assistance, the weather being very bad, the South Goodwin light ship had broken her moorings the night before and was lost after grounding on the Goodwins in the heavy seas. As the tide started to make, the *Contest* and *Napia* got hold of aft and the *Zurmand* forward, but two the *Zurmand*'s crew had been injured and she returned to Sheerness to land them.

The *Contest* and *Napia* refloated the *British Builder* the *Rumania* then got hold of forward and the three tugs towed her to safety into the River Medway. B.P. was so pleased with the performance of the tug crews in the adverse conditions that they gave a £500 gift to each crew on top of the salvage award.

The *Cutty Sark* was shifted from the East India Dock on 19th December to her final resting place: the dry dock especially built for her on the upper side of Greenwich Pier, William Watkins Ltd., supplying the *Gondia, Kenia* and *Java* free of charge to undertake the towage. Once berthed in her new home she was re-rigged and restored to her former glory as a Clipper ship and opened to the public by Her Majesty the Queen on 25th June 1957.

# 1955

The Elliott Steam Tug Co., had the *Vanquisher* built by Henry Scarr Ltd., Hessle, and placed under the management of Ship Towage (London) Ltd. This fine tug was placed under the command of Captain E. Mastin who had previously been Master of the *Atlantic Cock*. She was 294 gross tons, her dimensions being 113'3" x 28'9" x 12'7" the *Vanquisher* being the first diesel powered tug in the Ship Towage fleet, having eight-cylinder direct drive two-stroke British Polar engine developing 1,280 b.h.p. When new she created quite an impression on people seeing her for the first time. With the extra deck she had, the *Vanquisher* towered over the rest of the river fleet when laying alongside them. Her accommodation was far superior to the rest of the tugs: she had six cabins with maximum two to a berth, and two toilets with baths and showers. — a big step forward this when most of the other crews were living seven men to one communal cabin with a coal (bogie) fire in the centre for warmth and a galvanized bucket to wash in. At the time of her build she was advertised as 'the most powerful single screw tug on the thames'.

The *Cervia* returned to work in March after being repaired and refurbished at Ramsgate following her sinking at Tilbury the previous October.

The small Dutch Schoot *Urmajo* grounded on the Goodwin Sands in May. The *Ocean Cock* went to her assistance, refloating her on the 18th, then towing her into Ramsgate Harbour.

A collision occurred in July between the tanker *Cygnet* and the *Capitan Lucas*, twenty-five miles northeast of the East Goodwin light ship. The *Rumania* and *Vanquisher* made fast to the *Cygnet* and beached her in the Downs off Deal. She was later refloated by the *Vanquisher*, *Napia* and *Crested Cock* and towed to Sheerness. From Sheerness two Sun tugs towed her to

75

Tilbury Dock and later on to Hull. To finish this musical chairs of the ports the *Rumania* and *Vanquisher* left Hull with *Cygnet* in tow for Ymuiden. While on passage across the North Sea a strong northwest gale blew up, preventing the *Cygnet* from entering the Dutch port in the prevailing conditions. The tugs held the ship off the Dutch coast riding out the storm until first the *Rumania*'s tow rope parted followed by the *Vanquisher*'s. The *Cygnet* was later picked up by a Dutch tug and berthed in Ymuiden when the weather abated.

The *Rumania* ran round to Barrow-in-Furness in October from where she towed a lock gate to London.

# 1956

W.H.J.Alexander Ltd. took delivery of the *Sun XIX*, from Phillip & Son Ltd. of Dartmouth. She was a modern looking tug of 192 gross tons and having a length of 107'2" a beam of 25'11" and powered by a six-cylinder Rustin and Hornsby diesel of 1,210 b.h.p.

Sun tugs also sold two of the older tugs the *Sun II* and the *Sun III* to J.H. Piggott of Grimsby. They were identical sisters of 197 gross tons built in 1909 by Earl's Company Ltd. of Hull and powered by a 750 i.h.p. triple expansion engine. The *Sun II* was sold on 20th March being renamed *Lady Thelma*, the *Sun III* following on 31st May as the *Lady Sarah*.

On the evening of 10th February the Brazilian freighter *Loide Honduras* grounded on the North Longsand in the outer Thames Estuary. The *Rumania* left Dover and the *Cervia* and *Crested Cock* left Gravesend to go to her aid; it was blowing a force eight northeasterly gale and snowing at the time. The *Rumania* arrived in the vicinity of the ship in the early hours of the 11th and her services were accepted on Lloyds open form, no cure no pay. *Rumania* then anchored to await daylight and the flood tide before attempting to pass her tow rope to the *Loide Honduras* as she was not in any immediate danger. At 05.00 the *Rumania* grounded herself after dragging her anchor; all efforts by her Master Captain L. Belcher to get her off into deep water failed. The pounding the tug was taking on the sands holed her in the stoke hold port side to such an extent the pumps couldn't contain the influx of water.

The *Rumania* then sent a Mayday at 07.00 acknowledged by North Foreland Radio, that they were about to take to the lifeboats and abandon ship in approximate position, 51°43'N. 01°37'E. The tug had developed a port list that was increasing when the ten man crew attempted to launch a lifeboat. It turned out to be fortunate that the *Rumania* had sailed from Dover with only half her full complement of crew, some being left behind in the rush to sail, others being on leave. The crew attempted to launch the starboard lifeboat, the port boat being washed by the seas and not possible to get near. The starboard boat was swung out, but was smashed and torn from the falls by the rising sea; the wind had increased to force ten by this time. With the list increasing and the tide making, the ten crew were forced to hang on to the tugs frozen hand rails on her forecastle head and were in a completely exposed position. A full scale rescue operation had been put into operation by this time: Walton lifeboat had been launched, a R.A.F. Air Sea Rescue launch had left Felixstowe, the *Cervia*, *Crested Cock*, the Dutch tug *Maas* and the Royal Navy Cruiser *Superb* and Survey Ship *Vidal* were all making for the position of the *Rumania* at their best speed in the storm to give any assistance they could. Two Whirl Wind helicopters from the R.A.F. base at Martlesham Heath, Suffolk had also been scrambled and after a difficult job in the reduced visibility of driving snow found the stricken tug. The first helicopter picked up eight men, and the second which arrived soon after rescued the remaining two, all being safely landed at the R.A.F. base. It was a little after 10.00 when the rescue was completed five hours after the *Rumania* first grounded. The *Loide Honduras* was refloated by Smit's tug *Maas*, even though the *Cervia* and *Crested Cock* were on the scene belonging to the same Company as the *Rumania*. The Lloyds open form agreed with her being terminated with the loss of the tug, the contract going to the Dutch instead.

Her loss, the *Rumania* being the last of the true Ocean going tugs in the fleet, brought to an end William Watkins' latest attempt to keep a foothold in the Ocean towage market, the Company concentrating more on the River, Coastal and Continental towage from then on.

Also in February the *Vanquisher* towed the Greek Hellenic Line steamer *Germania* 2,106 tons from Pevensey Bay, Eastbourne, to Bremen. She had been damaged in a collision off Beachy Head and beached by the *Gondia*, *Water Cock* and the Newhaven tug *Foremost 22*. The *Rumania* was preparing for this tow, but with her loss the job was allocated to the *Vanquisher*.

The *Kenia* attended the Thames sailing barge match on 19th June. This was an annual event, the barges racing from the Ship & Lobster at Denton, to a turning point in the Estuary off Shoeburyness, and back to the Ship & Lobster in Gravesend Reach. The *Kenia* or *Gondia*, both having passenger licences, would be fitted with their canvas awnings and the owners and their guests could watch the progress of the race in comfort on the after deck of the tug.

The *Kenia* was also one of the tugs which towed the training ship *Worcester* from her permanent moorings at Greenhithe to Blackwall Dry Docks on 8th August, to have her bottom cleaned, it being ten years since she was first moored there.

The Indian vessel *Jalagolina*, of the Scindia Steam Navigation Co. Ltd., grounded on the Galloper in September, the *Vanquisher* and *Cervia* refloating her on the 21st.

Another grounding was T. & J. Brocklebank's *Manipur*, which went ashore off East Greenwich Power Station in fog on 13th October. The combined pulling power of the *Sunshine*, *Sun IV*, *Sun XI*, *Sun XII*, *Sun XV*, *Sun XVI* and *Sun XVII* was needed to refloat her.

# 1957

One new tug was added to the fleets in 1957, W.H.J.Alexander took delivery of the *Sun XX*, an identical sister to the *Sun XIX*. She was built at Dartmouth by Phillip & Son Ltd., was 192 gross tons, 107'2" x 25'11" x 11'9" and powered by a 1,210 b.h.p. six-cylinder Rustin and Hornsby diesel engine. These two tugs were fitted with a salvage pump and had a limited fire-fighting capability. One monitor being fitted fore side of the funnel on the flying bridge deck, foam could also be supplied. The *Sun XIX* and *Sun XX* were also issued with a passenger licence for seventy-seven passengers. One of the main uses of the tugs with a passenger certificate is to transport the 'Powder Monkeys' from Gravesend to the Chapman Anchorage where explosives are allowed to be loaded into ships. P.L.A. by-laws prohibit ships to load or discharge explosives in the docks up river.

Gaselee & Son scrapped the *Culex* on 17th January at Ward's Grays. She was a product of Alexandra Hall of Aberdeen, completed in 1924 having gross tonnage of 125. She had been laid up for a period of time on Gaselee's hulk *Apar* moored off the West India Dock pier in Limehouse Reach prior to being scrapped.

Sun Tugs also started a conversion programme of their older coal burning tugs. Between 1957 and 1962 the *Sun IV, Sun V, Sun VIII, Sun X, Sun XI*, and *Sun XV* were converted to burn oil at Sir Thomas Robinson yard at Grimsby and the *Sun XII* at Doigs of Hull. They were also modernised by having new funnels and their old radial davits replaced by luffing davits.

The *Sun XIX* also completed her first coastal tow in February by bringing the old train ferry *Essex Ferry II* from Harwich to be scrapped at Ward's yard at Grays.

*Back Row: Don Wyatt (deck hand), Alf Dartnell (2nd engineer), Bob Smallwood (cook), Percy Toms (fireman), Stan Jones (fireman).*
*Front Row: Denis Stedman (mate), Capt. Arthur Cooves (master), Huwie Dicks (chief engineer), Bert Chapman (deck hand).*

# 1958

One tug was added to the fleets in 1958, Gaselee & Son travelling to West Germany to have the *Culex* built by F.Schichou at Bremerhaven. The *Culex* was 97 gross tons, 80'4" x 21'6" x 10' and powered by a 660 b.h.p., eight-cylinder Deutz engine. She was towed to London by the *Serviceman* of the United Towing Co., Hull, and both were anchored at the Sunk for two to three days in dense fog, the *Serviceman* not being fitted with radar at that time. The first ship the *Culex* towed after delivery was the *Villegas* 1,216 ton belonging to MacAndrews & Co. Ltd., which she un-docked from London dock.

Ship Towage (London) Ltd., also started to convert their tugs to burn oil. Two tugs were sent to the Tyne for conversion, the *Contest* heading North in February followed by the *Tanga* on 3rd September.

In January a collision occurred at the lower end of Gravesend Reach between the North Thames Gas Board flat iron collier *Thomas Livesey* inbound with coal and the Royal Mail Lines *Loch Avon*. The *Thomas Livesey* was holed and beached in the Higham Bight assisted by the *Sun XVIII*, *Sun XIX* and *Sun XX*. Also in January the *Hartington* 7,325 ton grounded at Northfleet. She was refloated on the 9th by the *Kenia*, *Napia*, *Challenge* and *Water Cock*.

My own tugging career started in 1958, joining the *Racia* at North Woolwich Pier at 09.00 on 20th May, as cook. At that time four tugs of the Ship Towage fleet were based at Woolwich, these being the *Racia*, *Muria*, *Simla* and *Java*. The following day the *Racia* went to Clifton Slipways at Gravesend to have a strip of rubber fendering fitted to her stem, the *Racia* being used to test the strength and effectiveness of the fender. She was ideally suited for this with the large amount of dock work she undertook, which involved pushing through large numbers of drifting barges. Rubber hand fenders, some consisting of rings glued together with a line through the middle, were also put aboard for evaluation of the strength of the rubber and glue.

The *Kenia* attended on the needs of a film unit on 28th May in the Upper Pool. She assisted in the Riverside scenes being shot of the Alex Guinness film *The Horse's Mouth*.

The *Vanquisher* went to the assistance of the *Vori*, fully laden with grain, broken down and drifting with no anchors in the vicinity of the Smith's Knoll light vessel, the *Vanquisher* towing her to Newcastle-on-Tyne. The *Vanquisher* also assisted in the refloating of the *British Justice* 21,079 tons, at Thames Haven on 18th November, with the *Cervia, Napia, Water Cock*, and *Ocean Cock* and berthing her on No. 4 Jetty (now C jetty Shell Haven).

Culex (i).

# 1959

The modernisation of the fleets continued with three new tugs being delivered in 1959. William Watkins Ltd. took delivery of the *Dhulia* and Gamecock Tugs, the *Moorcock*. These two tugs were identical sisters and placed under the management of Ship Towage (London) Ltd. They were both built on the Humber by Henry Scarr Ltd., Hessle. They had a gross tonnage to 272 and dimensions of 113′7″ x 28′9″ x 12′6″ and powered by an eight-cylinder British Polar diesel developing 1,600 b.h.p. The *Dhulia* was the first of the pair completed arriving at Gravesend on 2nd September, the *Moorcock* in the middle of October. They were similar in design to the *Vanquisher* but without the middle deck so not having the lofty appearance of their predecessor. They were fitted with salvage and fire-fighting salvage pumps; late the following year or early 1961 the *Dhulia*, *Moorcock* and *Vanquisher* had their fire pumps altered to enable them to supply foam. From then on Ship Towage under contract to the oil companies kept a fire tug at Thames Haven 24 hours a day with a second tug being able to return to Gravesend between jobs. The *Vanquisher* and *Moorcock* were the mainstays of this work with the *Dhulia* standing in when a tug was at refit, etc.

The third tug completed was the *Sun XXI*, for W.H.J.Alexander Ltd. She was built by Phillip & Sons Ltd., Dartmouth, of 183 gross tons dimensions 107′2″ x 25′11″ x 11′8″ and powered by a six-cylinder Mirrless oil engine of 1,386 b.h.p. The *Sun XXI* was similar in appearance to the *Sun XIX* and *Sun XX* but with increased power and improved steering, the old rod and chain being replaced by hydraulic steering. The *Sun XXI* was not fitted with any salvage or fire-fighting pumps.

The P.L.A. did not have a fleet of ship towing tugs large enough to cover all of its dock work, the river tugs being used extensively in the docks at this time. They had the *Beam* and *Walbrook* in Tilbury Dock, *Plagal*, *Plangent*, *Plateau* and *Platina*, the four new diesels in the Royals, the *Beverly* in the West India Dock and the smaller *Plastron* in the Surrey Dock. Apart from the large volume of shipping towed within the enclosed docks, the tugs of Ship Towage (London) Ltd. were contracted to tow the P.L.A.'s fleet of heavy lift derricks in the river and docks. Three tugs were needed on the largest of them, the 200 ton lift the *London Mammoth*, when towing in the tideway, four at times when over the tide. The *London Ajax* was also a good provider of work when I was in the *Simla* and *Java* it was not unknown to complete a whole week's work towing the *London Ajax* alone from ship to ship around the West India Dock, two tugs being required for this. Sun Tugs on the other hand were contracted to tow the P.L.A.'s fleet of grain elevators in and around the docks. They also attended on the Dumb Wreck lighters and screwing lighters of the P.L.A. salvage department when they required a tug.

# 1960

There were two new tugs in 1960. W.H.J. Alexander Ltd. had the *Sun XXII* built by Phillip & Sons Ltd. She was an identical sister to the *Sun XXI*, had a gross tonnage of 183, dimensions of 107'2" x 25'11" 11'8½" and powered by a six-cylinder Mirrless diesel developing 1,316 b.h.p. William Watkins Ltd. took delivery of the *Ionia*, having been completed in Hessle by Henry Scarr Ltd., of 187 gross tons and dimensions of 99'9" x 26'2" x 11'7" and powered by a six-cylinder British Polar diesel of 960 b.h.p. The *Ionia* was smaller than the *Dhulia* and *Moorcock* and designed for their Woolwich base. Her hull being extremely strong, she was built to withstand the knocking about taken in the docks pushing through barges when towing ships to and from their berths.

Three tugs ended their days under the cutting torch at Thomas Ward's scrap yard at Grays. The first was the *Sunshine* on 13th February. She was one of the smaller Sun tugs built in 1889 by J.G.Fay & Co. Ltd., Southampton, having a gross tonnage of 103 and powered by a two-cylinder compound steam engine of 450 i.h.p. The *Sun VI* was next, arriving at Grays on 20th December, built at Preston by Allsup & Co Ltd. in 1902 for the Kings Lyne Conservance Board as a *Conservator*, 139 gross tons and powered by a 500 i.h.p. two-cylinder compound engine. Alexander's acquired her in 1915 renaming her *Sun VI*. Two days later on 22nd December the *Musca* of Gaselee & Son arrived at Ward's. She was Gaselee's last steam tug, dating from 1922 and having a gross tonnage of 75. Her last years had been spent in semi-retirement as the Tower Bridge tug. With her scrapping it became necessary to have changed the word 'steam' to 'motor' in the Act of Parliament that stated a 'steam' tug be kept on station at Tower Bridge to keep it clear of any obstructions. This enabled Gaselee to continue to maintain the service using a diesel tug.

The *Kenia* unshipped off the slipway at Ramsgate on 17th January, the last tug to be refitted there before the yard ceased trading the following year on 31st March 1961. William Watkins Ltd. had been associated with Claxton & Co. Ltd. since 1921 when Claxton's were expanded from repairing Trawler winches to be able to undertake tug refits. All Watkins' tugs were refitted in Ramsgate from that date.

The *Sunfish* was the victim of a tragic accident during the afternoon of 12th March. The *Sun VI* was forward and the *Sunfish* on aft of the Ellerman Wilson Lines' *Palermo* 2,838 gross tons, dragging through Tower Bridge inward bound in the Upper Pool. The *Sunfish* was dragged on the Northern Buttress of the bridge which her stern struck, rolling her over and she sank with the loss of her Chief Engineer. She was lifted by the P.L.A. Salvage department the next day and taken to Alexander's repair yard at Wapping, where she was refurbished and returned to work.

The Holland America Lines new liner *Rotterdam* paid a visit to London during August, berthing at the Tilbury Landing Stage assisted by the *Dhulia* and *Moorcock*. Having a gross tonnage of 38,615 tons she broke the *Mauritania*'s record as the largest liner to berth in the port by 3,000 tons.

A second tug was also sunk during March: the P.L.A. tug *Walbrook* capsized and sank in Tilbury Dock while assisting the Dutch freighter *Langkoeas* 9,200 tons on 21st March with her sister tug *Beam*. Fortunately no loss of life occurred, the *Beam* slipping her tow rope from the other end of the ship and with the aid of her search lights rescued all the six crew members from the murky water of the dock. The *Walbrook* was raised by the P.L.A. Salvage department, repaired and returned to service.

# 1961

Hibernia.

Two new tugs arrived on the River in 1961, W.H.J. Alexander Ltd. taking delivery of the *Sun XXIII* from Phillip & Son Ltd., Dartmouth. A handy tug of 143 gross tons 93'9" x 24'5" x 11'03/4" she was powered by a 1,400 i.h.p. six-cylinder Mirrless diesel engine and joined Sun Tugs up river fleet. The other new arrival was the *Fossa*, built on the Humber by Henry Scarr Ltd. Hessel, for

Gaselee & Son. She was powered by a six-cylinder Deutz engine of 1,000 b.h.p, 98 gross tons and dimensions of 85′9″ x 21′6″ x 10′9″.

As the new building programme was gaining momentum, the older tugs were becoming surplus and being scrapped. Sun Tugs sold the *Sunbird* to Ward's on 17th March, Dutch built in 1907 by Jonker & Stans Hendrikido, Ambacht, 64 gross tons 72′1″ x 18′5″ x 8′8″ and powered by a two-cylinder compound engine of 350 i.h.p.

William Watkins' veteran *Hibernia*, at the age of 77 years was finally scrapped at Grays on 13th April. A product of Maats De Maas, Delfshaven, Holland, the *Hibernia* was built in 1884 of iron and powered by a two-cylinder 850 i.h.p. compound engine. When built she had a length of 121′ and constructed as a seagoing tug towing as far afield as the Persian Gulf in 1908. During the First World War she served in the Dardanelles under the Royal Navy as H.M.S. *Hibernia III*. After World War I the amount of Ocean Towage undertaken by Watkins had decreased to an extent that it was decided to shorten the *Hibernia* to enable her to be used as a river tug. She was taken to Ramsgate on 22 September 1922, her bow cut off and a new stubby bow built on, shortening her length by 15′6″. This decreased her gross tonnage to 219 and her dimensions to 107′1″ x 22′1″ x 12′1″ the conversion being completed by 23 April 1923. An unusual feature of the *Hibernia* was that her boiler was fired from the foreside, most tugs stoke holds being the afterside of the boiler and their coal bunkers amidships, the *Hibernia*'s coal bunker being the foreside of the bridge. Her Master, Captain Bert Youseman retired at the same time as she was scrapped being presented with the tug's bell by the Company. He had been the *Hibernia*'s master since February 1927.

With the closure of Claxton's repair yard at Ramsgate, Ship Towage (London) Ltd. took over five dry docks and repair facilities of the closed Sheerness Naval Dock Yard, operating them under the name of the Medway Dry Dock & Engineering Co. Ltd. With the expansion of Sheerness as a port, the southern basin which contained three dry docks was filled in and reclaimed during the 1970s, leaving the Company with two dry docks and a slipway in the North Basin.

# 1962

Ship Towage (London) Ltd, took delivery of the first of two new fire tugs being completed by Cochrane's & Sons Ltd., Selby, built to take over from the *Vanquisher* and *Moorcock* as principal fire tugs at the Thames Haven Oil Refinery. Fully equipped to supply foam or water from hoses or from four monitors on a platform high on her mast, a salvage pump was also fitted. The first to arrive was the *Avenger* under the ownership of the Elliott Steam Tug Co. Ltd. on 21st November, powered by a nine-cylinder British Polar diesel of 1,800 b.h.p, 293 gross tons and dimensions of 118'5" x 30'5" x 12'11½".

The other new arrival in 1962 was the *Sun XXIV* for W.H.J. Alexander Ltd., built at Faversham by J. Pollock & Sons Co. Ltd. She was a fairly small compacted tug of 113 gross tons, 88'3" x 22'11" x 9'10¼" and powered by a 750 b.h.p. six-cylinder Mirrless diesel. She was designed principally for the Sun Tugs work in the Upper Pool replacing the ageing small tugs that were being scrapped.

Three tugs were sold. One the *Sun XVI* for further service was acquired by the Italian Company Societa Rimorchiatori Napoletana, Naples. The *Sun XVI* was the first of six Sun Tugs to be bought by them. She left the Thames under the name *San Cataldo*, this later being shortened to *S. Cataldo*. Of standard Empire Tug design the *Sun XVI* was built in 1946 by Alexander Hall & Co., Aberdeen and allocated the name *Empire Leonard*, but taken over by Sun Tugs on completion.

The following two tugs were both sold for scrap at Thomas Ward's, Grays. With the arrival of the *Sun XXIV*, the *Sunfish* became surplus and was towed to Wards by the *Sun XXIV* on 28th June, built in Holland in 1907 by Jonker &

Stans, Hendrikido, Ambacht, having a gross tonnage of 81 and powered by a 350 i.h.p. two-cylinder compound engine.

William Watkins' *Badia* was the other tug to end her days at Grays arriving on 14th November. She was built as the *Arcadia* by Cook Welton & Gemmel at Hull in 1895 and given the name *Badia* in 1952 when the P & O Line wanted the name *Arcadia*. A fine sea boat she had towed as far afield as Spain during the turn of the century. During World War I she served as H.M.S. *Chichester* under the Royal Navy and was bombed while coasting during World War II. She was of 180 gross tons 109′ in length and powered by a 700 i.h.p. triple expansion engine.

In 1962 six ships were laid up in the River Stour above Parkstone Quay Harwich, four old Greek steamers and two new British bulk carriers, one only being berthed two months previously by the *Contest* and *Watercock*. They were moored alongside each other with an anchor out each end of each ship. Three of the Greek ships broke adrift during a storm and grounded on the Essex shore. The *Dhulia*, *Napia* and *Contest* were sent round to Harwich in December to remoor them. The *Contest* was to supply steam, to the winches; this proved more difficult than it would appear, proving impossible at times to get steam from one end of the ship to the other. The steam pipes being rusted through, the only way to get steam to some of the winches was to connect the steam hose directly to it. The *Dhulia* relaid some of the anchors by lashing them to a foreward post and the *Napia* getting hold of her stern and towing her into position where they were dropped. After three days the ships were successfully remoored and the tugs returned to Gravesend.

Avenger *being launched 1962*.

# 1963

William Watkins Ltd. took delivery of the *Hibernia* from Cochrane & Sons Ltd., Selby, placing her under the management of Ship Towage (London) Ltd. A fully equipped fire tug, she was an identical sister to the *Avenger* of 293 gross tons and powered by an 1,800 b.h.p. British Polar diesel.

W.H.J. Alexander Ltd., also had a fire tug built, named *Sun XXV*, which arrived at Gravesend on 4th March from Dartmouth where she had been completed by Phillip & Son Ltd. Her pumps could be used in a salvage or fire-fighting capacity, supplying foam or water by hand lines or from three monitors, two on the mast and one on a platform abaft the funnel. *Sun XXV* was 116'1" x 28'5" x 11'10", 230 gross tons and powered by 2,000 b.h.p. six-cylinder Mirrless diesel engine.

Gaselee & Son Ltd. transferred the *Agama* 500 b.h.p to Felixstowe in early 1963, joining the *Hooligan*, a small tug of 105 h.p. and 55' in length, belonging to an associate company R.Lapthorn & Co. Ltd. of Hoo. There hadn't been any tugs stationed in the Haven ports since the sale of the *Empire Race* and *Empire Lucy*, of C.Rowbothan to Italy, apart from the Ipswich tug *River Orwell*. The two Empire tugs' main job had been to attend on the troop ships that ran from Parkstone Quay Harwich to the Hook of Holland, but when the movement of troops was transferred from sea to air the troop ships were withdrawn and the tugs subsequently sold, any towage being undertaken by tugs belonging to Ship Towage (London) Ltd., who ran round from the Thames when required. William Watkins had tugs stationed at Harwich during and after the Second World War.

One of the more frequent tows during this period was assisting ships to and from Ipswich with the *River Orwell* where they loaded scrap iron. When

Felixstowe was beginning to expand as a port and the Navy yard at Harwich about to be built, it was decided to station a tug in the port on a permanent basis, the *Agama* being sent round from London.

The death occurred of Mr J.R. Watkins, O.B.E., joint managing director of Ship Towage (London) Ltd., on 20th August aged 69 years. His ashes were scattered into the Thames at the Nore from the *Hibernia* on 27th August. He was succeeded by his son Mr William Watkins as joint managing director.

In October the *Sun XXV* was one of the tugs taking part in a P.L.A. exercise (Operation Play Fire). This was a simulated collision with fire on the water and was to test the efficiency and co-ordination of the emergency services.

Also in October the *Vanquisher* towed the Greek Steamer *Maraviki*, from lay-up at Harwich to Hull, assisted in the Humber by the *Lady Cecilia* of J.H. Piggott & Son Ltd.

Culex *with* Alice Bowater *in frozen River Swale.*

# 1964

W.H.J.Alexander Ltd., sold the *Sun XI* to Schelde Sleepvaarlbedrijf, M.V. Belgium, and was renamed *Schelde X*. Not lasting long under this ownership she was run down and sank shortly afterwards and resold in 1965 to Rimorchiatori Sardi S.V.A., Gagliari, Sardina and renamed *Andrea*. The *Sun XI* was a product of Earls Co. Ltd., Hull in 1925, 183 gross tons and powered by a 750 i.h.p. steam engine.

Sun Tugs also sold the *Sun*, going for scrap at Grays on 15th April. The *Sun* had been built at Appledore by R.Cox & Sons in 1906, 130 gross tons and powered by a 550 i.h.p. triple expansion engine. She was stationed at Gravesend soon after being delivered and was Alexander's first serious attempt as a permanent base there.

The Port of London Authority, sold the *Walbrook* in March to the Meeching Engineering (Marine) Ltd., Newhaven. A product of Ferguson Brothers, Port Glasgow in 1910, the *Walbrook* was one of a series of tugs ordered by the P.L.A. soon after its formation in 1908, a twin screw tug powered by two compound engines totalling 1,000 i.h.p. and in the later years of P.L.A. ownership was stationed at Tilbury Dock. It was resold to Lacmots Ltd. and scrapped at Queenborough.

William Watkins Ltd. veteran tug *Simla* was taken to the Medway Dry Docks at Sheerness on 10th April and put into number one dry dock where she was scrapped.

The *Simla* had been built on the Clyde by Lobnitz & Co., at Renfrew in 1898, 144 gross tons and powered by 500 i.h.p. triple expansion engine. 'Old Nell', as she was nicknamed by her crew spent the last few years of her life based at North Woolwich Pier.

The *Challenge* had her boiler converted to burn oil at Sheerness during the year and when completed her place was taken by the *Ocean Cock*, for the same conversion.

A spate of collisions occurred on the River during the year. At 09.15 on 18th April, the Norwegian Fred Olsen Line's *Bencomo* outward bound in foggy conditions collided with the fully laden tanker *Esso Cardiff* 31,659 tons inward bound for Thames Haven in the vicinity of the Shivering Sands Forts. The bow of the *Bencomo* was extensively damaged and she returned to Gravesend assisted from the Lower Hope by the *Sun XXV*, and moored at Gravesend upper swing buoy. The *Sun XXV* assisted in docking the *Bencomo* in Tilbury Dock without power on 20th April to undergo emergency repairs prior to leaving the Thames for Gothenburg, Sweden for permanent repairs escorted by the *Dhulia*.

During the afternoon of 12th October, the *Crested Cock* and the *Kenia* were undocking the *Maashaven* from Tilbury Dock New Entrance. The ship started her swing to starboard in the Bellmouth and the *Kenia* which was on the port bow when coming round the Maashaven went ahead and pinned her to the upper pier head before she cleared the ship's bow.

The *Kenia* was cut from the deck to the keel in the after end of the engine room starboard side. The crew were able to get a turn alongside the pier head enabling all hands to scramble to safety before she sank. She was raised by the P.L.A. Salvage Department and beached in Northfleet Hope above Tilbury Dock where she was patched. Pumped out by the *Muria* she was then refloated and laid alongside the coal hulk *Artemis* at Gravesend. Metal recovery (Newhaven) Ltd. purchased the *Kenia* and she left Gravesend on 12th November in tow of the tug *Sunnyside* bound for Sheerness. It was rumoured she was to be used in conjunction with the Channel Tunnel project, but this failed to materialise and she was scrapped. Built in 1927 by Cochrane & Sons Ltd., Selby, the *Kenia* was a passenger carrying tug of 200 gross tons and powered by 750 i.h.p. triple expansion engine.

In the early hours of 27th October the East German Vessel *Magdeburg* outward bound from Dagenham with a full deck cargo of new buses for Cuba was in collision off Broadness Point with the inward bound *Yamishiro Maru*. The *Magdeburg* was seriously damaged and beached on the Point by various tugs who had raced to her assistance, the *Hibernia* and *Sun XXV* amongst them. When grounded the *Magdeburg* rolled over onto her side and a full scale operation to rescue the crew was put in force. Fifty-six crew were saved including three women and the tugs launched their lifeboats to search for survivors, all being accounted for by 03.45. The salvage of the *Magdeburg* was a long, protracted affair and when raised she was taken to Tilbury Dock to be made seaworthy. Leaving the Thames in tow of Bugsier's tug *Albatross*, (I believe this to be her first tow) while crossing the Bay of Biscay, she developed a leak and sank.

Another collision occurred in fog during the evening of 11th December, in the vicinity of the Mid Blyth Buoy between the tanker *Statue of Liberty* and the *Sapporo Maru* in fog. The *Hibernia* and *Vanquisher* assisted the Statue of Liberty, the *Sapporo Maru* being beached by the *Avenger, Moorcock, Sun XVII, Sun XX, Sun XXII* and *Sun XXV*. The tugs were pushing up till 21.00 by which time the ship had settled. The *Sun XXV* commenced pumping in number 5 hold at 01.00 the following morning till 06.00; she then stood by the ship until the morning of 13th December when the *Sapporo Maru* was refloated and towed to Swanscombe buoys.

# 1965

Two new tugs were delivered to W.H.J. Alexander Ltd. The first arriving in the Spring from the Humber was the *Sun XXVI*, built by Charles D. Holmes Co. Ltd., at Beverly. A sister to the *Sun XXV*, built in 1963 at Dartmouth, the *Sun XXVI* had a gross tonnage of 230 and dimensions of 116'1" x 28'5" x 11'10" and powered by a six-cylinder 2,000 b.h.p. Mirrless diesel engine. She was fitted out with full fire-fighting and salvage pumps. The second tug delivered was the *Sun II* arriving at Wapping on 31st July from her builders Charles D. Holmes & Co. Ltd., Beverly. She was a smaller class of tug than the *Sun XXVI* joining the Sun Tugs up river fleet, the *Sun XXVI* being stationed at Gravesend. The *Sun II* is 28.58m x 3.74m, 150 gross tons and powered by a 1400 b.h.p. six-cylinder Mirrless diesel engine, a salvage pump also being fitted.

The Port of London Authority had four new (water tractor) tugs built by Richard Dunston Ltd., Hessel. They were given the names *Platoon*, *Plasma*, *Plankton* and *Placard* and were propelled by single Voith Schneider unit, the first tugs so equipped on the Thames giving these vessels excellent handling ability, a great advantage to ship towing in the enclosed docks. They were 122 gross tons 87'7" in length by 25'6" beam and powered by a sixteen-cylinder Lister Blackstone diesel engine 1,600 b.h.p. On delivery they were stationed in the Royal Docks and the twin screw tugs already there re-allocated to Tilbury and the West India Dock.

The P.L.A. also sold the *Beverly* for scrap on 19th February to Thomas Ward of Grays, the first of a trio of twin screw tugs ordered from Ferguson Brothers at Port Glasgow by the P.L.A. on its formation in 1908. Completed in 1910, 168 gross tons, 88' x 22'6" x 10'8" and powered by two two-cylinder compound engines of 1,000 i.h.p. total, the *Beverly* spent most of her career in the South West India Dock.

Java.

William Watkins Ltd. sold the *Java* for scrap in May to Southend Ship Breakers. It was resold to Belgium breakers and towed to the Continent by a tug belonging to J.P.Knight Ltd., Rochester. The *Java* was built in 1905 by Cochrane & Son Ltd., Selby, 128 gross tons 94′ x 19.6′ x 10.9′ and powered by 500 i.h.p. triple expansion engine.

On 1st May, Ship Towage (London) Ltd. acquired the *Fossa*, *Rana*, *Culex* and *Vespa* from Gaselee & Son Ltd., and all the Ship Towage contracts of the Company. Amongst the companies Gaselee towed for were the General Steam Navigation Company, MacAndrew & Son, the Brazilian, Loide Ships, and all the ships that supplied Bowater Lloyds, Kemsley paper mill at Ridham Dock on the River Swale. In August the Vespa 500 b.h.p. was stationed at Ridham

Dock, it being considered there was enough work to warrant a permanent tug in the Port. The *Fossa* and *Culex* were refitted soon after and their funnels painted with the Watkins' red band. The *Rana* and *Vespa* kept the Gaselee colours until after the new Ship Towage (London) Ltd. funnel colours were introduced in September.

This consisted of a black funnel with a broad red band, with a narrower blue band below it and the Dick & Page house flag each side on the red band. The four tugs also had their tall hinged funnels removed and replaced by a new short fixed funnel.

P.L.A. chartered the *Kent* 800 b.h.p. from J.P.Knight Ltd. for a short period around this time and placed her in the South West India Dock as a replacement for *Beverly*. The *Kent* was also chartered by Gaselee Felixstowe Ltd. in July as a replacement for the *Agama* when a more powerful tug was needed at Felixstowe; the *Agama* returned to London. I believe the *Kent* undertook the P.L.A. charter prior to her spell in Felixstowe. The P.L.A. also transferred the *Lord Devonport* from its dredging fleet to the dock tug fleet during this period: a single screw tug of 109 gross tons and built in 1959 at Faversham by J.Pollock & Sons Co. Ltd., and powered by a 900 b.h.p. British Polar Diesel. The *Lord Devonport* was also placed in the South West India Dock.

On 11th January the *Medicine Hat*, belonging to Canadian Pacific Steamship Co. inward bound collided with the outward bound *Esso York* rounding Stoneness Point off Greenhithe. The *Medicine Hat* received a large hole on her port side and was beached on the North shore above the Point light by the *Cervia*, *Napia*, *Crested Cock*, *Sun XVII* and *Sun XXIV*.

A series of fires occurred in 1965; on the 16th March the tanker *Erne* had a fire in her engine room while berthed at No 1 Jetty Thames Haven. It was extinguished with the assistance of the *Avenger*, *Hibernia*, *Dhulia*, *Napia* and *Vanquisher*.

The coaster *Vauban* caught fire and was abandoned on 2nd September near the East Tongue buoy off Margate. The *Vanquisher*, *Hibernia* and *Kestrel* of J.P.Knight went to her assistance and brought the fire under control. The *Vauban* was then towed to London and the *Culex* assisting the *Vanquisher* up river and berthing her in Lime Kiln Dock.

The *Esso Wandsworth*, one of four Esso tankers that were known to the tug crews as 'doodlebugs' and used to supply oil to the Thameside Power stations, was in collision in fog at the Ovens buoy in Lower Gravesend Reach on 23rd September. The ship was holed and taken in tow by the *Vanquisher*, *Cervia*, *Crested Cock*, *Hibernia* and *Sun XXV* and berthed at Commercial Wharf

Gravesend. While undergoing repairs the *Esso Wandsworth* caught fire on 12th October and the *Moorcock*, *Crested Cock* and *Challenge* assisted the Fire Brigade to extinguish it. The *Crested Cock* went to the assistance of the *Kweik* loaded with timber and anchored with engine problems at the Mid Barrow on 28th September. The *Crested Cock* towed her into the River Crouch where she berthed on the timber wharf. This is the only time I have known a Gravesend ship towing tug to enter the River Crouch.

The large *Tanker Ossa* was in trouble in the Channel in November and was towed from a position three and a half miles from Rye Harbour to Thames Haven by the *Vanquisher*, *Dhulia* and *Sun XXV*, via the Tongue and Knob anchorages. When discharged she was towed to Tilbury repair Jetty later being docked in Tilbury for dry docking.

The new extension of Tilbury Dock was being dug out at this time and the tugs were kept busy towing the loaded hoppers to the dumps at the Black Deep. On the coastal towing scene the *Moorcock* towed the *Rayjohn* from Rochester to Dundee, the *Vespa* assisting in the Medway as far as Sheerness.

In September the *Fossa* and *Culex* towed the paddle steamer *Medway Queen* from the East India Dock and handed her over to the *Dhulia* at Gravesend, who towed her to the River Medina, Isle of Wight where she was to become a floating restaurant. This venture was not very successful and in the late seventies was derelict and in a sinking condition. Various plans to try to preserve her were put forward and she was eventually towed back to the Medway in April 1984 on top of a pontoon by the tug *Patmore* owned by local Gravesend waterman Mr Mervin Street. It is hoped in time she can be restored to her former glory.

On Christmas Eve the *Cervia* left the Navy Yard at Harwich with the *Electra* in tow for the Hook of Holland. The *Cervia* handed over her tow at 06.15 Christmas morning and returned to Gravesend arriving late in the evening.

# 1966

Two new tugs were built in 1966. Ship Towage (London) Ltd. took delivery of the *Burma* from Richard Dunston Ltd., Hessel. The first of a pair ordered she was 166 gross tons, 30.71 x 7,83 x 3.81 m. and powered by a 1,050 b.h.p. eight-cylinder Ruston and Hornsby diesel engine. The *Burma* was rather old-fashioned in appearance with open bridge and with a large funnel, the bridge being enclosed by a fibre glass top a few years later. Designed for the up river base at Woolwich she was the only tug in the fleet not equipped with a lifeboat, apart from the four small tugs acquired from Gaselee the previous year.

The other new arrival was the *Sun III* built by J. Pollock & Sons Co. Ltd., Faversham for W.H.J. Alexander Ltd. An identical sister to the *Sun II* the *Sun III* was 150 gross tons and powered by a 1,400 b.h.p six-cylinder Mirrless diesel engine. The *Sun II* and *Sun III* were both fitted with a hinged mast to enable them to go under the bridges if required.

With the arrival of the new tugs more of the old steam tugs became surplus. W.H.J. Alexander disposed of three tugs. The *Sunrise* left Wapping on 12th May under tow of the *Sun II* to be scrapped at Antwerp arriving the following day. The *Sunrise* had been built in 1928 at Aberdeen as the *William Ryan*, Sun Tugs buying her in 1949.

The *Sun IV* and *Sun V* were both sold for further service to Societa Rimorchiatori Napoletani, Naples, Italy. The *Sun IV* left London under the name of *San Benigno* and the *Sun V* as the *Punta Alice*.

Both tugs were a product of Earls Co. Ltd. of Hull in 1915, were of standard Sun Tug design powered by a 750 i.h.p. triple expansion engine and having dimensions of 105' x 25'5" x 12'4".

Ship Towage (London) Ltd. scrapped the *Gondia* and *Watercock* at Antwerp. Both had been laid up alongside the coal hulk *Artemis*, the *Gondia* since 24th March, and the two tugs left Gravesend in tow of the *Moorcock* on 4th July. The *Gondia* had been a passenger carrying tug of 200 gross tons built in 1927 by Cochrane & Sons Ltd., Selby, for William Watkins Ltd. The *Watercock* was also built by Cochrane's as the *Masterman* for United Towing Company Hill, in 1923, Cock Tugs buying her in 1925. With the scrapping of the *Gondia* and *Kenia* the *Vanquisher* was brought up to D.T.I. standards to enable her to carry passengers.

One more tug was disposed of in 1966, the P.L.A. scrapping the *Beam*. Prior to her being sold the *Beam* had been stationed in Tilbury Dock. Built by Ferguson Brothers, Port Glasgow she was a 1,000 i.h.p. twin screw tug of 168 gross tons and was the last P.L.A. steam tug engaged in ship towage.

Another alteration in the fleets was the *Ocean Cock* being transferred to Felixstowe in the summer and chartered to Gaselee (Felixstowe) Ltd., an associate company of Ship Towage (London) Ltd. With her arrival at the East Anglian Port, the *Kent* was returned to J.P. Knight.

The *Ionia* had a coastal tow in April, taking a pontoon from London to Dawlish in Devon.

The *Crested Cock* and *Tanga* assisted in the salvage of the L.C.C. sludge vessel *Sir Joseph Rawlingson* during May. The *Rawlingson* had been sunk on 28th September 1965 after being in collision in fog with the mud hopper *Black Deep* under tow of the *Danube VIII* in the estuary in the vicinity of the Red Sand Towers. On being raised the *Cervia*, *Challenge* and *Crested Cock* towed her to the Nelson Drydock, Rotherhithe for repair, later being towed to Rotterdam and converted into a suction dredger and in 1973 became the heavy lift ship *Happy Pioneer*.

On 9th September the *Culex* represented Ship Towage (London) Ltd. in a River pageant from the Lower Pool to Chelsea with 200 other river craft. Part of the entertainment was a firework display from the grounds of the Royal Festival Hall to mark the 300th Anniversary of the Great Fire of London.

*Sun XXV* towed the Cunard Liner *Parthia* from Southampton to Glasgow on 30th March being relieved by two Clyde tugs on arrival at Greenock on 2nd April. The *Sun XXV* was also successful in refloating the Cory Collier *Corsea* ashore on the Northeast Gunfleet on 4th September. She was then engaged in two trips from Southampton between 9th and 12th September towing the Sand Dredgers *Sand Star* and *Sand Diver* to Ward's of Grays for scrap.

The *Moorcock* ran down to Brest and sailed on 11th November with the Norwegian vessel *Finse* with propeller damage in tow for Bremen.

American Challenger *with a steering defect being escorted to Rotterdam by* Sun XXII *183/60 and* Sun XXVI *230/65. As the tugs were not fast enough to keep up with the ship, the ship towed the tugs.*

# 1967

Ship Towage (London) Ltd. had one new building and one scrapped in 1967. The *Watercock,* the second of the pair, was built by Richard Dunston's Ltd., at Hessel, powered by 1,050 b.h.p. eight-cylinder Ruston & Hornsby diesel and having a gross tonnage of 161. The *Racia* and *Muria* were both scrapped at Antwerp, the *Muria* first, being towed by the *Ionia* on 11th April. The *Racia* had the distinction of being the last coal burner in the Ship Towage fleet going for scrap on 31st July towed over by the *Moorcock*. These two tugs were the last survivors in the company of the Ring Tugs (Gravesend United Steam Tug Company) absorbed by Watkins in 1937. Both had been built by Cochrane & Sons Ltd., Selby, the *Racia* in 1930 as the *Dilwara*, being renamed *Denderra* in 1935 and *Racia* in 1938. The *Muria* was completed in 1932 as the *Dongara* and renamed *Persia* in 1938 by Watkins. Burnt out at Thames Haven in 1941 and declared a total loss, she was taken to Ramsgate rebuilt and given the name *Muria* in 1946.

Two Sun Tugs suffered damage during the year. The *Sun III* undocked a Persian Ship out of the Southwest India Dock with the *Sun XVII*. When rounding Blackwall Point the ship had a complete engine failure and ran towards the North shore in the vicinity of the Orchard Dry Dock. Both tugs were broad off on the starboard bow attempting to drag the ship clear, when an inward bound Wilson Line vessel approaching the point forced the *Sun XVII* to slip her tow rope to avoid her. The *Sun III* was struck amidships and holed port side by the Wilson boat before being able to slip and get clear. The tug was beached but on inspection it was found she was not making water, the hole being in her port fuel tank.

The *Sun III* was taken to Alexander's repair yard at Wapping and from there to her builders at Faversham for permanent repair.

In December the *Sun XXII* sailed from Gravesend to assist the *Nimrods* with mechanical problems off the Danish coast and tow her to Harwich. When nearing the position of the ship the *Sun XXII* encountered a force eleven easterly gale causing structural damage and putting out of action her radios and radar. All contact with the tug was lost and there were fears at Gravesend for her safety. When the storm abated a little the *Sun XXII* was able to seek shelter and made landfall at Newcastle and put into the Tyne for essential repairs before returning to Gravesend. The *Nimrods* was I believe taken in tow by United Towing Company's *Welshman* and delivered to Harwich.

With the steady build up of Felixstowe as a major port, it became viable to have two tugs permanently stationed there. The *Ionia* was sent round by Ship Towage (London) Ltd. in July as a second tug and others were regularly sent from London when three or more tugs were required. Sun Tugs attempted also to establish a tug in the port when in August the *Sun XXV* was sent round, but after two weeks returned to London.

On the salvage side there were a few groundings involving a large number of tugs. On 25th January the American Steamer *Fenn Victory* went ashore on Shotly Spit at the mouth of the River Orwell in Harwich Harbour when bound for Ipswich. It was 29th January before the combined efforts of the *Cervia*, *Challenge*, *Dhulia*, *Iona*, *Ocean Cock*, the Ipswich tug the *River Orwell* and the Navy tugs *Resolve* and *Exspeller* got her into deep water.

The tanker *Statue of Liberty* was in trouble again, grounding on 12th October in the North Edinburgh Channel; she refloated the following day assisted by the *Moorcock*, *Hibernia*, *Dhulia* and *Sun XXV*.

On 20th November when the *Esso Westminster* went aground in Lower Gravesend Reach six tugs were needed to refloat her, the *Avenger*, *Vanquisher*, *Atlantic Cock*, *Tanga*, *Fossa* and *Sun XXVI*.

Also in November the tanker *Isanda* broke away from No. 10 Jetty Thames Haven; the *Avenger*, *Burma*, *Cervia*, *Challenge*, *Contest*, *Crested Cock*, *Hibernia*, *Moorcock*, *Napia* and *Vanquisher* all being employed to remoor her.

On the coastal towing side the *Dhulia* was sent round to Holyhead from where she towed the British Rail Ferry *St Andrew* to Antwerp in June.

The *Sun XXV* was employed towing the crane barge *Thor* around the coast. In May she towed her from Southampton to Calais, in July from Calais up the East Coast to Immingham and from Immingham to Liverpool in September.

The start of the run down of London Docks began in 1967 with the closure of the East India Dock. As the East India Dock shut the new grain terminal in Northfleet Hope was being built. Ship Towage (London) Ltd. had won the contract to supply the towage during the building of the jetty. The jetty was constructed by a number of concrete blocks built in one of the dry docks in Tilbury Docks. When completed they were towed out and stored in the dock. When required at the site three tugs towed them into position where they were sunk. The *Fossa* and *Culex* were used prior to the positioning of the blocks towing a crane barge up and down over the site dragging a large girder to level the foundations. This job occupied the tugs on and off for many months before it was completed.

The *Thorney* built in 1943 as the *Empire Percy* became surplus after delivery to the dredging department of the P.L.A. of the twin schottle pusher tug *Broodbank* 1,000 b.h.p. The *Thorney* was withdrawn and scrapped the following year by Scrappingco S.A., Belgium.

Watercock *being launched 1967*.

# 1968

One new tug was built in 1968: W.H.J. Alexander Ltd. had the *Sun XXVII* built at Faversham by J. Pollock & Sons Co. Ltd., having a gross tonnage of 226 and dimensions of 35.44 x 8.69 x 4.04m., power supplied by a six-cylinder 2,000 b.h.p. Mirrless diesel. Equipped with full fire-fighting and salvage pumps, her fire-fighting layout was an improvement of the *Sun XXV* and *Sun XXVI*. She is fitted with a derrick on the mizzen mast that can be laid on a ship or jetty for use as a ladder and fitted with hose connections each end, so hand lines can be run direct from it. Two super jet monitors also were fitted on a platform on the main mast.

Sun Tugs also sold the *Sun XVII* to Societa Rinorchiatori Napoletani, Naples, Italy, being renamed *Rania G* joining three ex-Sun Tugs already with the company. The *Sun XVII* was a product of Alexander Hall & Co., Aberdeen in 1946 and was of standard Empire Tug design of 233 gross tons and powered by a 1,030 i.h.p. engine.

The *Ocean Cock* was returned to Gravesend from her charter to Gaselee at Felixstowe in September after the arrival of Gaselee's new tug *Sauria* on 30th August from her builders Richard Dunston Ltd., Hessel. The *Sauria*'s hull and layout was the same as the *Burma* and *Watercock* but with a more modern appearance, the funnel and mast being combined and a lifeboat fitted athwart the deck abaft the funnel, and fitted with an eight-cylinder Ruston Paxman engine of 1,600 i.h.p. and also a limited fire-fighting capacity having a single monitor on the flying bridge deck supplying foam and water.

It was the end of an era on 24th October when the *Moorcock* towed the coal hulk *Artemis* away from her moorings off Denton in Gravesend Reach. The *Artemis* had been built as the *Woodwren* for the General Steam Navigation

*Coalhulk* Artemis *being towed to Sheerness for scrap by* Moorcock *24/10/68.*

Company. She was converted into a Coal Hulk at Ramsgate all her fittings above deck level being stripped out and a steam crane fitted amidships. With the demise of the coal burning tugs she became surplus, and towed to the Medway Dry Docks at Sheerness to be broken up.

The run down of the Docks continued with the closure of London Dock.

On 22nd March the South Eastern Gas Board flat iron collier *Dulwich* jammed under Wandsworth Bridge while outward bound light on the rising tide. The Dulwich received considerable damage to her engine room casing before being towed clear by the *Fossa* and *Rana*.

The *Ionia* was kept busy with salvage work at Harwich during the year. In June she refloated with the *Ocean Cock* the German coaster *Hermar* off the South Shipwash and towed her into Harwich. On 24th July, the *Ionia* left Harwich to go to the assistance of the *Don Juan* in the North Sea. The *Ionia* found the ship the next morning 58 miles east-northeast of Harwich and towed her shearing badly into harbour and berthed her at the Navy yard at 17.30. During the evening of 24th August the Harwich to Bremerhaven ferry *Prins Hamlet* grounded inside the Guard Buoy on the ebb tide after sailing with 650 passengers aboard. The *Ionia* and *Ocean Cock* immediately went to her aid but were unable to refloat her until five hours later on the following flood tide. The

*Ionia* also went to the aid of the Swedish vessel *Ihre* in trouble near the Sunk on 20th September in a southwest gale, and towed her into Harwich.

*Dhulia* went over to the Danish coast in October for the *Marmofjell* broken down off Edsberg towing her to Felixstowe and berthing her in the dock. On completion of cargo work the *Dhulia* then towed her to London berthing her in the Southwest India Dock, assisted from Gravesend by a Sun Tug.

The *Sun XXV* had a couple of coastal tows with dredging equipment: she towed the hopper *W.D.7* from Middlesbrough to Harwich in June and in November towed the grab dredger *Tilbury Toiler* from Gravesend to Newhaven.

Dulwich *stuck under Wandsworth Bridge, March 1968.*

# 1969

On 27th January the amalgamation took place between W.H.J. Alexander Ltd. and Ship Towage (London) Ltd. bringing together all the river ship towing tugs under the one company, London Tugs Limited. The new funnel colours were a black funnel with a broad red band edged by two narrow white bands, and the Dick & Page house flag each side of the red band. With the joining of the two companies' resources, Sun Tugs' Wapping repair yard at St John's Wharf was closed down and their tug moorings off Woolwich dockyard shifted across the water and moored off North Woolwich Park down stream from North Woolwich Pier, joining forces with Ship Towage's up river fleet. With thirty-six tugs under the new companies ownership the older steam tugs were soon being scrapped. The *Sun VIII* and *Sun X* were the first to go, leaving the Thames on 10th February for Antwerp in tow of the *Sun XXV*. They had both been built by Cochrane & Sons Ltd., Selby, the *Sun VIII* in 1919 and the *Sun X* 1920, being 196 gross tons and 750 i.h.p. They were followed two weeks later by the *Ocean Cock* and *Tanga*, also scrapped at Antwerp in tow of the *Moorcock* on 25th February. The *Ocean Cock* dated from 1932, a product of Alexander Hall & Co. Ltd., Aberdeen, 184 gross tons and 1,000 i.h.p. The *Tanga* was a year older built at Dartmouth by Phillips & Son Ltd. in 1931, her gross tonnage 203 and 850 i.h.p. The *Sun XII* and *Sun XV* were the final two tugs scrapped in 1969, again at Antwerp during May. They were sisters built by Earls Co. Ltd., Hull in 1925, 183 gross tons and 750 i.h.p. The only other changes in the fleet were the *Ionia* returned to Gravesend in March following her spell in Harwich, and the *Culex* took over from the *Vespa* at Ridham Dock for a short period. The *Vespa* returned to Woolwich where she was laid up.

The *Dhulia* towed the paddle tug *Reliant* from Seaham Harbour to the Thames in June on behalf of the National Maritime Museum. In August she was berthed at Cory's Barge Yard, Charlton where she was carefully cut up into sections and taken to the Maritime Museum and rebuilt in the Neptune Hall as a central exhibit, her side-lever engines and paddles being driven by electric motors for maximum effect.

The bulk carrier *Star Columbia* had engine problems and was towed to Tilbury Dock from the Warps anchorages by three tugs. When her London cargo was discharged she was towed to Rotterdam on 25th July by the *Dhulia* and *Sun XXVII*, *The Avenger* assisting as far as Southend. The *Dhulia* and *Sun XXVII* stayed with the *Star Columbia* towing her on to Ymuiden and then to Hamburg where she was repaired, the two tugs then returning to Gravesend.

With the opening of the Dartford Tunnel the Tilbury Gravesend car ferry was closed down and the passenger ferry moved from Gravesend's town pier to the West Street Pier vacated by the car ferry. The town pier was converted into a restaurant and the redundant floating pontoon was sold for further use at Gigha Island on the West Coast of Scotland. The *Sun XXV* was engaged to tow it north sailing from Gravesend on 14th August and arriving four days later and handing her tow over to the vessel *Sound of Islay*; she then returned to Gravesend.

In October the *Sun XXV* ran to a position thirty miles east of Start Point and took in tow the Stevy Clark collier *Portslade* and delivered her at Plymouth. The *Sun XXVI* went round later and towed her to the Bristol Channel for discharge and repair. The *Sun XXV* also had a tow from Skegness in November, with the dredger *Dragger* to Swanscombe.

Various ships were refloated during the year, amongst them the *Stafford* refloated by the *Ionia* and *Sauria* on 2nd January from Shortly Spit in Harwich Harbour. On 7th January the tanker *North Sands* with a draft of 43'6" had a complete engine failure while swinging for No. 10 jetty Thames Haven. Both the ship's anchors were dropped but she grounded inside the Western Dolphin of the berth. The *North Sands* was pulled clear with the combined efforts of the *Avenger*, *Hibernia*, *Dhulia*, *Napia*, *Atlantic Cock*, *Challenge*, *Sun XIX* and *Sun XXV* and safely berthed. Another ship to have trouble at No. 10 jetty was the *Zenatta* which broke adrift from the berth on 7th March and grounded. Refloated by the *Avenger*, *Hibernia*, *Dhulia* and *Sun XXVI* it reberthed at No. 9 jetty (now B jetty).

# 1970

With the steady decline of the upper reaches of the River, the Surrey Commercial Dock was closed. The Surrey Commercial Dock was the oldest dock system on the River and also the only enclosed dock on the south shore. The Greenland and Norway Docks had been built in the 1700s as a protection for the whaling ships. The Surrey Commercial Dock Co. was formed in 1807 and the dock was gradually expanded. The main commodity imported was timber but with the pattern of trade changing, timber was now being shipped packaged in large bulk carriers that berthed down river in Tilbury Dock. These ships were far too large for the Greenland Dock Lock leading to its inevitable closure.

With this decline three more tugs were sold: two, the *Atlantic Cock* and *Crested Cock* for scrap, and the *Vespa* for further trading. The *Atlantic Cock* and *Crested Cock* were towed to Antwerp in February. Both had been built by Alexander Hall & Co. Ltd., Aberdeen, the *Atlantic Cock* in 1932 and the *Crested Cock* in 1935 and had a gross tonnage of 182 and 177 respectively and each driven by a 1,000 i.h.p. steam engine. The *Crested Cock* was fitted with a very distinctive steam whistle, which easily identified the tug. This was rescued from her and fitted onto the *Fossa*. Operated by compressed air instead of steam it is still aboard her to this day. The *Vespa* was sold to Mr Harry Rose of Poole and renamed *Wendy Ann*, leaving in tow of the *Sun XXVI* on 6th July. The *Vespar* was the smallest of the four tugs transferred from Gaselee & Son in 1965, being 72 gross tons and 520 b.h.p. The *Ionia* had Westinghouse bridge controls fitted to her main engine in October. All British Polar engined tugs except the *Rana* were modernised in this way when they had their refits.

This enabled the company to reduce the engine room manning from four to two men bringing them in line with the rest of the fleet.

On the salvage side the tanker *Constellation* was refloated at the North East Knob on 9th January by the *Hibernia*, *Napia* and the Medway tugs *Knighton* and *Kennet*. In March the *Vanquisher* towed the *Lancing*, broken down in the Channel, from the Sandettee to Dover.

A dramatic collision occurred during the evening of 26th July when the Spanish cargo liner *Monte Ulia* inward bound off Hole Haven was forced to take violent avoiding action to miss a river tanker belonging to Union Lighterage Co., that had cut across the ship's bow. In avoiding the tanker the *Monte Ulia* crashed through the head of No.4 Jetty Coryton bringing down the oil booms and then cutting through the arm of the Jetty from west to east before finally grounding in Hole Haven. Oil from the fractured pipes ignited and there was a fear the fire would spread across Hole Haven to the oil and gas installations at Canvey Island. The fire was immediately tackled by the tugs *Sun XXVI* and *Moorcock* which were in the vicinity and the fire extinguished. The *Sun XXVI* went to the assistance of the *Monte Ulia* steaming through the holes in the jetty amongst the broken piles and later pulled her clear into the fairway. Fortunately, no lives were lost in this incident but the jetty was out of action for many weeks while temporary repairs were made to enable the jetty to be used while permanent repairs were in progress.

The *Sun XXVII* left London on 20th April with the training ship *Glen Strathallen* in tow bound for Plymouth to be scuttled. The *Glen Strathallen* had been built at Selby in 1928 as an Icelantic trawler, but in recent years had been a familiar sight on the river being run jointly by three colleges engaged in nautical studies, Norwood, King Edward VII and Poplar Tech., as a training ship. On the death of her owner it was requested that when no longer required the ship was to be scuttled and this was duly carried out on 27th April in the entrance to Plymouth Sound off Heybrook Bay, close to a large rock known as the Shagstone.

# 1971

Two tugs were sold in December 1971: the *Culex* sold to John G.Efthimion of
Piraeus, Greece and renamed *Atromitos*, and the *Napia* renamed *Tolmiros*. The
*Tolmiros* (*Napia*) sailed from Gravesend on 22nd December with the *Atromitos*
(*Culex*) in tow. All went well until the two tugs ran into bad weather in the Bay
of Biscay and the *Atromitos* broke adrift and all efforts by the *Tolmiros* to find
her failed. She was later found by a Spanish trawler and towed to northern
Spain. The *Culex* had been built in Bremerhaven in 1958 for Gaselee & Son
Ltd., powered by a 660 h.p. Deutz engine and was 97 gross tons. The *Napia* was
a larger tug of 261 gross tons built at Goole as the *Empire Jester* in 1943 and
powered by a 1,200 i.h.p. triple expansion engine.

A collision occurred off Coryton on 23rd January between the tanker *Border
Chieftain* and the Sludge vessel *Hounslow*. The *Hounslow* was holed in her side
and beached by tugs on the Blyth Sands. On examination it was found she was
holed in her cargo tank but in no danger of sinking, and was refloated again.
The *Avenger*, *Hibernia*, *Sun XXVI* and *Sun XXVII* assisted in this incident.

The tanker *Panther* grounded on the Goodwin Sands on 30th March; the
*Hibernia*, *Vanquisher*, *Sun XXVI* and *Sun XXVII* went to her aid from the
Thames as well as a large number of tugs from the Continent. It was 6th April
before she refloated.

Amongst the coastal tows completed in 1971 was a trawler towed from
Fleetwood round to Hull by the *Dhulia* in June. And on 2nd September the *Sun
XXVI and Vanquisher* sailed from Portsmouth with the cruiser H.M.S. *Belfast*
in tow for London. H.M.S. *Belfast* had been saved from the breakers and was to

be moored on permanent display in the Upper Pool off Hay's Wharf opposite the Tower of London. The two tugs arrived in the Thames with the cruiser on 3rd September and docked her in Tilbury Dock at 23.30.

Sun XXVI.

# 1972

Three more tugs were disposed of in 1972. The first to go was the *Cervia* in March; she had been laid up since May of the previous year. At the time of her sale it was believed she was to be preserved and was to steam out to Australia under her own power. This never materialised and she was put back to work under the ownership of International Towing Ltd., and was used engaged in coastal towing. This didn't go down too well with the tug crews at Gravesend who saw one of their old tugs which was supposedly sold for steam preservation competing against them on the coast. The *Cervia* had been built in 1946 as the *Empire Raymond* at Aberdeen and later transferred to William Watkins Ltd., and renamed. The *Cervia* was 233 gross tons and powered by a 900 i.h.p. triple expansion engine.

Next to go was the *Contest* which had boiler trouble and was sold for scrap to T.Ward at Grays. The *Challenge* was given the job of towing the *Contest* on her last trip to the breakers on 7th April. The *Contest* was built for the Elliott Steam Tug Company at Aberdeen in 1933, powered by a 1150 i.h.p. engine and having a gross tonnage of 213. With the scrapping of the *Contest* this left the *Challenge* as the last steam tug in the fleet.

The other change was the *Sun XVIII* which was sent round to Felixstowe under charter to Gaselee & Son (Felixstowe) Ltd.

On 20th March the *Sugar Refiner* outward bound light from Tate & Lyle's sugar refinery at Silvertown had a steering failure the lower end of Barking Reach off Crossness and collided with the *Artagen* moored at Samual Williams Jetty, Dagenham. The *Artagen* received extensive damage to her side and the *Sun II*, *Sun XXIII*, *Sun XVII*, *Sun XXIV* and *Fossa* all assisted in separating the two vessels.

The tanker *Chevron Antwerp* grounded in the estuary at the Tizard on 1st July and the *Moorcock*, *Vanquisher*, *Ionia*, *Sun XIX*, *Sun XXII* and *Sun XXVII* were all engaged to refloat her.

The *Sun XXV* had a tow from Southampton to Charlton at the end of February with a dredger and pontoon. She also towed the barge *Kingsnorth* loaded with beer vats from Sheerness to Leith and after unloading, towed her on to Aberdeen.

The *Plangent* suffered an unfortunate sinking after towing a ship into the lock of the King George V Dock in September. If a ship's beam was narrow enough to allow the tug to turn and pass between the lock wall and the ship's side, it would do so. This saved the delay of the tug having to lock out with the ship and wait while it was undocked by river tugs, and then lock back in again. The *Plangent* was doing such a manoeuvre, and as she slid past the inner lock gate, struck an obstruction protruding from it, which split the hull and the *Plangent* began to sink fast. The crew managed to get her clear of the lock and round the knuckle and were able to scramble ashore on the cross wall at No. 1 berth as she sank. Four wreck lighters from the salvage department soon had her lifted and she was refurbished and returned to work.

# 1973

The Port of London Authority disposed of two of its dock tug fleet, the *Platina* and *Plateau*, to the Holyhead Towing Company. They left the Thames on 16th April, the *Platina* under tow of the *Plateau* for the Anglesey Port. They were later renamed *Afon Goch* and *Afon Las* respectively. The *Afon Goch* name was changed again to *Afon Caradoc* in March 1976 when Holyhead Towing Co. purchased the Smit Tug *Schelde* and gave her the name *Afon Goch*. They were two of four identical sisters built at Hull in 1952, twin screw tugs of 1,200 b.h.p. and were 159 gross tons, the only difference being the *Plateau* had been built with fitted Kort nozzles.

The *Challenge* was sold by London Tugs Ltd. on 29th October to Taylor Woodrow for preservation in St Katherine's Dock. It was planned to keep her in a working condition and have her steaming on the river on occasions, and Taylor Woodrow had her boiler re-tubed at Erith. I also understood at the time she was going to be altered back as near as possible to her design when she was built; if this was the case it did not materialise. She is now one of the vessels on permanent display and open to the public in St Katherine's Dock representing an era now long passed. With the sale of the *Challenge*, the last steam tug in the fleet, it was also the end of an era for London Tugs stretching back to 1869 when Watkins first introduced the screw propeller to ship towing on the Thames, when he had the little *Era* of 30 gross tons built to test whether a tug driven by a screw propeller as against the paddle could be a success.

With the size of ships using the Port getting larger, it was apparent increased bollard pulls were required so the Company embarked on a modernisation programme to cope with this. The *Ionia* was first to be converted sailing from Gravesend on 1st June to the River Tyne where the work was undertaken by the

Tyne Dock and Engineering Company. There she had a gearbox fitted to her main engine and a Tow-master fixed Kort nozzle with three rudders fitted, increasing her bollard pull to 22 tons. She arrived back at Gravesend on 11th October on completion of her alterations, and on 31st October was once again stationed at Harwich.

The premature death occurred of Mr William Watkins, joint managing director of London Tugs Ltd., on 4th November at the age of only 47 years. The tugs had their white line on the bulwarks painted blue as a sign of mourning.

Amongst the salvage undertaken during the year was the *Sun XIX* which went to the assistance of the *Anita Schutt* on 2nd April anchored near the Shivering Sand Forts with her rudder damaged. This was caused when she was making her approach to Whitstable in heavy swell and she touched the ground. The *Anita Schutt* was carrying a cargo of stone at the time, and the *Sun XIX* towed her to Tilbury Landing Stage, from where she was shifted across the river to a drying berth at the Imperial Paper Mills, Gravesend for a survey of her damage. The Tug *Tudor Rose* later towed her to Whitstable to be unloaded.

During dredging operations at Shell Haven on 25th April the hopper *Augustas Manning* was being loaded but the dredger did not have the reach (these P.L.A. hoppers being quite beamy) to load the spoil evenly. One side of the hopper was filled causing it to list; it was then swung round alongside the dredger and the other side filled bringing it back onto an even keel. It was during one such manoeuvre that the tug *John White* (ex *Silvermark*) was swinging the hopper, but it had been loaded too much on the one side and it rolled over onto the tug crushing her engine room skylight and began to take water as she was being pushed under. The *Sun XIX* and *Sun XXV* were close by and immediately went to assist. The *Sun XIX* went alongside the *John White* took off the crew, put a rope on her and pulled her clear before the hopper sank her. As the *John White* was freed her main engines started and being direct drive was under way with nobody aboard her. The *Sun XIX* kept ahead of the *John White* steering her away from the oil jetties until the tug *Hembo* was able to catch the runaway up and put a man aboard her to stop the engine. The *Sun XXV*, meanwhile, had gone to assist the *Augustus Manning*, which had turned upside down by this time and get hold of it through its rudder frame and towed it clear of the fairway.

On the following day, 26th April, the American container ship *C.V. Staghound* grounded on her approach to Felixstowe at the Cliff Foot buoy. The *Sun XIX* and *Moorcock* ran round from Gravesend assisting the *Sun XXI*, *Sun XVIII*, *Sauria* and *Alison Howard* to refloat her on the tide of the following day.

*1973* — Cap San Antonio *on fire.* 127

At 01.53 on 17th November the *Sun XXVI* was running light down channel bound for Southampton for a tow when she received a Mayday from the West German Ship *Cap San Antonio* on fire and requesting immediate assistance in position 50°41′ 36″N. 00°41′ 06″E (10 miles south of Hastings).

*Sun XXVI* arrived at the ship at 02.20 and rescued two crew members who had jumped into the sea. The fire was in the midship accommodation, and as the crew were managing to contain the fire the *Sun XXVI* took her in tow bound for Dover. Hastings' lifeboat was on the scene soon after and returned the two survivors from the *Sun XXVI* back to the ship; the mate of the tug also went aboard for an assessment of the situation and on his return reported six crew members missing. The Bugsier tug *Hermes* arrived from her salvage station at Dover at 05.20 and made fast on the starboard side to assist in the fire-fighting. At 07.30 two fire brigade officers were airlifted aboard by helicopter and the Dover Harbour Tug *Diligent* also arrived on the scene and made fast to the port bow. At 09.40 the pilot boarded off Folkestone and with the ship developing a port list, which increased to 10°, the *Hermes* shifted aft to assist steering. The *Cap San Antonio* anchored 1¹/₂ miles west of Dover Harbour at 10.30 and the *Hibernia* arrived 10 minutes later with pumping gear and the fire brigade. The *Sun XXVI* then went alongside and commenced fire-fighting and pumping out the excess water. The large Bugsier tug *Oceanic, en route* to Germany through the Channel, arrived at the ship in the late afternoon and was engaged to supply foam. *Oceanic*'s prior commitments did not allow her to stay long and she dismissed herself at 04.00 the next morning. The *Avenger* arrived in the late evening and passed over extra pumping gear; she was bound for Southampton for the tow the *Sun XXVI* was to have done. At 19.30 on the 18th the fire brigade was satisfied that the fire was out and the tugs stopped pumping as the ship was on an even keel. The services of the *Hibernia*, *Diligent* and the fire brigade were all dispensed with leaving the *Sun XXVI* and *Hermes* in attendance. During the early hours of the 19th the *Sun XXVI* extinguished two pockets of fire that had re-ignited and was pumping again for a short period before removing all their equipment at 10.00, the tug then standing by.

At 15.30 the Dutch tug *Smit Enterprise* arrived alongside and prepared to tow the ship to Rotterdam. At 18.00 on 19th November the salvage was completed and the *Sun XXVI* returned to Gravesend. The *Cap San Antonio* was loaded with 2,000 tons of tin plate and chemicals, and had on board 45 crew members and three passengers of which four crew and two passengers lost their lives in the fire.

Amongst the coastal tows completed in 1973 was the barge *Kingsnorth* from Sheerness to Preston by the *Sun XXV* in February. This was one of a number of identical tows to Preston with the barge loaded with beer vats for a brewery in the northwest. The *Sun XXV* was forced to seek shelter at Dartmouth owing to adverse weather and caused a bit of interest locally by being visited by people who had been employed building her ten years before. The *Sun XXV* also towed the bucket dredger *Africa* from Gravesend to Portland Harbour on 27th and 28th December.

# 1974

The *Sun XVIII* was returned in September from her charter to Gaselee Felixstowe Ltd. to London and laid up at North Woolwich Pier. Her place at Felixstowe was taken by the *Rana* which worked there under Gaselee until November. She then returned to the Thames joining the *Sun XVIII* laid up on North Woolwich Pier.

Rana.

Following the success of the conversion of the *Ionia*, the *Avenger* was sent to the Tyne for modernisation at the Tyne Dock and Engineering Co., South Shields. The *Avenger* was fitted with a Towmaster fixed Kort nozzle, and a variable pitched propeller increasing her bollard pull from 18 to 32 tons, when completed the following year.

On the coast the *Sun XXV* towed a ro-ro pontoon from Harwich to Immingham in March and in April the *Avenger* ran to the Channel Islands to tow the grab dredger *Tilbury Toiler* and a hopper from St Hellier, Jersey to Southampton. Other coastal tows included a Humber paddle ferry *Wingfield Castle* from Hull to London by the *Sun XXVI* in July and the dredger *Beverwijk 5* from Middlesborough to Harwich by the *Sun XXV* in October.

On the salvage side the tanker *Cossicana* grounded at Coryton on 30th January and was refloated by the *Moorcock*, *Vanquisher*, *Burma*, *Hibernia*, *Dhulia*, *Sun XXV* and *Sun XXII*. The Suction dredger *Deepstone* suffered a breakdown at the Cross Sand Buoy northeast of Great Yarmouth in February, and the *Sun XXVI* towed her to Rotterdam for repair. A fire occurred in the accommodation in the West German coaster *Ellenora H* loaded with a cargo of bulk sugar in the vicinity of the East Goodwin on 16th October with the loss of two of her crew. An American warship and the British coaster *Frendo Spirit* went to her aid, and on the arrival of the *Hibernia*, a fully equipped fire-fighting tug, the warship handed over the fire-fighting to the *Hibernia* and left the scene. The *Hibernia* put into Dover and brought the fire brigade out to the ship. After the fire was extinguished the *Ellenora H* was towed to Dover Harbour; the *Frendo Spirit*, being relieved by a Dover Harbour tug, berthed on the eastern arm.

# 1975

On 1st January the Alexandra Towing Co. of Liverpool took control of London Tugs Ltd., the Medway Dry Dock & Engineering Co. Ltd. and Gaselee & Son (Felixstowe) Ltd. With this merger the direct links with the old established London tugs companies of William Watkins, Dick & Page and W.H.J. Alexander, which went back to the last century, was finally broken. London Tugs Ltd. now traded under the title of the Alexandra Towing Co (London) Ltd.

The *Sun XVIII* was sold in January soon after the take-over to A.N.Vogul and renamed *Ecclesbourne*. When built in 1951 she had been the first motor tug in the Sun tug fleet. Two more tugs left the Thames for other Alexandra operated ports; first to go was the *Rana* going to Swansea on 5th March followed in May by the *Sun XXII* to Felixstowe. The *Sun XXII*'s name was changed to *Deban* the following year. It was rumoured at the time that all the Gravesend fleet were going to have their names changed and be given local names in keeping with the method of naming tugs throughout the Alexandra fleet. But, as happens with many rumours, this failed to materialise, the tugs keeping their original names.

With the *Avenger* back on the River after her conversion on the Tyne the *Hibernia* was next to be modernised going to Sheerness in September, her Kort nozzle and variable pitched propeller being fitted by the Medway Dry Dock & Engineering Co. Ltd.

Among the various salvages undertaken was the refloating of the tanker *Nemeo* on 3rd January after she grounded in Long Reach by the *Sun XIX*, *Sun XXI*, *Sun XXV*, *Sun XXVII*, *Ionia*, *Vanquisher* and *Fossa*. On 17th May the *Sun XXV* ran to a position 10 miles west of Boulogne and took in tow the

*Magdelene Vinnen* with engine damage and handed her over to local tugs at the Hook of Holland the following day.

# 1976

The only change in the fleet in 1976 was the *Ionia* being transferred to Southampton from 25th May till 25th September when she returned to Gravesend.

Vanquisher *being raised after being sunk undocking* Jervis Bay.

While in the process of undocking the O.C.L. container ship *Jervis Bay* 28,876 gross tons from Tilbury Dock New Entrance stern first with the *Sun XIX* and *Sun III* during the afternoon of Thursday 8th January, the *Vanquisher* was girted and sank. This was more or less a carbon copy of the sinking of the *Cervia* in 1954, the *Vanquisher* being on the starboard quarter and being caught in the powerful wash of a steam-turbine powered vessel. With the ship going ahead with its helm to starboard the *Vanquisher* was unable to get round in time to run with the ship or to let go and was rolled over and sank. Fortunately, all the crew managed to get out of the tug and were picked up from the water by local waterman, Mr Hills, in his boat. The tugs were not fitted with the Britannia quick release towing hook at this time, and there was too much weight on the manual release hook for it to be knocked away. The *Vanquisher* was raised late on the following day by four wreck lighters of the P.L.A. Salvage Department, the *Hookness*, *Crossness*, *Broadness* and *Stoneness*. She was taken to Sheerness to be repaired and refurbished, returning to work on 10th June.

His Royal Highness, the Prince Phillip, Duke of Edinburgh, visited the newly completed Alexandra House on 1st June and unveiled a sculpture in welded bronze of the sea god Poseidon by Mr C Rice on the forecourt to mark the occasion.

The Duke of Edinburgh was given a guided tour of the building and presented with a scale model of the sculpture by the Company. Alexandra House is situated on the eastern side of the entrance to the Royal Terrace Pier and consists of five floors; the top two are leased to Trinity House as the Pilot Station for both River and Channel Pilots at Gravesend, the lower two floors house the offices of tug movement control of Alexandra Towing, and the bottom floor houses the store and keeps the tugs supplied with all their day to day requirements.

The *Sun XXV* left Southampton on 16 January for Ardyne Point on the Firth of Clyde with the barge *G.W. 132* in tow. Storms in the Irish Sea forced her to seek shelter at Dublin for 8 days, sailing on 26th January but, with the weather still far from good, put into Belfast later the same day. The *Sun XXV* safely delivered the barge to Ardyne Point the following day and then returned light to Gravesend.

In February the *Sun XXVII* towed the pontoon *G.W. 135* from Southampton to Flotta Island in the Orkney Islands. This was one of a number of tows to Flotta undertaken by various units of the fleet at this time with equipment for the oil terminal being built at Scapa Flow to receive North Sea oil. The

Liverpool based Alexandra tug *Huskinson* was based there while the building was taking place assisting the contractors.

Other coastal tows completed included the Brazilian submarine *Tonelero* towed from Chatham naval base in March by the *Avenger* to Barrow-in-Furness, the *Moorcock* accompanying as escort tug.

The *Avenger* also had a tow in August of a pile barge from Portland Harbour to Milford Haven Dock. From there she ran down to St Nazaire in the Bay of Biscay for two Westminster dredging hoppers that she had delivered to St Nazaire in February to be taken to Rotterdam. The *Avenger* left on 26th August with the *W.D.842* and *W.D.843* in tow; she sheltered behind the Isle of Wight for weather for a day and arrived Rotterdam on 30th August. In October *Sun XXV* towed the *Pointe Du Tovlinquet* from Le Harve to Greenhithe. The ship was owned by F.T.Everard Ltd., and was being returned to Greenhithe at the end of a charter to a French firm.

The tanker *Golar Nichu* grounded on the Mucking while swinging to berth at Shell Haven on 17th January. This ship had minimal stern power and did not manoeuvre easily, and when attempting to round off the berth two years later she grounded in the same place. On this occasion she was refloated with the combined efforts of the *Ionia*, *Dhulia*, *Moorcock* and *Sun XXVII*.

During the late afternoon of 29th July a fire started on the end of Southend Pier and quickly got out of hand. The *Vanquisher* and *Moorcock* had just unberthed a tanker at Shell Haven and proceeded immediately to the fire as did the *Avenger* who was in the vicinity of the Pier at the time. A very fierce fire was burning on the tugs' arrival and they set to work fighting the fire with monitors and hand lines. The *Sun XXVII*, *Hibernia* and *Dhulia* ran down from Gravesend and the *Keverne* arrived from the Medway. A crop-spraying aircraft also made repeated flights over the Pier dropping its load of water onto the fire. To us tug-hands fighting the fire, it appeared that the plane succeeded in soaking us each time it went over as much as its attempts to extinguish the blaze.

Southend lifeboat was used transporting the fire brigade from the shore side of the fire round to the tugs fighting the fire on the outside of the pier. The fire was finally put out during the early hours of 30th July and the *Moorcock* and *Vanquisher* were retained damping down and at 07.00 were the last two tugs dismissed.

# 1977

Three new tugs were ordered from Richard Dunston Ltd. at Hessel soon after the Alexandra Co. took control of London Tugs, and all three were delivered in 1977. First to enter the water was the *Sun Essex* on 22nd March and after fitting out arrived at Gravesend on 22nd July followed by the *Sun Kent* launched on 4th April and arriving Gravesend on 7th October. They were identical sisters of 272 gross tons, 32.92 x 9.61 x 4.91m. and powered by Vee twelve-cylinder Ruston Paxman diesel engine of 2,000 b.h.p. driving a variable pitched propeller in a steerable Kort nozzle developing a bollard pull of 35 tons. The pair were also fully equipped fire-fighting tugs able to supply foam or water from three monitors, one on top of the main mast and the other two from a platform on the mast above the bridge. The pump is also able to be used in a salvage capacity. The *Sun Essex* and *Sun Kent* were also fitted with a towing winch for coastal towing, the first tugs so fitted in the Gravesend fleet. The third tug delivered was the *Sun London*, launched on 19th July and arriving at Gravesend from the Humber on 17th November. The *Sun London*'s dimensions were 32.92 x 9.61 x 4.91m., 265 gross tons and powered by a Ruston Paxman twelve-cylinder Vee engine of 2,640 b.h.p. driving a variable pitched propeller in a steerable Kort nozzle producing a bollard pull of 45 tons. The *Sun London* is also one of a pair her sister being the Wallasey part of Alexandra's Liverpool fleet, both also fitted with towing winches.

With the arrival of the *Sun Essex* the *Fossa* became surplus and was sold in July, after a spell laid up in the K.G.V. dock. Her buyers were Darling Brothers, a London Lighterage Company, and was renamed *Kilda*.

The *Fossa* was the last of the four tugs from Gaselee & Son to remain in the Gravesend fleet.

The *Sun XXV* was next in line to be modernised, dry docking at Sheerness on 15th June for the fitting of her Townmaster Kort nozzle by the Medway Dry Dock & Engineering Co. Her's is a fixed Kort nozzle and her single rudder being replaced by three smaller ones placed side by side.

Coastal towing was still on the increase and among the tows completed in 1977 was the barge *Flotta Queen* from Aberdeen to Gravesend in February by the *Vanquisher*. Also in February the Greek tanker *Panaghia A* was towed from lay-up from the King George V dock to Rotterdam by the *Dhulia* and *Moorcock*. The *Dhulia* also had a tow of the bucket dredger *Africa* from Gravesend to Southampton in April. In July the *Moorcock* towed two Lykes Seebee barges the *LY 109*, *LY 204* from Gravesend to Great Yarmouth. These barges were from the barge carrying vessel *Doctor Lykes* which was one of three ships which regularly berthed on buoys off Gravesend. The two barges were loaded with drilling equipment for use in the North Sea and it was the first time that any of the barges had been towed round the coast. The tugs *Hector Reed* and *Gulf Ace II* assisted the *Moorcock* to berth the barges in Great Yarmouth. After being unloaded and reloaded with cargo for the States, the *Moorcock* towed the pair back to Gravesend where they were loaded into the *Tilly Lykes* for passage to the U.S.A.

In November the large bulk carrier *Triton* dragged her anchor from the Warps anchorage below Southend in a storm and grounded. The *Sun Essex*, *Hibernia*, *Vanquisher* and *Sun XXVII* were all employed to get the *Triton* afloat again and back to her anchorage.

*1977* — Sun Kent, Sun Essex.

# 1978

The *Sun XXV* returned to Gravesend after the fitting of her Kort nozzle and had bollard pull trials on 2nd March, her pull having increased from 22 tons to a useful 35 tons. The *Sun XXVI* went to Sheerness soon after for an identical conversion as the *Sun XXV* and was the last tug in the fleet to be modernised in this way. During the refits the *Sun XXVI* was bought up to D.T.I. standards for carrying of passengers and was issued with a certificate the following year for a maximum of 65 passengers to be carried as far seaward as the Southend anchorages. Passengers were being carried up to this time by the *Vanquisher* and *Sun XX*.

In June the Royal Terrace Pier was formally reopened after being renovated and bought back to its original form. The Royal Terrace Pier was first built in 1844 and is now a listed building. The reopening ceremony was undertaken by Mrs H.B.Bicket, wife of the chairman of the Alexandra Towing Co., Mr Henry Bicket.

Violent storms raged over the southeast of England on 12th January resulting in various ships getting into difficulties in the Thames. The large liquified gas tanker *L.N.G.Aries*, 83,646 gross tons started to break her moorings at the North Thames Gas Board Jetty at Canvey Island during the afternoon and called for tug assistance. The *Sun Essex* was Shell Haven duty tug and the *Sun London* was at No. 4 Sea Reach running back from Harwich, both going immediately to the *L.N.G.Aries* and pushing to keep her on the berth. The *Moorcock*, *Sun XIX*, *Sun XXI* and *Dhulia* ran down from Gravesend and were all pushing but the wind increased and, despite the combined power of all the tugs, a violent gust of wind broke her adrift.

The ship was swept across the channel and she grounded on the south side breaking the chains holding the collar barges of the Egypt Bay barge moorings, spinning one of them in the air and knocking them adrift; they ended up aground on the sea wall of the Kent shore. After the ship had grounded the *Sun London* and *Sun Essex* managed with extreme difficulty in the extreme weather conditions to get hold of forward and, with the other tugs pushing, to refloat her. The *L.N.G.Aries* then proceeded to the Warps to anchor with the *Sun London* and the *Sun Essex* towing forward. The weather was so bad that it was necessary to increase the length of the tugs tow rope. This was achieved by the crew getting a towing spring from the after hold into the engine room via the escape hatch and dragging the rope up the engine room ladder onto the deck where it was connected on. The seas were far too rough to be able to open the hatch to the after hold. When the ship had anchored the two tugs remained in attendance throughout the night until the storm had abated. The *Silverforce* also got into difficulties during the storm, dragging her anchor at Southend, the *Vanquisher* and *Hibernia* assisting her. During the early hours of the following morning 13th January the *Thordrache* broke adrift from Swanscombe buoys and the *Dhulia* went to her aid towing her off so she could be re-moored.

The tugs were engaged in two large oil pollutions during the spring: the first after the grounding on the French coast of the *Amoco Cadiz*, the *Vanquisher* and *Sun XXV* being chartered by the Government and left Gravesend bound for Plymouth on 18th March. Both arrived at Portland on 21st March for shelter and were fitted out with the oil dispersing equipment there and shifting to Weymouth the following day to await orders.

The Southampton based Alexandra tug *Coburg* was also standing by in Weymouth. The three tugs left Weymouth on 25th March in an attempt to get to Guernsey but it was blowing a force eight gale and with the risk of damage to the dispersant gear all returned to Weymouth. They finally left on 30th March for St Peter Port, Guernsey from where they left daily to an area designated to that tug for spraying. Other tugs working from Guernsey were *St Mawes* (Falmouth Towing Co.) *Avongarth* and *Point Spencer* (Cory Ship Towage) *Calshot* (Red Funnel Tugs) *Coburg* (Alexandra Towing Co.) *Pullwell Victor* (Frank Pearce Tugs) and the *Lady Sarah* and *Lady Alma* (Humber Tugs). The *Vanquisher* and *Sun XXV* were dismissed on 8th April and arrived in the Thames the following day, landing the spraying gear at Tilbury Landing Stage.

Less than a month later on 6th May a collision occurred in the vicinity of the Haisborough Sands off the Norfolk Coast with the result the Greek tanker *Elani V* broke in two foreside of the bridge. The stern section remained afloat and was towed to Rotterdam, but the bow section capsized and was floating upside down. The ship was loaded with heavy fuel oil and a large volume was floating on the sea. A fleet of tugs and trawlers was chartered by the D.T.I. to try and stop as much oil as possible from polluting the holiday beaches of East Anglia. The *Moorcock* sailed from Gravesend late the same evening for Great Yarmouth where the anti-pollution vessels were to be based, arriving the following morning. The *Sun Kent* arrived from Middlesbrough from where she had delivered her tow from Odense, Denmark. The *Scotsman*, *Irishman*, and *Guardsman* of United Towing Company of Hull were engaged in trying to salve the fore part of the *Elani V*.

The *Sun Kent* was also made fast to the *Elani V* for a few days assisting the salvers. The *Sun XXV* and *Hibernia* arrived on 9th May swelling the ranks of the tugs that were arriving from ports on the east and south coast. Alexandra Towing also contributed the *Egerton* from Felixstowe and the *Romsey* from Southampton, Tyne tugs the *Cragsider*, Tees Towing the *Ralph Cross*, Humber Tugs *Lady Alma* and *Lady Sarah*, Red Funnel Tugs, Southampton *The Calshot*, the Great Yarmouth Tug *Hector Reed*, the American Tug *Miss Natalie* and some small tugs and trawlers from Lowestoft formed the fleet chasing oil slicks up and down the east coast. The Royal Navy had a mine sweeper and later a frigate co-ordinating the anti-pollution vessels; a helicopter from the frigate was used seeking out the oil slicks and directing the tugs to them. The wreck was eventually blown up in the vicinity of the Cross Sands buoy, all the Gravesend's tugs were gradually dispensed with and were all off hire by 5th June.

The tanker *Golar Nichu* again grounded on the Mucking Flats while attempting to swing to berth at Shell Haven. As previously mentioned she grounded in January 1976 while doing the same manoeuvre. In this incident it required the services of the *Sun Essex*, *Sun Kent*, *Moorcock*, *Ionia*, *Avenger* and *Sun XXVI* to refloat her and get her berthed safely.

During 11th and 12th September the *Sun XXV* went to the assistance of the *Lys Blink* broken down 25 miles northeast of North Foreland in a force eight gale and towed her to Sheerness for repair.

Coastal towage was still increasing in volume and amongst the tows undertaken were, in February the *Sun London* towed the sheerlegs *Amsterdam* from Ymuidem to London for heavy lift work on the Thames Barrier. While returning the *Amsterdam* to Ymuiden on 12th February, the *Sun London* stood by the *Sea Lion* broken down twenty-seven miles east of Southwold until the arrival on the scene of the *Sauria* from Felixstowe.

On the 30th March the *Sun London* left Ymuiden with a submersible barge *M.G.338.2* in tow for Calshot, Southampton Water where it was anchored by the Dutch salvage vessel *Hulp-in-Nord*. The *Sun London* stood by the barge until its cargo had been floated off and then returned the barge to Ymuiden arriving 14th April.

The *Sun Kent* ran to Plymouth at the end of June to tow the preserved three masted topsail schooner *Kathlene and May* to St Katherine's Dock, London. The *Kathlene and May* had been opened to the public at the Barbican, Plymouth but had not proved a very viable proposition there. It was decided to shift her to London to join other Maritime Trust Ships on show in St Katherine's Dock, and she left Plymouth in tow of the *Sun Kent* on 30th June. A five knot speed and force five wind restriction was in force for the tow and the *Sun Kent* arrived at Gravesend on 3rd July and handed the schooner over to the *Sun XXIII* and *Sun XXIV* for the passage up river.

On 8th July the *Sun XXVII* and *Vanquisher* assisted the Dutch tug *Temi IV* away from Greenhithe with the training ship *Worcester* in tow. With the building of the new nautical training college ashore the old *Worcester* was no longer required and was scrapped in Belgium. Built in 1905 as the *Exmouth* she was built in the style of a 'Wooden Wall' and had trained hundreds of Merchant Navy cadets since she replaced the old *Worcester* at Greenhithe in 1946. With her scrapping one of the familiar sites of the Thames disappeared.

# 1979

The Alexandra Towing Co. (London) Ltd. took delivery of the large twin screw tug *Formidable*, arriving at Gravesend on 17th May. The *Formidable* was second of a pair built by Richard Dunston Ltd. of Hessel, her sister *Indomitable* being delivered in January and is part of Alexandra's Liverpool fleet. The *Formidable* is 406 gross tons, dimensions of 35 x 10.26 x 4.9m. and is powered by 2 eight-cylinder Ruston Paxman V engines of 1,760 b.h.p. each, 3,520 b.h.p. total, driving variable pitch propellers in steerable Kort nozzles producing a bollard pull of 55 tons. Both tugs were built for working in open waters, having a large raised fo'c's'le and fitted with a towing winch, but still being small enough to be used as a harbour tug when not required at sea.

The *Waterloo* was the next edition of the Gravesend fleet being transferred from the Swansea fleet and arriving in the Thames on 7th June. She was also a high-powered tug built with coastal towing in mind, having a slightly raised fo'c's'le and a high housing giving a very lofty top heavy appearance. Built by Richard Dunston Ltd., Hessel in 1977, along with her sister *Wellington* which was based at Liverpool, were 315 gross tons, dimensions 33.86 x 9.61 x 4.81m. and powered by identical engines as the *Formidable* twin eight-cylinder Ruston Paxman V engines total 3,520 b.h.p. driving a single variable pitch propeller in a steerable Kort nozzle producing 54 tons bollard pull. The *Waterloo* was also a fully equipped fire tug able to supply foam or water from three monitors on the mast or hand lines, the fire pump also doubling as a salvage pump. Also fitted was a twin barrelled towing winch for sea and coastal towing.

Four tugs were also deleted from the Gravesend fleet, two being sold and two redeployed at Southampton. The latter pair was the *Sun XXIV* going to

147

Southampton during April, followed by the *Sun XXI* on 30th June. There was usually one small tug in the Alexandra Southampton fleet and the *Sun XXIV* was a replacement for the *Cherry* (ex-*Cherrygarth*) that had capsized on 18th December of the previous year while assisting the *Tanafjord*.

The two sold were the *Sun XIX* and *Sun XX* going to Societa Rimorchiatori Napoletani Naples, Italy, and joining other ex-Sun tugs already in the fleet. The *Sun XIX* had been laid up in the King George V Dock since 1st March 1978 and was the first to leave, sailing from Gravesend on 13th April under the name *Sole Primo* (Sun One) arriving Naples on 24th April. The Italian crew then returned to Gravesend to prepare the *Sun XX* renamed *Sole Secondo* (Sun Two) for her voyage South, leaving the Thames on 26th May.

Coastal towing was still on the increase especially with the larger tugs now in the fleet and a large proportion being related to the oil exploration in the North Sea. The *Sun XXV* towed the Stephenson Clark collier *Aldrinton* to the River Tyne from Harwich with engine damage during 15th – 16th May. The *Sun XXV* followed this by towing three barges from Dunkirk to Bremerhaven with the *Formidable*. The *Sun XXV* sailed on 4th June and arrived on 6th June with one barge, followed the next day by the *Formidable* (her first coastal tow) with two barges arriving Bremerhaven 7th June.

Also in June the *Avenger* towed the trawler *St Martin* from Southampton to Lowestoft handing her over to the tug *Ala* outside the Suffolk port. In July the *Waterloo* towed the suction dredger *Marinex V* from Amsterdam to Swansea to be scrapped. She then proceeded across the Bay of Biscay to Le Verdun at the mouth of the River Gironde, France. The *Waterloo* took in tow the containership *Eurobridge Link* anchored off the port after sustaining a crankshaft explosion and took her to Rotterdam arriving 1st August where her cargo was unloaded. The *Formidable* had returned the barges she towed to Bremerhaven back to Dunkirk and from there she ran to Rotterdam, relieved the *Waterloo* of her tow and towed the *Eurobridge Link* on to Hamburg for repairs, the *Waterloo* returning to Gravesend from Rotterdam. The *Sun London* was also busy on the coast towing the *Maesk Barge 9* from Rotterdam to Cherbourg during July; she then ran to Swansea to tow the *Rana* to the River Medway. As mentioned earlier, the *Rana* had been transferred to Swansea in 1975 and had now become surplus to requirements in the Welsh port and was sold to the London Lighterage Company, Humphrey Grey Ltd. The *Sun London* delivered the *Rana* to the Medway on 5th August. She was then refitted on the slip at Strood and fitted with a new wheelhouse, her name changed to *Redriff* during September. The *Formidable* towed the barge *Moreland No 7*

148

from the River Schelde to Bordeaux in August and on completion of it being loaded, the *Formidable* returned to Bordeaux to act as escort tug to her sister the *Indomitable* which was to tow it to Stavanger, Norway. The convoy sailed on 17th October; a weather restriction was in force for the tow and bad weather forced the tugs to seek shelter in Cherbourg, the River Tyne and Leith before safely delivering at Stavanger during November.

Amongst the other coastal tows completed was the *Maersk Barge 3* from Rotterdam to Cherbourg in August by the *Sun London*, which the following month towed the *W.D. Challenger* from Gravesend to Brest returning to Portland to tow the dredger *Afrika* to Southampton. The *Formidable* also towed the *Bargeman* from Ardersier to Rotterdam during September.

*November 1979 — Fire on* Portal III *put out by* Hibernia *and* Sun XXVI.

On the salvage side the *Waterloo* was involved in another oil pollution prevention job from 6th–17th July. The German tanker *Tarpenbek* was in collision in the vicinity of Selsey Bill with the R.F.A. logistics ship *Sir Geriant* on 21 June and capsized. The *Waterloo* joined tugs from Southampton and Portsmouth in preventing oil from reaching the beaches of the South coast and Isle of Wight while a salvage operation took place.

The Spanish container ship *Candamo* had a steering failure on 28th August when outward bound at the Thames Barrier, and struck one of the buttresses, causing slight damage. The *Sun II* was the safety tug at the barrier; Alexandra's were contracted by the G.L.C. to supply a tug 24 hrs a day while the barrier was being built to guard against such an eventuality. The *Sun II* immediately got hold of the *Candamo* assisted by the *Sun XXVII* which was duty Woolwich fire tug and pulled her clear before any serious damage was done. The *Candamo* was in trouble again in October when anchored off Gravesend; she swung on the high water and a mooring buoy fouled her propeller. The *Formidable* pulled her clear without damage.

On 27th November a serious fire occurred on the pontoon *Portal 3* engaged in the building of the extension to Tower Wharf, Northfleet. A ruptured pipe from a diesel tank fuelled the fire and gas cylinders stored on the deck were exploding and some shooting across the water like torpedoes. A spirit tanker unloading petrol at the adjacent Robins Wharf was forced to shut down and leave the danger area. The *Hibernia* went to the scene and fought the fire with foam and bought it under control before it spread to the crane and other machinery on the barge. The *Sun XXVI* then arrived with the Kent Fire Brigade who boarded the barge and completely extinguished the blaze.

# 1980

The only change in 1980 was the *Dhulia* being transferred to Great Yarmouth on 16th July. She replaced the smaller *Canada* (ex-*Pea Cock*) which returned to Liverpool; Alexandra Towing had established a tug in Great Yarmouth for approximately a year and crews to man the tug being supplied from Felixstowe when required.

Ramsgate was being extended into a Ferry Port with new jetties being built outside the existing harbour and a new breakwater to be constructed to protect them. The *Sun XXIII* was sent to Ramsgate during May and she and other tugs on occasions worked in the port for a period of months assisting the ferries when they required a tug.

The *Sun XXV* was bought up to D.T.I. standards for the carriage of passengers and was issued with a licence to carry sixty-five passengers to as far seaward as the Southend anchorages. This bought the number of passenger carrying tugs back to three following the sale of the *Sun XX* the previous year. The passenger tugs were used at times as a replacement of the Gravesend to Tilbury ferry when the ferry was out of commission.

Further run-down of the ports took place with the closure of the South West India Dock to commercial traffic. The only ships that continued to dock there were the wine tankers, (the P.L.A. had shifted the bulk wine store from London dock on its closure in 1968 to South West India Dock) and timber ships bound for Montique Myers timber berth in the Milwall Dock.

The *Formidable* was engaged on a number of tows well outside the near continental trading area during the year. On 14th March she sailed from Sarpsborg in the Oslo Fjord, Norway bound for Santander, Spain with the L.P.G. tanker *Aegis Diligence* 7,937 gross tons, that had been fire damaged in

October 1975, for scrap. Bad weather was encountered all the way and after delivery of the tow returned to Brest. From Brest the *Formidable* towed the hoppers *W.D. 681* and *W.D. 684* to Southampton going via Cherbourg owing to bad weather again arriving on 31st March. From Southampton she sailed back across the Bay of Biscay to Bayonne near the Franco-Spanish border and left on the 5th April with the Dipper dredger *W.D. Doha* in tow for Dover. On arrival at Dover the sea fastenings were removed and the *Formidable* then towed the dredger on to Ramsgate where it was to be used digging the new deep water channel to enable the new ferry service to operate at any state of tide. The following month the *Formidable* left Flushing with the *Atlantic Freezer* in tow for Vigo arriving on 8th May. She then ran to Leixoes in Portugal and took in tow Wijsmullers heavy lift semi-submersible barge *Ocean Servant 2* and towed her to Ymuiden arriving on 22nd May.

In June the *Sun London* towed the *I.T.M.1* from Middlesbrough to the Thames loaded with the gates of the Thames Flood Barrier. This was one of many tows from the Tees where the gates and arms to operate them had been built, loaded on barges belonging to I.T.M. for transportation and towed to the Thames by tugs of the Gravesend fleet. The tugs were also involved in the towages of the sills that the gates were to lie in on the river bed.

These concrete sills were constructed at the barrier site and when completed towed to the King George V Dock to be stored until needed. When each sill was required on site four tugs would tow it from the Dock, one made fast on each corner and it would be positioned between the buttresses and sunk in the required position. The Schottel driven tug *Grey Lash* of Humprey & Grey Ltd., was also used on the final positioning being moored up alongside the sill and being able to push or pull in any direction as the sill was eased between the buttresses. The towage associated with the Thames Barrier were carried out over a period of approximately five years from 1978 – 1983.

The *Sun London* towed the *G.W. 135* from Woolwich to Southampton and the *Grand Turtle* from Woolwich to Great Yarmouth in August. In September she towed two hoppers from Lowestoft to Southampton, the *Koggen* from Holehaven to Ymuiden and *Karen Winther* with a wire in its propeller from Dover to the Hook of Holland, handing the ship over to the *Hoeksebank*. The *Sun London* also towed the dredger *W.D. Europe* from Harwich to Liverpool sailing on 10th October. Rough seas were encountered down channel and tug and tow put into Southampton and Falmouth for shelter before arriving at Liverpool on 20th October after a very stormy voyage. Also in October she towed the *Clever Turtle* from Rotterdam to the King George V Dock, London.

Of the salvages undertaken the collier *Aldrington* had an engine room fire in the vicinity of the Shipwash Sands during January. The *Hibernia* left Felixstowe to assist and took the ship, which was fully laden with coal, in tow for the Thames.

The *Sun Kent* ran down to assist from the Estuary and the two tugs berthed the *Aldrington* on Tilbury Power Station for unloading. On completion the *Sun XXV* left on 28th January with the ship in tow for the River Tyne for repairs, the *Sun XXV* handing over the tow to local tugs off the Tyne pier heads during the morning of 30th January.

The large car carrier *Helenus* broke adrift from her berth at Sheerness during a strong gale on 29th March and collided with the *Montaquce* which then struck the ship on the next berth smashing one of her lifeboats and setting off a smoke flare, which gave a first impression that the ship was on fire. J.P. Knight Ltd. requested two tugs from Gravesend to assist their tugs at Sheerness. The *Sun Kent* and *Sun XXV* left Shell Haven immediately and on arrival assisted the *Helenus* with the *Keston*, *Keverne* and *Kennet*. This ship was later swung and she put to sea. The *Sun Kent* then went to the *Montaquce* and with the *Kemsing* pulled her clear.

# 1981

A higher powered tug was required at Felixstowe with the larger container ships using the port and the *Sun London* was transferred there from Gravesend on 6th April as a stopgap measure while a new tug was being built. The number in the Gravesend fleet remained the same with the return to the Thames of the *Sun XXI* after her two years spell at Southampton arriving at Gravesend after

Sun XXI.

being refitted at Sheerness on 20th April. In September Alexandra Towing, Gravesend acquired a second-hand single Voith Schneider tug from the French. She was the *Clairvoyant* of Societe De Remorquage, and De Sauvetage Du Nord, Dunkirk, was renamed *Sun Swale* and arrived Gravesend on 8th September. Built in 1968 by Ziegler Freres at Dunkirk, she has a gross tonnage of 195, dimensions of 27.01 x 8.01 x 6.3m. and powered by an eight-cylinder Crepelle of 1,500 b.h.p. With the arrival of the *Sun Swale,* the *Moorcock* became surplus and was scrapped. Her last towing job was the large container ship *S.A. Sederberg* 53,023 gross tons away from Northfleet Hope container terminal to Gravesend on 21st October. The *Moorcock* was then laid up on the buoy where any useful engine spares were stripped from her, after which she was towed to Queenbrough ship breakers in December by the *Watercock* and scrapped.

During the year the P.L.A. closed down the Royal Group of Docks to commercial traffic. These were the last of the up river docks and it left Tilbury as the only enclosed dock in operation, apart from the small Regent Canal Dock at Limehouse, operated by the British Waterways Board. The Regents Canal connects with the Grand Union Canal and the Lee Navigation.

The Royals were not totally shut though, the King George V Dock being used for laying up some of the many surplus ships that could not find cargoes with world trading in recession. So in a space of just fifteen years five of the P.L.A. six enclosed docks and most of the up river wharves had closed down and gave the upper part of the river an air of dereliction. Gone also were most of the craft tugs and barges that could be counted in thousands that used to transport the cargos around the port, a sad sight to the people who remember the river when it was a thriving industry.

With the river continuing to decline, the Company was looking more and more to sea towage to fill the gap. In January Alexandra Towing won a contract to supply two large fire tugs to operate in the Mediterranean port of Arzew, Algeria as harbour tugs. The *Waterloo* from London and *Wellington* from Liverpool where chosen for this job and the *Waterloo* left Gravesend on 22nd January for Arzew. The *Wellington* and *Waterloo* worked successfully in the port until August when both tugs returned to the United Kingdom. While in Arzew the crews worked for a spell of six weeks at a time before being relieved by air. In February the *Formidable* towed a barge from Rotterdam to Seville in southern Spain. On her return to the North Sea the *Formidable* towed the jack-up drilling rig *Penrod 80* from the Placid Gas field off the Dutch coast to Rotterdam assisted by the *Indomitable*, *Lady Moira* and *Indusbank*, the same tugs towing the rig to a new position five miles east of Scarborough, Yorkshire. In February the *Sun London* towed the pontoon *Clever Turtle* from Rotterdam to the Tyne. After being loaded with Modules at Wallsend the *Clever Turtle* was towed to Lock Kishorn on Scotland's West Coast by the *Formidable* escorted by the *Wallesey* during April, the *Formidable* returning the barge to the Tyne after unloading. She then had a tow of the canal narrow boat *Bonjour* from Gravesend to Calais on 11th May, followed by the *Clever Turtle* again to Loch Kishorn from the Tyne in the same month. Another tow to Loch Kishorn was completed in June with the barge *Giant 12* from Lowestoft. In September the *Formidable* attended on the cable ship *Cable Venture* in Lyme Bay and the Western Approaches. The *Cable Venture* was doing tests with a cable burying plough towed on the sea bed; these tests were hampered by extremely bad weather. The following month she towed the *Anna Becker,* broken down at the Sunk, to Rotterdam, the tow carried away in adverse conditions but was soon reconnected and delivered to the Hook of Holland. In November the *Formidable* was in Norway to tow the *I.T.M. Mariner* from Grimstad to Middlesbrough. In December the *Formidable* sailed on the longest tow to date. Leaving Gravesend on 5th December, light tug to Seville in Spain arrived on the 10th and sailed two days later with the barge *Dracaza XIII* loaded with a well-head for Abidjan on the Ivory Coast. Tug and tow arrived at Dakar on 24th December and spent Christmas there sailing on Boxing Day, and then delivered the tow at Abidjan on 3rd January 1982. The *Formidable* then returned north calling at Las Palmas and arrived at Brest on 22nd January.

Amongst the salvages carried out was the refloating of the *City of Plymouth* by the *Formidable* on 20th April following her grounding below Southend Pier. The *Sun Essex* went to the assistance of the Greek freighter *Aegis Blaze* loaded with grain, with a cracked hull and making water off Margate on 15th July. The ship was beached and, after emergency repairs were carried out, was refloated by the *Sun Essex* and *Sun Kent*, which then escorted her to the Southend Anchorages and was docked later in Tilbury Dock.

Reef (Underwater Services) Ltd. set up a company offering towage on the Thames. Three tugs were acquired: the *General VI*, a craft tug of 90 gross tons and 450 b.h.p. from Cory Lighterage Ltd. and renamed *Barra Reef*; in June two tugs were chartered from the fleet of Harpag Lloyd A.G., Bremerhavn the *Centaur* and *Lowe* both 160 gross tons and 1,060 b.h.p. and renamed *Daunt Reef* and *Carrig Reef* respectively; a fourth, the *Luchs* 95g.t. 450 b.h.p. Voith Schneider tug was also chartered and renamed *West Reef*, but was not delivered to London before the company ceased trading. The *Barra Reef* returned to Cory and the *Daunt Reef* and *Carrig Reef* were towed back to Bremerhavn in October by the German tug *Gavant*.

# 1982

The *Sun XXI* was again withdrawn from the Thames fleet, going to Sheerness on 22nd February to be refitted prior to being transferred to Gibraltar. The *Sun XXI* was to join her sister the *Deban* (ex *Sun XXII*) at Gibraltar where commercial shipping had increased sufficiently to warrant a second tug in the port, independent of the Royal Navy dockyard tugs. The Masters for the *Sun XXI* were sent out from Gravesend for approximately one year, the *Deban*'s Master coming from Liverpool.

Sun Thames.

A new twin Voith Schneider tug was ordered by the Alexandra Towing Co. from the Mctay Marine Ltd., Bromborough. Named *Sun Thames* she was launched on 10th March and arrived at Gravesend from the Mersey on 1st May. The *Sun Thames* is 369 gross tons, dimensions of 31.02 x 9.52 x 3.81m. and powered by twin six-cylinder Ruston Paxman diesels with a total output of 2,640 b.h.p. producing a total bollard pull of 30 tons. She is fully equipped as a fire tug enabling her to supply foam or water from three monitors and or hand lines, also fitted is a towing winch for her harbour towing gear. This allowed any length of tow line to be selected at will.

The *Vanquisher* was withdrawn from service on 3rd May two days after the arrival of the *Sun Thames* and sold to Medway Secondary Metals for scrapping at Bloors Wharf, Rainham, Kent. *The Avenger* towed her to Sheerness on 3rd June, a small tug towing her up the Medway to Rainham. So after a life of twenty-seven years this well-known and well-liked tug was scrapped. Advertised as the most powerful single screw tug on the Thames when built, but with the large increases in power required in river and coastal tugs in recent years, she was now regarded as obsolete and disposed of.

The Alexandra Towing Company of Felixstowe took delivery of their new tug *Ganges* 281 gross tons 2,640 b.h.p. with a bollard pull of 42 tons from Richard Dunston Ltd., Hessel, arriving Felixstowe on 15th May. With her delivery the *Sun London* was returned to the Thames fleet, arriving back at Gravesend on 30th June.

I.T.M., the heavy lift and transportation Company, had one of its North Sea barges the *I.T.M. Mariner* converted into a crane barge during March in the Royal Albert Dock. The *Formidable* towed the *I.T.M. Mariner* to the Thames with a dismantled crane on its deck. In the Royal Albert Dock the 200 ton crane was erected and the accommodation for ninety-four men, a helicopter pad and life-saving equipment all being built onto the barge. Ten men from Alexandra Towing Gravesend were transferred over to the crane barge for a year; they were a mate and four deckhands on each watch. The *I.T.M. Mariner* left Gravesend during April towed by the *Waterloo*. Trials with the eight anchor mooring system were carried out off Southend. The anchors were laid by the *Redoubtable* (ex-*Chambon Alice*) '81 (ex-*Sea Husky*) '80 an anchor handling tug built in Yugoslavia in 1975 and powered by two Burmeister and Wain Alpha diesels of 4,960 b.h.p. with a bollard pull of 70 tons. The *Redoubtable* had been acquired by the Alexandra Marine Transportation Ltd. in 1981 and manned by a Liverpool crew.

After trials the *I.T.M. Mariner* was towed to the West Sole Gas Field, thirty-eight miles east of the River Humber, where she was to renovate the production Platforms there for B.P. On 2nd May during a southwest gale, one of the anchors carried away and swung the *I.T.M. Mariner* athwart of the sea. Attempts were made to get her back head to sea by adjusting the other anchors, but she began to drift while this was being attempted. The Wijsmuller tug *Typhoon* was working nearby with another barge and was sent to assist and made fast to the *I.T.M. Mariner*; the anchors were then slipped and she started towing towards the Humber for shelter. The *Formidable* left Gravesend to assist and was diverted to the Humber and relieved the *Typhoon* at the Bull anchorages and towed the *I.T.M. Mariner* to the Tees for repairs arriving on 4th May. The *Redoubtable* assisted by the *Formidable* then recovered the anchors and wires from where they had been abandoned at sea and returned them to the *Mariner*. All repairs were completed and she left the Tees in tow of the *Formidable* back to the West Sole Gas field on 13th May. The two tugs then stayed in attendance with the *I.T.M. Mariner* towing and assisting her when required until the job was completed and the *Formidable* towed her to Newcastle arriving on 17th August; the *Formidable* then returned to Gravesend.

Other tugs in the fleet were also busy on the coast; the *Sun London* towed the barge *Tunny* from Gravesend to Rotterdam in May followed by the *I.T.M. Voyager* from Middlesbrough to London. In June she towed two Thames lighters to Sullom Voe, Shetland Isles, assisting the *Sun Essex* with the *G.W. 224* alongside the *I.T.M. Mariner* on her way home. The *Waterloo* was towing the barge *Nysel* loaded with two well-head modules from Stornaway to Lerwick, when the wire parted in heavy swell on 8th July north of the Scottish mainland.

The *Waterloo* reconnected to the barge's emergency towing wire, put into Sandside Bay to sought out the broken gear and make a permanent connection before continuing to Sullom Voe where the *Nysel* was safely delivered. Also in July the *Sun Essex* towed the *I.T.M. I* from London to Dundee where two loads were driven aboard with low loaders bound for B.P. refinery at Grangemouth, sailing 30th July and handing over tow in the Firth of Forth off of Inchkeith the following morning to local tugs from towage to Grangemouth. The *Waterloo* ran down to Falmouth in August for B.P.'s new fire fighting and support rig *Iolair*, the Waterloo escorting her through the English Channel and up the North Sea as far as the Humber.

During the early hours of 7th September a fire broke out in the engine room of the Portuguese fish factory ship *Ave Maria* in the vicinity of the Galloper. Two Royal Navy Frigates, H.M.S. *Leander* and H.M.S. *Euryalus*, went to her assistance and rescued the forty-five crew members by helicopter. The *Waterloo* left Gravesend and arrived at the abandoned ship at 11.30 and commenced towing her to Margate Roads anchoring her at 19.30. The *Waterloo*, assisted by fire-fighting teams from the Frigates, continued fire-fighting and pumping out the build-up of water in the hold. The *Ave Maria* was of wooden construction making fire a much more serious hazard than if she was built of steel; a hole had already burnt through the ship's side. The salvage vessel *Kinloss* and the tug *Mastiff* arrived from Chatham Dock Yard relieving the *Euryalus*. The fire was finally extinguished at 22.00 on 9th September. The *Waterloo* then towed the disabled ship to Chatham Dock Yard delivering her there at 06.00 on 10th September.

In October the *Formidable* ran to the Forties Field attending on the *Iolair* while she was engaged in fire-fighting and manoeuvring trials round the platforms. The *Formidable* then ran to Felixstowe for the *I.T.M. II* to Middlesbrough and when returning to Gravesend went to the assistance of the tanker *Cableman* broken down 9 miles northeast of the Sunk Light Vessel on 16th November. The *Formidable* towed her to C Jetty Shell Haven and was assisted in berthing by the *Sun XXVII*.

To round the year off the *Formidable* ran to Hamburg and sailed on 12th December, towing the tanker *Stylis* with stern damage bound for San Esteban, Spain for scrap. When in the English Channel in the vicinity of the Owers on 15th December, a force ten southwest gale was encountered. The *Formidable* was hove-to and the force of the wind and the sea was gradually pushing tug and tow in a northeasterly direction. The T.H.V. *Siren* was in the vicinity at the time and recorded winds of 60 knots. On the following day the weather had abated sufficiently to enable the *Formidable* to put into Southampton for shelter assisted to berth by the *Albert* and *Romsey*. The *Formidable* sailed on 27th December with the *Stylis* and arrived off San Esteban on New Year's Eve. Orders were received to proceed to Gijon. This being again changed to Aviles, the *Formidable* finally berthed the ship assisted by three local tugs during the evening. She then returned to the Thames.

162

# 1983

In 1983 the Alexandra Towing Company (London) Ltd. celebrated the 150th anniversary of towage on the River Thames. It started when Mr John Rogers Watkins, a London waterman and sailing shipowner, founded the River's first successful towage company in 1833 with his son William when they had the *Monarch* built at North Shields. The vast majority of tugs built during this period came from Tyne Ship Builders and the *Monarch* was typical of tugs from this era. She was 26 gross tons, a wooden clench built hull of 64'10" and powered by a single side lever engine of 20 nominal h.p., steam being supplied by a flue boiler with a jet condenser; bunkers of 7 tons of coal were carried. By today's standards this boiler would be thoroughly inefficient but was the best available at that time. It was 1845 before she was re-boilered with a more efficient tubular boiler. Her success can be gauged by the fact she was in Watkins' ownership for 33 years being broken up in 1876. Watkins prospered as did other tug owners on the River in keen competition with each other. After the Second World War the remaining ship towing companies gradually amalgamated or were taken over (as set out in greater detail on previous pages) until just one company, London Tugs Ltd., remained, in 1969 this company becoming part of the Alexandra Towing group of companies in 1975. To mark the occasion of the 150th year of towage the Alexandra Towing Company commissioned Mr David Cobb, president of the Royal Society of Marine Artists to paint an oil painting depicting famous towing events in the company's history on the Thames. This painting was presented to the Honourable Company of Watermen & Lightermen, accepted by the Master and Wardens and hung in their main hall. The tugs crews and shore staff were each presented with a case containing six bottles of special brew beer by the company.

In this anniversary year changes in the fleet were still taking place. Alexandra Marine Transportation Ltd. purchased the anchor handling tug *Chambon Sirocco* from Compagnie Chambon Marseilles renaming her *Implacable*, arriving at Sheerness on 10th February from Dunkirk to be refitted prior to entering service. Although not part of the Gravesend fleet I have entered her in this history because she was manned by five Gravesend crews. A sister tug to the *Redoubtable*, the *Implacable* was built at the Tito shipyard Yugoslavia in 1975 for Bugge Supply Ships A/B, Norway as the *Sea Setter* and sold to Chambons in 1980, dimensions of 39.62 x 9.9 x 5.31m. 300.36 gross tons and twin variable pitch propellers in Kort rudders powered by two sixteen-cylinder Burmeister & Wain Alpha diesels with a total output of 4,960 b.h.p. producing a bollard pull of 70 tons. A bow thrust unit of 200 b.h.p. developing a thrust of 2 tons was also fitted. A clear deck for anchor handling she was also capable of carrying loads of up to 150 tons on it. The *Implacable* was used extensively all around the coast during the short time she was in Alexandra's ownership, most of her work being related to the oil industry. One of her more spectacular jobs was in December 1983 when she towed the new oil rig *Sovereign Explorer* from the builder's yard at Birkenhead to Holyhead, assisted by the Voith Schneider tugs *Canada* and *Collingwood*, berthing the rig in the Holyhead Harbour on 8th December. A violent storm blew up the following day and at 09.00 the *Sovereign Explorer* began to break adrift and a barge between her and the quay was holed and in a sinking condition.

The *Implacable* under the command of Capt. D. Webb immediately made fast to the rig followed by *Canada*, *Collingwood* and the Holyhead tugs *Afon Las* and *Afon Goch*. More tugs were needed and the tug supply *Suffolk Progress* was released from her duties in the Morecombe Bay gas fields, and the tugs *Brackengarth* and *Hollygarth* of Rea Towing Company left Liverpool, battling through force 10 winds to get to Holyhead to assist. All tugs battled against the elements to bring the rig under control and the following morning the *Implacable* handed over her towing gear to the *Brackengarth*; the *Implacable* then began to run the rig's anchors away. It was late on 11th December before the *Sovereign Explorer* was safely moored and the tugs stood down. The *Implacable* remained in attendance at Holyhead to the rig, until it was towed to the River Clyde by Alexandra's new large tug supply vessel *Invincible* in January 1984.

*1983* — Waterloo *making fast to* Penrod 92 *in North Sea.*

The Gravesend fleet lost one of its principal coastal tugs when the *Waterloo* together with her sister *Wellington* from Liverpool were both sold to the Iranian National Shipping Company, Bandar Abbas, Iran. The *Waterloo* was withdrawn on 19th April and sent to Sheerness for a refit prior to sailing for the Persian Gulf. The *Waterloo* left Gravesend on 7th May, and arrived Gibraltar on 12th May, meeting up with the *Wellington* there. Both tugs left Gibraltar the following day for the 1,900 mile run through the Mediterranean to Port Said, through the Canal to Suez, then down the Red Sea, Gulf of Aden, Arabian Sea and into the Persian Gulf arriving at Bandar Abbas on 4th June after a voyage of 6,352 miles. The *Waterloo* and *Wellington* were renamed *Ghorban* and *Ghader* respectively and when accepted by their new owners the crews flew back to the U.K. arriving on 14th June.

Another deletion to the Thames fleet was the transfer of the *Sun III* to Alexandra Towing at Swansea leaving Gravesend on 23rd June for the Welsh port. In the following year she was renamed *Fabians Bay*, a local name more in keeping with her new area of work.

With Tilbury as the only enclosed Dock the *Plangent* became surplus to the Port of London Authority's dock tug fleet and was transferred to the dredging department, changing her maroon colour casing of the dock tugs to the grey of the dredging fleet. This left the four tractor tugs to cover the docks towage with the remaining twin screw tug *Plagal* laid up.

Plagal.

# 1984

1984 saw a further reduction in the fleet with the sale of the *Sun XXIII* on 6th April to Havelet International Ltd., Guernsey and renamed *Sunwind*. A product of Philip & Son Ltd., Dartmouth in 1961, the *Sun XXIII* was built for W.H.J.Alexander's up river fleet, of 143 gross tons and 93'9" long and powered by 1,400 i.h.p. six-cylinder Mirrless diesel. She was a versatile tug ideally suited for the up-river dock and jetty work that was still in abundance in the sixties. When sold it was rumoured she was bound for Canada but this never materialised and worked at Plymouth for a short while before being laid up there. Acquired in August 1985 by Street and Henderson Ltd., Gravesend, she returned to the Thames arriving at Gravesend on 5th August 1985 and was renamed *Suncrest* in November.

The Felixstowe based Alexandra tug *Sauria* manned by a Gravesend crew got into difficulties during the evening of 30th July while getting hold of the port bow of the Cuban ship *Julio Antonia Mella* in the vicinity of the Pitching Ground Buoy in the Harwich approach channel. While the tugs tow rope was being hove aboard, the ship contacted the starboard quarter of the *Sauria*,rolling her round the ship's bow and laying her on her port side. Her Master, Mate and Deckhand were all washed from the tug into the sea. As the *Sauria* came clear from the ship's bow, she righted herself and the three men in the water managed to swim back to the tug and re-board her. The propeller was damaged and she had water damage inside but fortunately no one was hurt. The *Langton* had come to their assistance and towed her back to the Navy Yard at Harwich, later being towed to Clifton Slipways at Gravesend for repair to the damage sustained in the incident.

Two ships grounded during June which required large numbers of tugs to refloat them. The Elder Dempster Line container ship *Sekondi* had steering failure and grounded inside the Ovens Buoy off Coal House Point, East Tilbury on 8th June. The combined power of the *Watercock*, *Burma*, *Avenger*, *Sun Essex*, *Sun Kent* and *Sun London* was required to refloat her and the *Sekondi* was then escorted to anchorage at Southend.

During the early hours of 19th June, the *Texaco Norge* was in the process of shifting her berth at Wouldhams Jetty, Grays, assisted by the *Sun Essex* and *Watercock*. While in the process of swinging it shut in dense fog, the ship grounded on the Black Shelf down stream of the berth. More tugs rushed to her aid but were unable to refloat her on the falling tide. The *Sun Kent* also grounded while attempting to get hold of the ship and the crew were taken off for a while as a precaution. As the tide made during the afternoon the *Sun Kent* refloated herself and then assisted the *Sun Essex*, *Watercock*, *Sun Swale*, *Sun London*, *Hibernia* and *Sun Thames* in the safe refloating of the *Texaco Norge* which was fully laden with spirit at the time.

The *Implacable* was kept busy during the year around the coast and near continent, a large percentage of her work being involved in towing barges to and from the Morecambe Bay gas field. The Alexandra Towing Co. secured a contract from the Ministry of Defence for the *Implacable* in the Falkland Islands. She was dry docked on the Tyne in November for a refit and modifications required for her to undertake a long spell in the South Atlantic. On completion she sailed on 19th December towing H.M.S. *Rame Head* to the Naval Base at Rosyth on the Firth of Forth arriving the following day, and from there sailed south on 21st December. During the morning of 24th December when in the English Channel 27 miles south of the Isle of Wight, the *Implacable* developed a list, capsized and sank, the crew abandoning ship in the tug's two inflatable life rafts. On receiving the Mayday call a Royal Naval rescue helicopter was scrambled from its base at Lee-on-Solent and was soon over the area and winched the survivors to safety, two from the sea and the remainder from the rafts, the only exception being the Chief Engineer who was lost with the tug. A sad and premature end to the tug's short spell under the Red Ensign.

For many years London's rubbish had been towed down river in barges and used for reclamation on the Essex marshes at Rainham, East Tilbury, the Mucking and Pitsea. In 1985 the transporting of this rubbish was containerised and this required the building of new barges designed for this service. Around twenty of these barges were built for Cory Waste Management by James Cook

& Son at Wivenhoe on the River Colne in Essex. The Alexandra Towing Company was contracted to tow them from Brightlingsea to Cory's Barge Yard at Charlton. They were towed round over the period from late 1984 through the middle of 1985 as they were completed by the builders. The *Sun XXVII* delivered the first one, but the majority were towed round by the *Sun II*, usually two at a time. These barges revived names that had previously been held by Cory's large but now defunct fleet of colliers, *Cormist* and *Cormead* to name two of them.

Burma.

# 1985

More changes took place to the Alexandra fleet in 1985 with the arrival of the *Hendon* at Gravesend on 30th June from the Southampton fleet. The Hendon had been built by Richard Dunston Ltd. at Hessle for the account of France Fenwick, Tyne & Wear Co. Ltd. in 1975. She was never accepted from the builders and on completion was laid up in Hull Docks and put up for sale. Purchased by the Alexandra Towing Company in 1978 and stationed at Swansea, she was engaged in many long distance tows while in the Welsh port. She was transferred to Southampton in 1984 and on to Gravesend in 1985. The *Hendon* is a single screw tug on 153 gross tons dimensions of 29 x 9.15 x 4.9m. and powered by a six-cylinder Mirrless Blackstone diesel engine of 3,180 b.h.p. driving a single screw in a steerable Kort nozzle having a bollard pull of 45 tons. The *Hendon* worked for a short while before being towed to Sheerness by the *Sun XXVI* in late October for the repositioning of her sea towing winch. When built her towing winch was placed on the after deck, which made the handling of tow ropes for normal river towing difficult. When she returned to the River it had been replaced amidships leaving the after deck clear for river work.

The *Sun Swale* was stationed at Ramsgate in June on a permanent basis providing towage and fire-fighting services in the new harbour being built for the Sally Line. The *Sun Swale* being a Voith Schneider propelled vessel was the ideal choice of tug for the nature of the work in the confines of the new harbour.

Another deletion to the fleet took place in October with the sale of the *Avenger* to Purvis Marine of Canada for work on the Great Lakes. Renamed *Avenger IV* she sailed from the Thames on 31st October. After refuelling and rectifying an engine problem she left St Michaels in the Azores on 28th

November bound for Halifax. A television news item concerning the bad weather that was being experienced in North America at the time showed her arriving at the Canadian port completely covered in ice. The *Avenger* had been built in 1962 by Cochrane & Sons Ltd., Selby for Ship Towage London Ltd. as a fire-fighting tug at the Shell Haven refinery.

The *Avenger* was soon replaced by a new vessel from the builders Mctay Marine Ltd., Bromborough in November. Named the *Sun Anglia* she is a twin Voith Schneider tractor tug of 339 gross tons, dimensions being 33.33 x 9.50 x 3.80m. and powered by two six-cylinder straight Ruston R.K.270 diesel engines with a combined b.h.p. of 3,444 producing a bollard pull of 38.5 tons. She is a sister to the Liverpool based *Bramley Moore*. She is fitted with two towing winches, one for her harbour tow rope and the other for sea work, enabling her to undertake rig shifts or any work that requires a tug of her versatility. Her keel was laid down on 22nd April and completed in November. After running trials she left Liverpool on 20th November and arrived Gravesend on the 23rd and went to show to the firm's customers on 26th November in Upper Pool at Tower Pier.

During the afternoon of 23rd April the large Polish bulk carrier *Powstaniec Wielkopolski* 20,593 gross tons, fully laden with grain, broke adrift from the Grain Terminal buoys in Gravesend Reach. The ship was lying moored head up river and her foreward moorings carried away on the ebb tide, the ships head swung to the north across the river and would have probably collided with the Tilbury Landing Stage if it hadn't been for the quick response of the tugs that raced to her aid. The *Sun London* and *Ionia* began pushing on the ships starboard bow and the *Hibernia* got hold of the port bow and the *Powstaniec Wielkopolski* was eased back into mid-stream. The tugs remained in attendance swinging her on the low water and when the flood tide had risen sufficiently to allow her to pass over the Diver Shoal at the lower end of Gravesend Reach, the ship then proceeded down river to anchor at Southend.

On the upper side of the East India Dock Lock a memorial stone stood until recently removed which read 'To 105 brave souls who sailed from near this spot on 19th December 1606 in three vessels *Sarah Constant* 100 tons, *Godspeed* 40 tons and *Discovery* 20 tons and arrived at Cape Henry, Virginia 30th April 1607 and James Town 17th May 1607'. Voyages had been made to the New World since 1585 to try to establish a colony in North America but it was the emigrants on these three small ships that founded the first successful settlement. To mark the 400th Anniversary of these voyages a replica of the *Godspeed* was constructed at James Town to recreate the voyage from England. The

*Godspeed* was shipped to Felixstowe in March aboard Hapag Lloyds container ship *Stuttgart Express*. She was re-rigged in Felixstowe dock and towed to Ipswich dock by the Tug *Gray Alpha*. The settlers were all from Norfolk and Suffolk and after being on show at Ipswich and Harwich was towed to Gravesend by the *Sun II*. On 19th April *Godspeed* was towed from Gravesend to St Katherine's Dock by the *Sun Swale* where she was officially welcomed to London. The *Godspeed* was seen off on the start of her voyage on 30th April by the Duke of Edinburgh from off Island Park, Isle of Dogs, opposite Greenwich Naval College. She was towed down river by two whalers under oars and, when rounding Saunders Ness out of site of the dignitaries, *Godspeed* was handed over to the *Sun II* for towage down river, arriving at Gravesend at 15.30 and moored off the Promenade. Last minute stores were taken aboard the vessel and she sailed under tow of the *Sun II* at 19.30. The *Sun II* was to tow the *Godspeed* to a position south of the Isle of Wight from where she was to proceed under sail alone. A good passage was had out of the Thames Estuary and through the Dover Straits but when in the vicinity of the Greenwich Buoy off Beachy Head a choppy head sea built up and the *Godspeed* began shipping water. It was decided to put into Newhaven for shelter arriving at 18.30 the 1st May. Tug and tow left Newhaven in the morning of 3rd May and, as the winds were from a westerly direction and the *Godspeed* could not sail very close to the wind, the *Sun II* towed her to St Helen's Roads, Isle of Wight, where she anchored to await more favourable conditions. The *Sun II* was then dismissed and returned to Gravesend. The *Godspeed* sailed from the anchorage on 5th May and, after calling at Tenerife, arrived in the Virgin Islands on 13th July but with the hurricane season approaching it was too late to make Virginia, so the barque waited at San Juan, Puerto Rico, until the hurricane season had passed.

During the summer various tugs were engaged attending on the crane barge *I.T.M. Mariner* which was laying the inshore ends of the Electricity Cables to join the British and French grids being laid across the English Channel from Folkestone to Sangette near Calais. The *Formidable, Sun London* and *Sun XXVI* were amongst the tugs that attended her on the English side. The *I.T.M. Mariner* was towed back to Middlesbrough by I.T.M.'s own tug *I.T.M. Seafarer*, and on 16th July the *Formidable* and *Sun London* ran from Gravesend to rendezvous with the *I.T.M. Mariner* which was under tow of the *Smit Lloyd 117* off Sangette. The two tugs took hold of the barge, the *Smit Lloyd* then let go and proceeded to lay the *I.T.M. Mariner*'s anchors. When this was completed the two tugs were dismissed and the *Sun London* returned to Gravesend and the *Formidable* ran to the River Tyne and sailed towing an I.T.M. barge from

South Shields to Harwich. The *Formidable* then ran to Dover and towed the barge *G.W. 225* from the Eastern Docks to Folkestone where it was beached and loaded with two mechanical diggers. She then towed the loaded barge across the Channel to Calais and then out to the site at Sangette where the barge was again beached to unload the diggers. The empty barge was taken back to Dover Harbour being assisted to berth by the tug *Anglianman*. The *I.T.M. Mariner* had now finished her work off the French coast and the *Formidable* returned to Sangette, and with the *Sun Kent* and *I.T.M. Seafarer* held the *I.T.M. Mariner* while the *Smit Lloyd 117* then took over the tow and returned it back to the River Tees, the *Formidable* and *Sun Kent* returning to Gravesend arriving on 26th July.

Amongst the other coast tows the *Formidable* was engaged in was in shifting the oil rig *Penrod 92* in September to a new location off the Norfolk coast, assisted by the tugs *Yorshireman* and *Union Two*.

# 1986

The Gravesend fleet was strengthened by the transfer from Swansea of the anchor handling tug *Indefatigable*. A sister to the *Redoubtable* and the ill-fated *Implacable*, the *Indefatigable* arrived at Gravesend on 18th August after being refitted at Sheerness and had her name changed to *Avenger* on 2nd September: a twin screw tug of 299 gross tons with dimensions of 39.88 x 10.11 x 4.61m. and powered by 2 sixteen-cylinder Alpha Vee diesel engines total 4,960 b.h.p. coupled to two variable pitch propellers in steerable Kort nozzles; a 200 h.p. bow thrust is also fitted. The *Avenger* had been built in Yugoslavia in 1975 as the *Sea Diamond* for Bugge Supply Ships, London, and sold in 1980 to Compagnie Chambon, Marseilles being renamed *Chambon Bora*. Purchased by the Alexandra Towing Co. in 1984 she was stationed at Swansea and given the name *Indefatigable* and worked for an extended period in the area of Douala in the Cameroon, West Africa.

The other changes at Gravesend began with the *Sun Thames* replacing the *Sun Swale* at Ramsgate from March until the end of July while the *Sun Swale* was under repair.

An extra tug was needed at Gravesend for a short period and the *Egerton* was transferred from Felixstowe in April to strengthen the fleet and worked on the Thames until 21st May when she was no longer required, and she was returned to Felixstowe. The *Egerton* was stationed at Felixstowe soon after the Alexandra Towing Co. took control of Gaselee & Son (Felixstowe) Ltd. in 1975. She dates from 1965 and has a gross tonnage of 172 built at Northwich by W. J. Yarwood & Sons and powered by an eight-cylinder Crossley diesel of 1,200 b.h.p.

*Egerton* was the last of a group of six identical tugs ordered by the Company in the early sixties, three from Richard Dunston Ltd. and three from W.H. Yarwood & Sons.

The last remaining links with the up-river bases was severed on 9th June with the sale of North Woolwich Pier for demolition. With the run down of the upper river the pier had become surplus.

The Port of London Authority disposed of the *Plagal* during the summer for scrap, being broken up in Barking Creek. The *Plagal* was the first of the four twin screw diesel tugs built in 1951 – 2 for the large volume of towage that was prevalent in the docks at that time.

The *Plagent* was also sold late in December to owners in Piraeus and renamed *Cerberus*. She left Tilbury Dock on 8th January 1987 under tow of the *Ektor* (ex *Masterman*) for Greece. The *Ektor* had just been purchased from the United Towing Co., Hull, and called in at Tilbury for the *Plangent* on her delivery voyage to the Mediterranean.

A number of long-distance tows were completed during the year. The first, undertaken by the *Formidable*, was of the *Egton* 9,958 gross tons from Hartlepool to Naantali, Finland for scrap. Laid up at Hartlepool since April 1977 she was the last ship in the ownership of the Old Tramping Co. of Headlam & Sons of Whitby. The *Egton* sailed under tow of the *Formidable* on 6th January on her final voyage. Tug and tow put into Copenhagen on 11th January for shelter and later, after pushing through the ice that was still surrounding the Finnish coastline, delivered the *Egton* to Naantali on 17th January.

Soon after the return of the *Formidable* from Finland she went to Lowestoft to have a bow thruster fitted to improve the versatility of the tug; her sister the *Indomitable* was similarly converted at Lowestoft after the *Formidable*.

The *Formidable* ran round to the Medway and sailed on 21st April towing Townsend Thorenson's ro-ro *Gaelic Ferry* away from Chatham dockyard, from where she had been in lay-up to Southampton. At Southampton she was loaded with two link-spans, one weighing 198 tons, in the Alexandra Dock by the ports new 200 ton lift floating crane. The link-spans had been made redundant with the transfer to Townsend Thorenson's ferry service to Portsmouth and the Alexandra Dock was now being converted into a yacht marina called Ocean Village. The *Formidable* then towed the *Gaelic Ferry* to Zeebrugge, Belgium where the link-spans were to be used at Townsend's berth, arriving on 26th April; the *Gaelic Ferry* was then to be scrapped.

The *Formidable*'s next job was with the *Sun Anglia* assisting British Telecom's cable ship *C.S.Alert* in the laying of the first fibre optic underwater telephone cable from Broadstairs to Ostende. The cable is buried in the sea bed by a plough towed astern of the *C.S.Alert* and various tugs had been engaged with the cable ship over a period of time testing the plough and the ability of the tugs to hold the ship on its course. The *C.S.Alert* ploughs the cable into the sea bed at approximately one knot and the tugs were positioned at the bow and quarter holding her broadside to the tide, changing sides every six hours as the tide turned enabling her to keep to the predetermined surveyed track across the sea bed. After arrival at Ostende the *Formidable* laid two stern anchors from the *C.S.Alert* to hold the ship while the cable was spliced into the end laid from the shore. This was successfully completed on 5th May and two tugs returned to Gravesend.

In June the *Sun Essex* towed the bucket dredger *S'Gravenhage* from Felixstowe to Ramsgate where it was to deepen the approach to the Ramsgate Channel. When off Ramsgate the *Sun II* relieved the *Sun Essex*, positioned the dredger and ran the anchors away. The *Sun II* then attended to the needs of the *S'Gravenhage*, shifting anchors and running crews, etc. On completion the *Sun London* towed the dredger back to Felixstowe in July.

The *Formidable* set off on her longest voyage to date when she ran to Bremen in July and sailed towing a submersible barge *Fairalp 3* to Augusta, Sicily. On delivery the *Formidable* ran to Crete and anchored off for a week awaiting orders, before proceeding to Piraeus, Greece for a crew change. She sailed the following day 1st September up the Aegean Sea through the Dardanelles and Bosporus into the Black Sea and berthed at Sulina, Romania on the Delta of the River Danube. The *Formidable* left Sulina on 12th September towing a links-span pontoon the *Oslo Havne Vesen* bound for Oslo, Norway. Gibraltar was reached on 26th September where the *Formidable* bunkered. Sailing on the 29th, Oslo was reached on 12th October after a tow of 3,939 nautical miles; the *Formidable* then returned to Gravesend.

Another long tow took place starting in September when the *Hendon* ran to Bremen and towed the barge *P.7* loaded with gas storage cylinders via the Kiel Canal into the Baltic and up to Hamina, Finland. These cylinders were to be used for the storage of natural gas from Russia. When unloaded the barge was to be towed to the Mediterranean, the *Hendon* returning through the Kiel Canal into the North Sea. She put into the Thames Estuary on 4th October and handed her barge over to the *Avenger* which completed the tow to Augusta, Sicily.

Tug and tow arrived Gibraltar on 12th October and handed the barge *P.7* over to the *Sun XXI* while the *Avenger* bunkered, sailing later the same day for Sicily arriving at Augusta on 18th October. The *Avenger* then returned to the Thames arriving at Gravesend on 2nd November.

# 1987

The Gravesend fleet was further reduced on 10th August, when the *Hibernia* was withdrawn from service, towed to Sheerness dry docks by the *Sun London* on 21st August for minor repairs before being sold to Ahilleus II Shipping Co. of Thessaloniki, Greece, together with the *Sauria*. The *Sauria* had been transferred to Swansea from Felixstowe earlier in the summer and after being sold, ran to Sheerness and sailed on 24th September renamed *Triton*, towing the *Hibernia* renamed *Atrotos* bound for Piraeus arriving during the second week of October.

The *Ionia* was next to leave the Thames, sailing 24th November bound for Falmouth. Her new owners were the Falmouth Towing Co.

The *Formidable* ran to Flushing and sailed 7th February on one of the longer tows undertaken in 1987, with the tanker *Rio Euphrates* in tow for Lisbon. The vessel had extensive bottom damage and after a stormy tow across the Bay of Biscay was drydocked for repair at the Lisnave yard; the *Formidable* then returned to Gravesend.

Alexandra Towing were engaged in a number of coastal tows of preserved ships during the summer. In June the *Formidable* and *Sun Anglia* ran to Hartlepool to tow H.M.S. *Warrior* to Portsmouth. The *Warrior* had just completed a seven year £5 million rebuild restoring her as near as possible to how she was when completed. Her keel had been laid on 25th May 1859 at the Thameside yard at Ditchburn & Mare at Blackwall and launched on 29th December 1860, William Watkins tugs attending at the launch.

On completion she was the most powerful ironclad warship in the world, the pride of the Royal Navy, but technology was advancing fast and by the turn of the century was in the reserve fleet. Between 1904 and 1924 *Warrior* was renamed *Vernon III* as base ship for the Torpedo Training Establishment. On 13th March 1929 she was taken out of lay-up and towed to Milford Haven and became Oil Fuel Hulk C77 and there she stayed until September 1979 when the *Hendon*, then based at Swansea, sailed with her in tow for Hartlepool.

When the *Warrior* left Hartlepool on 12th June practically the whole town turned out to give her a tremendous send-off, the ship being prominent in the town for the last seven and a half years. Once clear of the fairway the *Sun Anglia* let go and escorted the *Formidable* and *Warrior* on the tow south. On reaching the Nab Tower at the entrance of the Solent on the 16th the *Sun Anglia* made fast to the stern of the *Warrior* for berthing at Portsmouth, the *Flying Breeze* from Southampton also assisting. The *Warrior* was escorted the final few miles by an armada of welcoming yachts, ferries, pleasure craft and dockyard vessels. The following day the *Formidable* sailed from Gosport towing the wooden steam sloop *Gannet* to the River Medway to be rebuilt and preserved at Chatham. Completed in 1878 at the Sheerness Naval Dockyard, the *Gannet* was one of a class of fourteen ships. During her lifespan she became the *President*, headquarters ship of the R.N.V.R. and at a later date became naval training ship *Mercury*. On arrival in the Medway the *Gannet* was handed over to Cresent Shippings tugs *Lashette* and *Shovette* and berthed in dry dock at the Chatham Historic Dockyard.

The World War II vintage destroyer *Cavalier* was towed to the River Tyne from Brighton Marina by the *Sun Anglia* during June. The *Sun II* assisted the *Sun Anglia* out of the marina at Brighton and the *Seasider* and *Tynesider* assisted in berthing on arrival in the Tyne on 16th June. H.M.S. *Cavalier* was first opened to the public at Southampton before being towed along the coast to Brighton. Completed in November 1944 by J. Samuel White & Co.Ltd., Cowes, I.O.W., being one of thirty-two ships of the Ca, Ch, Co, & Cr, class, she was the last destroyer in the Royal Navy to have seen service in World War II. Her active service lasted until April 1973 when she became part of the reserve fleet at Chatham. After completion of a refit, *Cavalier* will be part of a maritime museum at Newcastle.

The *Avenger* left Gravesend on 2nd June for Rotterdam and sailed the following day towing the large semi-submersible barge *Goliath Pacific* to Bremen. On arrival at Bremen, the barge was submersed, loaded with dredging equipment and sailed for Flushing. Orders were changed *en route* and the *Avenger* put into Southend anchorage for a crew change and repairs to the barge's sea fastenings. Tug and tow set sail the same day 11th June for Abu Kammash in Libya, bunkering at Ceuta on 20th June. On arrival at Abu

Kammash on 1st July the *Goliath Pacific* was submerged and the hoppers and barges floated off in one and a half hours. The *Avenger* then set sail on the return tow to the U.K. with the barge, arriving at Portsmouth on 20th July. At Portsmouth the *Goliath Pacific* was again submerged and loaded with the training ship *Foudroyant* and the World War I monitor *C23*, ex-*Minerva*, to be towed to Hartlepool. Once there the expertise of the workforce that transformed the *Warrior* will be used on the two ships. The *Foudroyant* had been built at Bombay in 1817 as the frigate *Trincomalee* and is the second oldest ship afloat in the world at this time. Her career as a training ship at Portsmouth is planned to continue on completion of her renovation. The two vessels were floated off the barge in the River Tees and towed into Hartlepool.

A collision took place in the Dover Strait 25 miles off the Kent coast, during the early hours of 30th May in fog. The tanker *Skyron* loaded with 136,879 tonnes of crude oil, collided with the Polish freighter *Hel* in position 51° 25′ N 002° 00′E. A large number of vessels answered the Mayday call, the *Hel* having a large hole in her port side and the *Skyron* a hole in her bow and on fire in the fore peak. The *Sun Swale* left Ramsgate and on arrival started to fight the fire in the bow of the abandoned *Skyron*. The tugs *Sun Kent, Sun Thames,* and *Avenger* ran from the Thames and the *Deft* brought out the fire brigade from Dover. The *Sun Swale* followed later by the *Sun Kent* made fast aft to try and stop the drift of the *Skyron* onto the sandbanks, as she was in danger of grounding. The fire was extinguished and part of the crew reboarded and the ship was got underway again and proceeded to Rotterdam, with the *Avenger* escorting. The *Hel* was escorted into Flushing by Dutch tugs.

On Friday 16th October a hurricane swept across the south of England uprooting trees by the million and causing extensive damage to property. Shipping also suffered in the Thames estuary: four ships in the Southend anchorages, the *Manjoya, Ajax A.S., Othoni* and *Lux Arbitrator* grounded on the north shore after dragging their anchors in the violent storm. The Polish Liner *Stephen Batory* also got into difficulties in the outer estuary and called for tug assistance. The *Sun Anglia* went to her aid and managed to make fast to the ship in the heavy seas. The liner lost both her anchors but was later able to proceed and safely berth at Tilbury Landing Stage. On the following flood tide tugs were able to refloat the grounded ships. The *Manjoya* was first to be refloated assisted by the *Sun London, Sun Kent, Sun Essex* and *Avenger*. The *Formidable, Sun II* and *Sun London* refloated the *Lux Arbitrator* and the *Sun XXV* with the Hull tugs *Salvageman* and *Lady Vera*, the *Othoni*. The *Ajax A.S.* was able to get herself afloat without assistance.

Sun Mercia.

# 1988

A new work pattern was implemented in September by the Gravesend fleet and ties with Felixstowe also came to an end with the transfer of crews to the East Anglian port. Gravesend tugs had supplemented the towage needs of the haven ports since the withdrawal of the troopship *Empire Parkstone* and the tugs *Empire Race* and *Empire Lucy* that attended her in 1958. With the new work system the *Burma* and *Watercock* were laid up and two small Voith Schneider tugs, the *Adept* and *Agile* were added to the fleet from Liverpool to increase the versatility of the Gravesend fleet. The two tugs were towed to London in a most economical fashion, by tugs changing their bases. The *Wallasey* left Liverpool with them in tow to Swansea, where she was to replace the *Victoria*. The *Victoria* then towed them to Gravesend arriving on 19th September, and after delivering them ran on to Felixstowe, her new base. The *Agile* and *Alerte* had been acquired by The Alexandra Towing Co., Liverpool in 1978 from Soc. Boulonnaise de Remorquage, Boulogne, the *Alerte*'s name being changed on 17th May to *Adept*. They were placed in the A.T.C.L. subsidiary company of Bulk Cargo Handling Services Ltd., and were used mainly in the towage of grain barges from Seaforth to Manchester. They had been built in 1971, having a gross tonnage of 48.59, a length of 55.35' and powered by a single Voith Schneider unit of 580 b.h.p. These tugs first jobs on the Thames were in the berthing and unberthing, in a mud berth, of the large North sea barges *A.M.T. Voyager* and *A.M.T. Traveller* at the Mobil Oil refinery at Coryton. These barges were loaded with modules for a cracker, for refining lead free petrol being installed at the plant, and had been towed back and forth from Rotterdam, by the *Formidable* and *Hendon*. Barges were also being towed from Flushing by the *Hendon* to the South West India Dock in conjunction with the massive

183

building project being undertaken at Canary Wharf. One of the small tugs would assist in the berthing of these barges into the dock.

The *Avenger* and *Formidable* both met in Algiers during March. The *Avenger* had sailed from Gravesend on 11th February bound for Augusta, Sicily, arriving on the 22nd. From Augusta she sailed with the semi-submersible barge *Goliath Caribic* in tow for Algiers where it was loaded with three Dutch canal tanker barges. The *Formidable* sailed from Felixstowe towing a North Sea barge, north about to the River Clyde arriving 22nd February. She then ran to Falmouth changed crews and sailed for Algiers arriving 5th March. Both tugs sailed on 13th March, the *Avenger* bound for Rotterdam with the *Goliath Caribic*. The *Formidable* towed the cement distribution barge *Seament II* to Viana Do Castelo in northern Portugal to be drydocked and then on to Tilbury Dock to join the *Seament VI* which had been distributing cement from there since arriving from Piraeus in tow of the tug *Schotland* in June 1986. The *Formidable* sailed from Viana Do Castelo on 25th March and orders were then changed and she was diverted to Brest arriving 1st April. While the eventual destination of the barge was decided, the *Formidable* remained in attendance until 13th May when she was released and returned to Sheerness where she was refitted. The *Avenger* put into Gibraltar for stores and delivered the *Goliath Caribic* at Rotterdam on 23rd March, and then returned to Gravesend. The *Seament II* was later returned to Algiers in September, towed by the Spanish tug *Punta Tarifa*.

The *Sun Kent* was engaged to tow two lightships for Trinity House during February: one from Harwich to the Tyne and a return tow back to Harwich.

The *Hendon* ran down to Lisbon in May and sailed on the 11th towing the luxury classic yacht *Jezebel*, 996 gross tons, with engine damage to Falmouth. On arrival the *Jezebel* was berthed in the River Fal on the lower ship tier in King Harry Reach, assisted from Falmouth by the tug *St Piran*. The *Jezebel* had been built in 1930 as the *Reveler*, became the *Chalena* in 1931 and served the U.S. Navy in World War II and armed with 2 three-inch guns as the U.S.S. *Beaumont* stationed at Pearl Harbour. In 1949 she became the *Elpetal*, and *Jezebel* in 1983.

During October and November three tugs were employed assisting cable layers. The *Formidable* and *Avenger* with the *Bramley Moore* and *Waterloo* from Liverpool were working with the *Cable Venture* belonging to Cable & Wireless, in the laying of a new fibre optic transatlantic cable from the Bristol Channel to the edge of the continental shelf. This section was being ploughed in and required tugs to hold the ship on her designated track. The *Sun Anglia* also was working with the *Waterloo* and the Hull tug *Seaman* assisting British Telecom's *Bar Protector* in the ploughing of a fibre optic cable from Guernsey to Dartmouth.

The year ended with the *Avenger* towing the *Seament VI* from Tilbury Dock to Liverpool on 29th December. With the large amount of building taking place in Docklands and the South East, a larger capacity vessel was required at Tilbury, so the *Seament VI* was replaced by the cement ship *Alkazar* from Liverpool. The *Avenger* delivered her tow on 2nd January and returned to Gravesend.

# 1989

Two tugs were disposed of in 1989: the *Burma* and *Watercock* were towed away from the tug moorings at Gravesend on 19th November by the *Sun London* and taken to the Medway drydock at Sheerness, where any equipment of use was removed. Both had been laid up on the buoy at Gravesend since 19th September 1988, these two being the last representatives of the Ship Towage (London) Ltd. fleet prior to the amalgamation with Sun Tugs in 1969, when it became London Tugs. Also they were the last holders of a long line of William Watkins and Gamecock names that were familiar on the river for well over a century.

An order for a new Voith Schneider tug was placed on Merseyside with Mctay Marine Ltd., Bromborough. This tug due for delivery in July 1990 will have a raised fo'c's'le, duel towing winches, one river and one sea. Engine power will be approximately the same as the *Sun Anglia*, with a bollard pull of 38 plus tons, but with a larger fresh water and bunker capacity to increase her endurance. Extra accommodation will also be provided for supernumeries who are at times required to be carried when working with cable ships.

From 3rd July a large number of sailing vessels gathered in London for the *Cutty Sark* Tall Ships Race from London to Hamburg. Some of the larger square riggers were berthed in the South West India Dock, but the vast majority were moored in the Upper Pool, which was a sea of masts and spars. This is probably the last time so many large square riggers will be seen in the heart of London. When the Dartford Thurrock bridge is completed, it will restrict the height of vessels able to pass under it. The *Sun Thames*, *Sun Anglia*, *Sun Kent*, *Sun Essex* and *Sun II*, together with the *Agile* and *Adept* which were stationed in the Pool for the week, were kept busy attending on the various movements of naval vessels and sailing craft in the upper reaches. On 8th July all the sailing ships took part in a parade of sail down the river, carrying as much sail as possible. The tugs had a few hectic hours work getting the ships out of the dock and off of the various tiers, to take their place in the parade.

Cable laying formed a large part of the sea work during 1989. The *Sun Anglia* with the *Anglian Knight* and *Seaman* were engaged, assisting British Telecom's *Bar Protector* during February and March, ploughing a fibre optic cable from Dieppe to Brighton. The *Sun Anglia* and *Seaman* then assisted the *Flexservice III*, ploughing a cable from Aldeburgh, Suffolk to Domberg in Holland during April. Also in April the *Formidable* and *Avenger* were working with the *Cable Venture* in laying a spur to Cork, Eire from the Atlantic cable laid the previous year from the Bristol Channel to New York. Again in August the *Sun Anglia* and *Avenger* assisted the *Northern Installer* to plough a power cable to the Amethyst Gas Field from Easington, North Humberside. This type of work is not by any means new to the Gravesend tugs. William Watkins' tugs were involved in a lot of work laying and repairing the various telegraph cables around the coast during the 1860s. Of the conventional sea work undertaken the *Avenger* and *Formidable* had various oil rig movements and tows of barges loaded with modules out to platforms being constructed in the North Sea. In August the *Avenger* had a tow from Zeebrugge to Lisbon with the barge *Ram I* loaded with a jack up barge, following during September and October with tows from Holy Loch and Loch Kishorn to the River Tyne and the same two barges from the Tyne to Harwich. The *Formidable* ended the year with a tow of the Dutch bucket dredger *Edax* from Conwy, North Wales to Rotterdam during December.

On the salvage side the self-unloading collier *Telnes* 6,794 gross tons owned by Jebsons, grounded on 27th December on the Kentish Knock Sands in the outer Thames estuary. The combined efforts of the *Hendon*, *Formidable* and *Sun Thames* refloated her on the evening tide, and she was then able to proceed to Tilbury Power Station the following morning to discharge her cargo of coal.

*1989* — Avenger.

# 1990

Fleet changes took place in the first week of 1990. A fire-fighting tug was required at the Shell Oil terminal at Hamble on Southampton Water. The *Sun Essex*, being transferred to the Southampton fleet of Alexandra Towing, sailed from Gravesend on 3rd January. Her place at Gravesend was filled by the *Waterloo* being consigned to the Thames from Liverpool, arriving on 6th January. The *Waterloo* is a twin Voith Schneider tug build in 1987 by Mctay Marine Ltd., Bromborough and powered with two Ruston engines developed 3,444 b.h.p. with a bollard pull of 38 tons. She is fitted with twin towing winches placed side by side, one for river, the other for sea towage, but is not equipped for fire-fighting.

The *Sun XXVII* drydocked at Sheerness on 25th January until 21st March to be upgraded. A Kort nozzle and Becker rudder being fitted and her tall mizzen mast being removed, the Kort nozzle increased her bollard pull from 22 tons to 33 tons. The Becker rudder greatly improved the handling characteristics of the tug when towing.

The Gravesend fleet was further strengthened with the arrival of the *Sun Mercia* on 20th August from her builders Mctay Marine, Bromborough, Merseyside. The *Sun Mercia* is a twin Voith Schneider tug of 3,860 b.h.p. with a bollard pull of 43 tons, a gross tonnage of 449 and dimensions of L.O. 33.015 m. beam 10.46 and a summer draft of 5.26 m. She is a fully equipped fire-tug capable of supplying foam or water from twin monitors on her mast or from handlines, whatever is required and is also fitted with a double-barrelled towing winch, one for harbour and the other for sea towage. A Voith Schneider tug of this power is an extremely useful unit of the river fleet and ideally suited for specialist sea towage such as fine positioning of oil rigs and assisting cableships when engaged in ploughing cables into the sea bed. Her first commercial tow was undocking the Russian container ship, *Professor Tovetykh* from Tilbury Dock on 6th September.

The coastal tugs were kept busy during the summer months. British Telecom Marine won a contract to lay two 33 K.V. electric cables from the Isle of Skye to the Outer Hebrides for Scottish Hydro Electric. A cable ship was not suitable for this, so Alexandra Marine Transportation Ltd. were sub-contracted to supply a barge and tugs. The *Hendon* towed the *A.M.T. Traveller* from Chatham Docks to Southampton in April, where the barge was rigged for laying large power cables. On completion one cable was loaded at Southampton and was then towed to the A.E.I. jetty at Gravesend by the Liverpool based *Redoubtable* for the loading of the second cable. *Redoubtable* then towed the barge to the Isle of Skye, where the cables were laid along a narrow predetermined track between Skye-Harris and Skye-South Uist during May-June. The *A.M.T. Traveller* was held on its narrow track by the *Sun Anglia* and Liverpool's *Bramley Moore* with *Redoubtable* running the moorings and *Huskisson* assisting where required. On completion the *A.M.T. Traveller* was towed to Newcastle for decommissioning by the *Redoubtable* and then to Felixstowe by the *Sun Anglia*.

The *Formidable* sailed from Gravesend on 12th June through the Kiel Canal to Arhus on the east coast of Denmark for the towage of *Drydock No.2* to Malaga to Spain's Mediterranean coast. Course was set through the Kattegat and Skagerrak into the North Sea. Bunkers were taken at Falmouth and tug and tow arrived at Malaga on 12th July after a rather stormy and arduous tow. The dry dock had to be pumped out on numerous occasions during the voyage.

The *Formidable* was also engaged during September and October with the *Redoubtable* and United Towings' *Guardsman* assisting B.T.'s cableship *C. S. Alert*, ploughing from Cornwall to the edge of the continental shelf of a new fibre optic telephone cable laid between northern Spain and Cornwall.

The *Avenger* was also fully employed towing the rock barge *Safe Astoria* from Uddevella, Sweden and Larvik, Norway, to Fairlight, Sussex, from June till November. This rock was to arrest the serious erosion that was taking place in this section of the south coast. When off Fairlight the barge was taken from the *Avenger* and beached by small shallow draft tugs to be unloaded, one being the *Sun XXIV* that was sold by Alexandra Towing Co., Southampton to Subsearch Marine Services Ltd., Newhaven during April.

One salvage of note during the year was the refloating of the tanker *Golconda 1*, 7302/78 from the Margate Sands. Fully laden with spirit the

*Golconda 1* had grounded during the night of 7–8th February in a violent storm. The *Formidable* sailed from Gravesend at 05.00 and on arrival made fast to the tanker and refloated her under the terms of Lloyds Open Form. The *Golconda 1* was undamaged and proceeded to the Thames and berthed at Grays on the following tide.

The contract to supply the towage needs at Ramsgate came to an end on 30th April, and the *Sun Swale* returned to Gravesend. She was then transferred to the Alexandra Towing Co. fleet at Gibraltar, sailing from Gravesend 18th May to be refitted at Milford Haven prior to proceeding to her new base.

# 1991

On 1st January the P.L.A. reduced its participation in dock towage to one tug with one spare, the Alexandra Towing Co. (London) Ltd. supplying additional tugs within Tilbury Dock when required. The *Platoon* and *Plasma*, both single Voith Schneider tugs of 1,600 b.h.p. built in 1965, were put up for sale and acquired by the Alexandra Towing Co. (London) Ltd. being towed from Tilbury Dock on 8th & 9th January and moored on the tug moorings at Gravesend. On being refitted at the Medway Dry Docks, Sheerness, they were renamed *Dhulia* and *Burma*, reviving on the river names from the William Watkins' fleet.

With the acquisition of the *Burma* and *Dhulia* Alexandra had a very versatile Gravesend fleet of 8 Voith Schneider propelled tugs, from the small *Agile* and *Adept*, 6 tons bollard pull, through to the *Sun Mercia*, 43 tons bollard pull, and 9 screw tugs ranging from the *Sun II*, 16 tons bollard pull, to the *Avenger*, a twin screw anchor handling tug of 70 tons bollard pull.

The *Avenger* was involved in a dramatic salvage operation on 24th February when running light down Channel. At 13.50 she intercepted a Mayday from the coaster *Breydon Merchant* 425/71 on fire 12 miles south of Newhaven and loaded with 120 tonnes of munitions bound for the army in Northern Ireland. The crew were rescued by a helicopter from Manston; the fire was located in the stern of the ship, burning out the engine room, accommodation and bridge. With the risk of a violent explosion a six mile exclusion zone was placed round the ship and the minehunter H.M.S. *Kellington* was ordered to sink the *Breydon Merchant* if she drifted inshore threatening the coastal resorts. The *Avenger* with considerable fortitude put a man aboard to make her wire fast and towed her away from the coast. At 08.40 the next morning H.M.S. *Kellington* confirmed that the fire was out. Course was set down Channel while the authorities decided what to do with her. When off Portland, her course was reversed and she was towed to the Sunk anchorage while it was decided what port would accept her. On 28th February the *Avenger* towed the ship to the Chapman explosives anchorage off Canvey Island where the cargo was assessed for damage. The cargo had been stowed 30 feet from the bulkhead and had not suffered any damage. The ship was then shifted to the Mucking explosive anchorage and the munitions transhipped into the *Breydon Enterprize*. The *Breydon Merchant* was towed to Denton buoys and handed over to her owners and was later declared a C.T.L. and arrived at Otterham Quay, Rainham on 18th June to be scrapped.

The *Burma* and *Dhulia* went out of the river for the first time since being delivered from the buildings. On 3rd June the *Burma*, *Waterloo* and *Deban* (from Felixstowe) ran to Lowestoft to berth the large flat top barge *H108* in the Waverney Dock to load a module for the North Sea. With little clearance between the pierheads it required precision handling with highly manoeuvrable tugs. On 1st August *Dhulia*, *Waterloo* and *Trimley* (from Felixstowe) towed the loaded *H108* out of Lowestoft Harbour and handed her over to the sea tug *Njord* for on towage to its destination.

Alexandra Marine Transportation Ltd. won a contract from the Shell Oil Company to supply tugs and barges for the transport of a new cracker unit in eight barge loads from Sunderland and Rotterdam to Shell Haven over a period from May to September. A pad had been constructed at the western end of the Shell refinery in the Mucking bight and a narrow channel dredged out for the barge. The *Avenger*, *Formidable* and *Sun Mercia* carried out the bulk of the sea towage and when off Shell Haven the four small voiths, *Burma*, *Dhulia*, *Agile* and *Adept* would take the barge *A.M.T. Traveller* from the sea tug for berthing. When unloaded the same four tugs would manoeuvre the barge from the pad down the dredged channel and hand it over to the tug waiting to take it to sea.

The Honourable Company of Master Mariners' headquarters' ship *Wellington* was towed from her permanent moorings in Kings Reach alongside the Albert Embankment to Sheerness on 29th July for its first drydocking in over 25 years. The Wellington built in 1934 as a Leith class sloop served as a convoy escort on Atlantic convoys during World War II. The *Agile* and *Adept* towed her down through the bridges, handing her over to the *Waterloo* below Tower Bridge for towage down river. Towage had to be undertaken in daylight, so the *Wellington* was moored on Gravesend swing buoy overnight and drydocked the next day assisted by the *Waterloo* and *Dhulia*. On completion of her refit the *Wellington* was returned to her moorings in Kings Reach on 29/30th October by the *Waterloo*, *Agile* and *Adept*.

The long-awaited new bridge over the Thames at Dartford build to ease the chronic congestion at the Dartford Tunnel was opened by the Queen and named Queen Elizabeth II Bridge at midday 30th September. The *Sun Mercia*, *Sun Thames* and *Sun Anglia* added to the celebrations by putting on a water display with their fire monitors.

The two remaining P.L.A. dock tugs *Placard* and *Plankton* were sold to Port of Tilbury London Ltd. and in September were renamed *Orsett* and *Linford* after villages in Essex. This brought to an end the P.L.A.'s involvement in dock towage that they had carried out since its conception in 1908.

J.P. Knight Ltd., the Medway tug owners, acquired a new Z peller the *Kuroshio*, which was shipped from Japan on the heavy lift ship *Project Arabia* to Southampton. The *Sun Mercia* took charge of the *Kuroshio* when she entered the water on 9th February, towing her to Sheerness where she had handed over to Knight's

Four Alexandra tugs, the *Sun Mercia*, *Formidable*, *Endurance* (Liverpool), and *Wallasey* (Swansea), were employed assisting the *Northern Installer* plough a fibre optic telephone cable from Winterton Ness, Norfolk to the German Fresian Island of Juist during April and May. The *Sun Mercia* and *Formidable* held the ship athawt the tide while the *Northern Installer* laid the cable along a predetermined track. The *Endurance* grappled along the route ahead of the ship for any obstructions, while the *Wallasey* acted as guard ship.

The *Sun Mercia* had another cable laying contract in August, this time in the Bay of Biscay assisting the French Cable ship *Vercors* ploughing a cable from St Hilaire De Riez to the edge of the continental shelf.

The *Avenger* towed the car carrier *Simbad* that had sustained engine damage from Sheerness to Hamburg at Easter. From there she ran to Schiedam and towed a stinger to the pipelaying barge *Semac 1* that was to lay a gas pipe from the Dogger Bank to Zeebrugge. The Italian pipelaying barge *Castoro II* was contracted to lay the shore end of this pipe and the *Avenger* towed her from Rotterdam to Zeebrugge during June. The *Avenger* and an Italian tug then laid the *Castoro II*'s anchor pattern of ten anchors and was employed for a further three weeks walking the *Castoro II*'s anchors as she laid the pipe from the beach out into the North Sea.

The Alexandra Towing Co. (London) Ltd. ordered two twin Voith Schneider river tugs from Richards Shipbuilders at Great Yarmouth: the first being launched on 11th November and named *Sun Surrey* for delivery during March 1992; the second will be named *Sun Sussex* for completion in July-August 1992.

# 1992

The *Formidable* carried out a tow with the barge *A.M.T. Explorer* from Chatham to Invergorden and back to the River Tyne. She then ran to Felixstowe where the containership *Zim Antwerpen*, 11,858/83 had sustained propeller and rudder damage and, assisted by the Z pellar *Deban* as steering tug, towed her to Rotterdam on 6/7th March for repair.

Cable work was also keeping the tugs employed in the spring and summer, the *Sun Mercia* assisting the French cable ship *Vercors* in the Bay of Biscay during March. The *Sun Mercia*'s next job was to assist B.T.'s *C.S. Alert* lay eleven short cables from the beach at Newquay, Cornwall out to sea with the *Avenger* and *Flying Spindrift* from the Clyde. In May-June the *Avenger* and *Sun Mercia* were working with the *Stena Seaspread* and the *Cable Carrier* laying the southern North Sea section of a cable from the Fresian island of Nordeney to the U.S.A. During July the *Avenger* was again assisting the *Stena Seaspread* laying cables in the Irish Sea from the U.K. mainland to the Isle of Man and Ireland. Also in July the *Formidable* was assisting the *Flexiservice III* laying cable in the North Sea. When not employed with the cable ships the *Avenger* and *Formidable* were employed in the North Sea with tows related to the oil industry.

The *Sun Surrey*, a twin Voith Schneider fire-fighting tug of 2,880 b.h.p.and 378 gross tons, arrived at Tilbury Dock on 18th March from Lowestoft where she had been completed by her builders Richards (Shipbuilders) Ltd. The following day bollard pull tests were carried out and a pull of 40 tons was achieved. The *Sun Surrey* was handed over to The Alexandra Towing Co. (London) Ltd. on 20th March and integrated into the Gravesend fleet. With her arrival the *Waterloo* was withdrawn from service on 6th April prior to being returned to the Liverpool fleet, sailing from Gravesend on 22nd April. With her return the *Egerton*, a 1,500 b.h.p. single unit Voith Schneider tug and near sister to the *Sun Swale* now stationed at Gibraltar, was transferred from Liverpool to the Gravesend fleet, arriving 21st May. She was built in 1969 as the *Subtil* for Societe De Remorquage & Du Sauvatage Du Nord, Dunkirk until sold to The Alexandra Towing Co. Ltd. on 1st October 1991 and renamed *Egerton*. A smaller class of Russian container ships running to Tilbury Dock preferred to have smaller less powerful tugs for docking, the *Egerton* being ideal for this type of work and also the berthing of naval vessels in the Upper Pool and South West India Dock.

Port of Tilbury London Ltd. fitted the *Linford* with an A frame with a mud dragger to her stern. They were experimenting to see the effectiveness of keeping the berths clear of mud by dragging it from the dock walls into the middle of the dock to be removed by a suction dredger. This method had been used with good effect in the river, dragging the mud from riverside wharfs into the tideway where the tide carried it away. The A frame is detachable and is lifted ashore when not required for dredging so as not to interfere with her towing capabilities.

The Port of London Authority transferred the remaining two dredging tugs *Lord Devonport* and *Lord Waverley* to Port of Tilbury London Ltd. in January; they were two of a quartet built by James Pollock & Sons, Faversham in 1959 and 1960 respectively. The *Lord Devonport* had been used as a ship-towing dock tug for a short period during the 1960s, the *Lord Waverley* spending her whole career in the dredging department.

The *Sun Sussex* arrived at Tilbury dock on 20th July to undergo bollard pull trials and was handed over to The Alexandra Towing Co. (London) Ltd. on 23rd July. Built at Great Yarmouth by Richards (Shipbuilders) Ltd. she was a twin Voith Schneider fire-fighting tug and sister to the *Sun Surrey*.

With the addition of the *Sun Sussex* the *Sun London* was transferred to Felixstowe on 25th July. The *Sun II* was sold to Greek owners along with her Swansea-based sister *Fabians Bay*, ex-*Sun III* in September. The *Sun II* was taken to Sheerness on 11th September being joined there by the *Fabians Bay*, and both tugs sailed on 13th October, one towing the other bound for the Mediterranean. Thames Towage entered a new era when on 17th November Howard Smith (U.K.) Ltd. made a £52 million cash offer for the Alexandra Towing Co. Ltd. Group, which was recommended by the directors and accepted by the shareholders. Howard Smith Ltd. is a major Australian towage and salvage company. It entered into U.K. towage in 1987 with the acquisition of United Towing Co. and Humber Tugs Ltd., and in 1991 the Medway Fleet of J. P. Knight Ltd. after clearance by the Office of Fair Trading and the Monopolies Commission, A.T.C. Ltd., became part of Howard Smith (U.K.) Ltd on 1st March 1993.

In the sixty years that this book has attempted to portray, great changes have taken place in both the tug fleets and the Port of London. Neither bear much resemblance to pre-war days: ship size has increased dramatically since the introduction of containerisation with a corresponding decrease in ship numbers, and tugs now have power and methods of propulsion undreamed of sixty years ago, with bollard pulls of 30,40 and 50 tons plus, being the norm in the river tugs of the nineties.

What the next century holds in these changeable times is impossible to predict. I just hope that London remains a major port and there is still a towage industry on the River Thames in the year 2033 and it can then celebrate its 200th anniversary.

# William Watkins Ltd.
# Fleet List 1933–1950

Canada                        1880–1935
Official No. 82785
Gross Tons 72          Built 1880
by Thames Iron Works, Blackwall.
80.5′ x 16.9′ x 9.8′

2 cylinder high pressure engine with both cylinders the same diameter. Re-engined 3-1884 with a compound 2 cylinder engine. 1888 re-engined with a 350 i.h.p. triple expansion engine.

5-1935 sold for scrap for £110 to G. Cohen & Son, & scrapped at Canning Town.

Hibernia (ii)              1884–1961
Official No. 89622     Call Sign JPWG
                                   later MGSR
Gross Tons 219        Built 1884
by Maatschappij De Maas, Delfshaven, Holland.
121′ x 22.1′ x 12.9′
107.18′ x 22.1′ x 12.9′ after being shortened in 1922–3.

825 i.h.p. 2 cylinder compound engine by the shipbuilder.

2-8-1914 requisitioned by Royal Navy & renamed H.M.S. *Carcass*.

1915 renamed H.M.S. *Hibernia III*

1919 returned to owners & renamed *Hibernia*.

1-2-1950 to Ship Towage (London) Ltd.

13-4-1961 sold to T. W. Ward Ltd., Grays, Essex for scrap.

*Nubia*                          1890–1935

Official No. 98149              Call Sign MQGP

Gross Tons 102                  Built 1890

by Westwood, Baillie & Co., Poplar, London.

87.6′ × 18.6′ × 10.7′

350 i.h.p. 3 cylinder triple expansion engine by J. Stewart & Son, Blackwall. 5-1935 sold to G. Cohen & Son for £140, & scrapped at Canning Town.

*Scotia* (ii)                   1893–1935

Official No. 102862             Call Sign MQPW

Gross Tons 136                  Built 1893

by Anderson, Laverick & Co. Ltd., Newcastle.

97.5′ × 19.5′ × 11.2′

493 i.h.p. 3 cylinder triple expansion engine by J. Stewart & Son Ltd., Blackwall. 5-1935 sold to G. Cohen & Son for £160, & scrapped at Canning Town.

*Arcadia* 1895–1962
Official No. 105766    Call Sign MQTJ
Gross Tons 180    Built 1895
by Cook, Welton & Gemmel, Hull.
109′ × 21.5′ × 11.8′

700 i.h.p. 3 cylinder triple expansion engine by Earles Shipbuilding & Engineering Co. Ltd., Hull.

4-8-1914 requisitioned by the Royal Navy & renamed H.M.S. *Chichester*.

29.5.1919 returned to owners & renamed *Arcadia*.

1-2-1950 to Ship Towage (London) Ltd.

6-1952 renamed *Badia* (ii) when P. & O. required former named for a new liner being built.

14-11-1962 sold to T. W. Ward, Grays, Essex for scrap.

*Simla* 1898–1964
Official No. 108343    Call Sign MQZX
Gross Tons 144    Built 1898
by Lobnitz & Co. Renfrew.
100.4′ × 20.1′ × 11.3′

500 i.h.p. 3 cylinder triple expansion engine by the shipbuilder.

Requisitioned by Royal Navy 7-1914–7-1915.

1-2-1950 to Ship Towage (London) Ltd.

10-4-1964 scrapped by Medway Drydock & Engineering Co. Sheerness.

*Java* (ii)                          1905–1965
Official No. 120611      Call Sign MCGX
Gross Tons 128            Built 1905
by Cochrane & Sons, Selby.
94′ × 19.6′ × 10.9′

500 i.h.p. 3 cylinder triple expansion engine by G. T. Grey & Co., South Shields.

Name changed to H.M.S. *Carcass* when requisitioned by Royal Navy 21-7-1915–14-5-1919.

Requisitioned by Royal Navy 1940–1945.

1–2–1950 to Ship Towage (London) Ltd.

Sold to Southend Shipbreakers, May 1965 for scrap who stripped vessel, hull resold to continental shipbreakers, Metaalhandel En Sloopwerken H. P. Heuvelman N.V. Krimpen A/D, Ijssel, Holland.

*Badia* (i)                          1909–1947
Official No. 125778      Call Sign MGXY
Gross Tons 150            Built 1909
by Phillips & Son., Dartmouth.
96.2′ × 20.6′ × 10.9′

500 i.h.p. 3 cylinder triple expansion engine by the shipbuilder.

Name changed to H.M.S. *Chester* when requisitioned by Royal Navy 31-7-1914–7-9-1917.

2-10-1947 sold to Fowey Tug & Co. & renamed *Penleath*.

Sold 1961 and scrapped at Rotterdam.

*Doria*                                    1909–1947
Official No. 125767          Call Sign MCXT
Gross Tons 150                 Built 1909
by Philip & Son Ltd. Dartmouth.
96.2′ × 20.6′ × 10.9′

500 i.h.p. 3 cylinder triple expansion engine by shipbuilder.

30-7-1914–2-1-1919 requisitioned by the Royal Navy.

Requisitioned by the Royal Navy during W. W. II & served at Southampton under the management of Risdon Beazley.

1947 sold to Societa Rimorchiatori Riuniti, Genoa & renamed *Euro*.

29-11-1947 departed from Ramsgate under tow of *Empire John*.

1954 renamed *Venezuela*.

1956 renamed *Cile*. 1957 scrapped.

*Vincia*                                   1909–1947
Official No. 129004          Call Sign MCYZ
Gross Tons 150                 Built 1909
by Philip & Son Ltd., Dartmouth
96.2′ × 20.6′ × 10.9′

500 i.h.p. 3 cylinder triple expansion engine by the shipbuilder.

30.7-1914–15-12-1919 requisitioned by the Royal Navy & renamed H.M.S. *Chub*.

Requisitioned by Royal Navy during W.W.II.

1947 sold to Societa Rimorchiatori Riuniti, Genoa & renamed *Eolo*.

1954 renamed *Peru*.

1957 scrapped.

*Palencia*                1920–1939
Official No. 137528
Gross Tons 95            Built 1916
by I. J. Abdela & Mitchel Ltd., Queensferry,
for The Alexandra Towing Co. Ltd.,
Liverpool as *Sloyne*.
76.6′ × 18.1′ × 10.2′

350 i.h.p. 2 cylinder compound engine by A. Dodman & Co. Ltd., Kings Lynn.

Acquired by William Watkins Ltd., 1920.

Acquired by James Towing Co. Southampton 1939.

Later acquired by Shell Oil Co., Gibraltar.

Requisitioned by Royal Navy on harbour service 9-1939–1-1946.

Believed scrapped late 1960s.

*Rumania* (ii)            1928–1935
Official No. 145733       Call Sign MPDN
Gross Tons 148            Built 1919
by Phillips & Son, Dartmouth, for the Royal
Navy as *H.S.79*.
86.2′ × 21′ × 10.4′

450 i.h.p. 2 cylinder compound engine by the shipbuilder.

Acquired by Guy of Cardiff & renamed *Welsh Rose*.

Acquired by William Watkins Ltd., 1928.

Acquired by Nash Dredging Co 14-5-1935 for £4,500.

1940 sold to Government of Trinidad & renamed *St David*.

1954 deleted from the register without explanation.

*Muria* (i)                 1920–1940

Official No. 136308         Call Sign GTVM

Gross Tons 192              Built 1914

by Scott & Sons. Bowling, for Steel & Bennie Ltd., Glasgow, as *Wrestler*.

106.3′ × 23.1′ × 11.7′

450 i.h.p. 2 cylinder compound engine, by Aitchison, Blair & Co. Ltd., Glasgow.

Acquired by Royal Navy on completion & renamed *Hotspur*.

Acquired by William Watkins Ltd., 1920 & renamed *Muria*.

Requisitioned by Royal Navy 1940 & stationed at Harwich as rescue tug. Sunk by mine and lost with all hands off North Foreland in position 51° 26′ 30″N. 01° 27′ E. on 8-11-1940.

*Fabia*                     1920–1946

Official No. 144445         Call Sign MJXP

Gross Tons 151             Built 1919

by Edwards & Co. Ltd., Millwall for the War Dept. as *H.S.85*, renamed *Wendy*. Transferred to Royal Navy 1919 & renamed *Early* 1920

Acquired by W. Watkins Ltd., April 1920 & renamed *Fabia*.

85′ × 20.9′ × 10.6′

3450 i.h.p. 2 cylinder compound engine by Plenty & Son Ltd., Newbury.

Requisitioned by Royal Navy 1939–1946 & served in Thames Estuary under the R.A.F. & at Londonderry under the Navy.

1946 sold to Hemsley Bell & Co., Southampton for £7,500.

1947 sold to Liverpool Screw Towing Co. & renamed *Moorcock*.

12-4-1956 sold for scrap to T. W. Ward, Preston.

*Gondia*            1927–1966
Official No. 149941     Call Sign MDWJ
Gross Tons 200        Built 1927
by Cochrane & Sons Ltd., Selby.
100′ × 25.1′ × 11.8′

760 i.h.p. 3 cylinder triple expansion engine by Crabtree & Co. Ltd., Great Yarmouth.

Passenger licence for 200 passengers.

Requisitioned by Royal Navy on harbour service 1940–1946.

To Ship Towage (London) Ltd., 1-2-1950.

Towed Antwerp for scrap by *Moorcock* July 1966.

Demolished by Scrappingco S.A., Belgium.

*Kenia*            1927–1964
Official No. 149891     Call Sign GQCX
Gross Tons 200        Built 1927
by Cochrane & Sons Ltd., Selby.
100′ × 25.1′ × 11.8′

760 i.h.p. 3 cylinder triple expansion engine by Crabtree & Co. Ltd., Gt. Yarmouth.

Passenger licence for 200

Requisitioned by Royal Navy 8-1939 on examination service.

Rescue tug at Harwich with Pennant No. W47 after *Muria* was mined 11-1940, until 1945.

1-2-1950 to Ship Towage (London) Ltd.

12-10-1964 sank undocking *Maashaven* from Tilbury Dock new entrance.

Sold to Metal Recovery (Newhaven) Ltd.

12-11-1964 towed to Sheerness by tug *Sunnyside* & scrapped by Lacmots Ltd., Sheerness.

*Tanga*                       1931–1969
Official No. 162531    Call Sign MPYN
Gross Tons 203          Built 1931
by Phillips & Son Ltd., Dartmouth
100′ × 25.3′ × 11.7′

850 i.h.p. 3 cylinder triple expansion engine by Earle's Shipbuilding & Engineering Co. Ltd., Hull.

Requisitioned by Royal Navy & served at Iceland 1940–1943.

1-2-1950 to Ship Towage (London) Ltd.

27-1-1969 to London Tugs Ltd.

25-2-1969 towed Antwerp for scrap by *Moorcock* for Scrappingco S.A. & demolished at Klein Willebroek, Belgium.

*Napia* (i)                   1937–1939
Official No. 136661    Call Sign MFDC
Gross Tons 155          Built 1914
by J. P. Rennoldson & Sons, South Shields, for The Gravesend United Steam Tug Co. as *Doralia*.
90.3′ × 22.1′ × 10.7′

550 i.h.p. 2 cylinder compound engine by the shipbuilder.

Served at Le Havre for the army during W.W.1.

1929 fitted with fire-fighting pumps.

Acquired by William Watkins Ltd., June 1937.

Renamed *Napia*, June 1938.

Requisitioned by Royal Navy 6-12-1939 on examination service. 20-12-1939 lost by mine with all hands in Ramsgate Channel.

*Cervia* (i)                    1937–1946

Official No. 148586      Call Sign MNLG

Gross Tons 157.05        Built 1925

by J. P. Rennoldson, South Shields. for the Gravesend United Steam Tug Co. as *Tamesa*.

90′ × 22′ × 10.6′

550 i.h.p. 2 cylinder compound engine by the shipbuilder.

Acquired by William Watkins Ltd., June 1937.

Renamed *Cervia*, 17th June 1938.

Requisitioned by Royal Navy 1942–1945 and served at Methil & Londonderry.

24-5-1946 sold to Ridley Tugs, Newcastle & renamed *Monty*.

1954 sold to J. H. Pigott, Grimsby & renamed *Lady Elsie*.

1962 renamed *Lady Hazel*. 1963 scrapped by Arie Rijsdijk Boss & Zooms.

*Racia* (ii)                    1937–1967

Official No. 162492      Call Sign MDLX

Gross Tons 163           Built 1930

by Cochrane & Sons Ltd., Selby for The Gravesend United Steam Tug Co. as *Dilwara*.

95′ × 24.1′ × 11.2′

750 i.h.p. 3 cylinder triple expansion engine by Earles Shipbuilding & Engineering Co. Ltd., Hull.

1935 renamed *Denderra*.

Acquired by William Watkins Ltd., June 1937.

Renamed *Racia*, June 1938.

Transferred to River Clyde during W.W.11.

To Ship Towage (London) Ltd., 1-2-1950.

Scrapped Antwerp 31-7-1967, being sold to Van Den Bossche & Co., Belgium & demolition commenced at Boom, 2-8-1967.

*Persia* (ii)          1938–1967

Official No. 162684     Call Sign MLNF

Gross Tons 165         Built 1932

by Cochrane & Sons, Ltd., Selby for The Gravesend United Steam Co. Ltd. as *Dongara*.

95′ × 24.1′ × 11.2′

750 i.h.p. 3 cylinder triple expansion engine by Earles Shipbuilding & Engineering Co. Ltd., Hull.

Acquired by William Watkins Ltd., June 1937.

Renamed *Persia*, June 1938.

C.T.L. after being gutted by fire, when tanker *Lunula* mined at Thames Haven, 9-4-1941.

Rebuilt at Ramsgate and returned to work 1943.

Renamed *Muria* (ii) 1946.

To Ship Towage (London) Ltd., 1-2-1950.

Towed Antwerp by *Ionia* for scrap, 11-4-1967. Sold to Scrappingco. S.A.

*Napia* (ii)          1946–1971

Official No. 169087     Call Sign MLSV

Gross Tons 261         Built 1943

by Goole Shipbuilding & Repairing Co. Ltd., Goole.

105.8′ × 30.1′ × 12.5′ × 12.5′

1,200 i.h.p. 3 cylinder triple expansion engine by McKie & Baxter Ltd, Paisley, for Ministry of Shipping as *Empire Jester*.

Acquired by William Watkins Ltd., 1946 & renamed *Napia* (ii).

1-2-1950 to Ship Towage (London) Ltd.

27-1-1969 to London Tugs Ltd.

December 1971 sold to John G. Efthinou, Greece & renamed *Tolmiros*.

1973 sold to Locus Matsas, Piraeus, Greece. 19-2-1986 sold to M. Tzonis & Co. & scrapped at Perama.

*Cervia* (ii)        1946–1972

Official No. 180997    Call Sign GDPM

Gross Tons 233        Built 1946

by Alexander Hall & Co. Ltd., Aberdeen for Ministry of Shipping as *Empire Raymond*.

$105.2' \times 27.1' \times 11.7'$

900 i.h.p. 3 cylinder triple expansion engine by the shipbuilder.

1946 acquired by William Watkins Ltd. & renamed *Cervia*, December 1946.

1-2-1950 to Ship Towage (London) Ltd.

25-10-1954 sank undocking P.& O. Liner *Arcadia*, 5 lives lost.

27-1-1969 to London Tugs Ltd.

March 1972 sold to be preserved.

1973 returned to commercial towing by International Towing Ltd.

1985 preserved at Ramsgate by East Kent Maritime Trust.

*Zealandia* (ii)       1946–1952

Official No. 169177    Call Sign MGRS

Gross Tons 479        Built 1944

by Clelands (Successors) Ltd., Willington Quay-on-Tyne for Ministry of Shipping as *Empire Winnie*.

$137.1' \times 30.1' \times 15.3'$

1,250 i.h.p. 3 cylinder triple expansion engine by George Clark (1938) Ltd., Sunderland.

1946 acquired by William Watkins Ltd. & renamed *Zealandia*, 1947.

1-2-1950 to Ship Towage (London) Ltd.

1952 sold to Adelaide S.S. Co. Ltd. & renamed *Yuna*.

1971 sold to Coral R. Rotondella, Australia.

1972 sold to M.C. & A. Michela, Australia.

1973 stripped and reduced to a barge.

1974 scrapped at Bunbury Harbour, Western Australia.

*Rumania* (iii)　　　　　1946–1956
Official No. 169185　　Call Sign MDFC
Gross Tons 592　　　　Built 1944
by Clelands (Successors) Ltd., Willington Quay-on-Tyne.
137.1′ × 33.1′ × 15.1′

1,250 i.h.p. 3 cylinder triple expansion engine by Ailsa Shipbuilding Co. Ltd., Troon, for Ministry of Shipping, as *Empire Susan*.

Placed under the management of William Watkins Ltd.

Acquired by Williams Watkins Ltd., 1946.

Renamed *Rumania*, 1947.

To Ship Towage (London) Ltd., 1-2-1950.

Lost on North Longsand 11-2-1956 assisting *Loide Honduras*.

*Empire John*　　　　　1946–1951
Official No. 169171　　Call Sign MQVJ
Gross Tons 479　　　　Built 1943
by Clelands (Successors) Ltd., Willington Quay-on-Tyne.
136′ × 30.1′ × 15.3′

1,275 i.h.p. 3 cylinder triple expansion engine by Swan Hunter & Wigham Richardson Ltd., Newcastle for Ministry of Shipping.

Acquired by William Watkins Ltd., 1946 on long term charter.

Returned to Ministry of Shipping, 1951.

Sold to Dominion Coal Co. Ltd., Montreal, Canada, without change of name or British Registry.

1965 sold to Commonwealth Metals Inc., Canada for demolition. Resold to Cia Espanola De Demolicion Naval, Madrid. 26-11-1965 arrived Bilbao for scrap.

# Tugs placed under the management of William Watkins Ltd. by the Ministry of War Transport during World War II

| | |
|---|---|
| *Empire Piper* | 1942–1957 |
| Official No. 165836 | Call Sign MKZZ |
| Gross Tons 250 | Built 1942 |

by Clelands (Successors) Ltd., Willington Quay-on-Tyne.

107.8' × 26.2' × 12.5'

1,000 i.h.p. 3 cylinder triple expansion engine by Swan Hunter & Wigham Richardson Ltd., Newcastle.

Served in Iceland under Watkins.

Acquired by John Cooper Ltd., Belfast & renamed *Piper*, 1947.

1971 sold to A. P. Papayani, A.E., Greece, & renamed *Sotiros*.

1984 sold & renamed *Lalrion*.

1987 scrapped at Rafina.

| | |
|---|---|
| *Empire Spruce* | 1942–1947 |
| Official No. 168780 | Call Sign BDRB |
| Gross Tons 129 | Built 1942 |

by Richard Dunston Ltd., Thorne.

95.5' × 20.5' × 8.4'

500 i.h.p. 3 cylinder triple expansion engine by McKie & Baxter Ltd., Paisley.

Coastal tug under Watkins. Transferred to Admiralty, March 1947 & renamed *Emulous*.

1958 sold to J. D. Irvine Ltd., St John, N.B., Canada, & renamed *Irvine Oak*.

1961 fitted with a 16 cylinder General Motors V diesel engine.

*Empire Jean*        1945–1946

Official No. 169193    Call Sign MNLQ

Gross Tons 593        Built 1945

by Clelands (Successors) Ltd., Willington Quay-on-Tyne.

137.1′ × 33.1′ × 15.1′

1,250 i.h.p. 3 cylinder triple expansion engine by D. Rowan & Co. Ltd., Glasgow.

1946 sold to Metal Industries (Salvage) Ltd., & renamed *Metinda III*.

1961 sold to Spanish Navy & renamed *R.A.3*.

*Empire Susan*      1944–1946

Official No. 169185    Call Sign MDFC

Gross Tons 592        Built 1944

by Clelands (Successors) Ltd., Willington Quay-on-Tyne.

137.1′ × 33.1′ × 15.1′

1250 i.h.p. 3 cylinder triple expansion engine by Ailsa Shipbuilding Co. Ltd., Troon.

Sold to William Watkins Ltd., 1946, & renamed *Rumania* (iii), 1947.

To Ship Towage (London) Ltd., 1-2-1950.

11-2-1956 lost on North Longsand assisting *Loide Honduras* which was aground.

*Empire Winnie*      1944–1946
Official No. 169177      Call Sign MGRS
Gross Tons 479      Built 1944
by Clelands (Successors) Ltd., Willington
Quay-on-Tyne.
136′ × 30.1′ × 15.3′

1275 i.h.p. 3 cylinder triple expansion engine by George Clark (1938) Ltd., Sunderland.

Sold to William Watkins Ltd., 1946, & renamed *Zealandia* (ii) 1947.

To Ship Towage (London) Ltd., 1-2-1950.

1952 sold to Adelaide S.S. Co. Ltd., Adelaide, Australia & renamed *Yuna*.

1971 sold to Coral R. Rotondella, Australia.

1972 sold to M. C. & A. Michela, Australia.

1973 stripped & reduced to a barge.

1974 scrapped at Bunbuay Harbour, Western Australia.

*Empire John*      1943–1946
Official No. 169171      Call Sign MQVJ
Gross Tons 479      Built 1943
by Clelands (Successors) Ltd., Willington
Quay-on-Tyne.
136′ × 30.1′ × 15.3′

1,275 i.h.p. 3 cylinder triple expansion engine by Swan Hunter & Wigham Richardson Ltd., Newcastle.

Chartered by William Watkins Ltd., 1946–1951.

1951 sold by Ministry to Dominion Coal Co. Ltd., Montreal, Canada without change of name or British registry.

1965 sold to Commonwealth Metals Inc., Canada for scrap.

Resold to Cia Espanola De Demolicion Naval, Madrid.

Arrived in tow of *Praia D'Adraga* at Bilbao 26-11-1965.

*Empire Martha*  1945–1947
Official No. 180459  Call Sign GSQZ
Gross Tons 296  Built 1945
by Cochrane & Sons Ltd., Selby.
116′ × 27.6′ × 12.7′

750 i.h.p. 3 cylinder triple expansion engine by Franklin Machine & Foundry Corp., Providence, Rhode Island, U.S.A.

1947 sold to James Contracting & Shipping Co. Ltd. & renamed *Foremost 106*.

1949 sold to Remorquage Letzer, Antwerp & renamed *Georges Letzer*.

*Empire Humphrey*  1944–1945
Official No. 169344  Call Sign MGRG
Gross Tons 274  Built 1944
by Cochrane & Sons Ltd., Selby.
105.2′ × 26.6′ × 12.2′

850 i.h.p. 3 cylinder triple expansion engine by Amos & Smith Ltd., Hull.

1945 transferred to Admiralty.

1946 sold to Netherlands East Indies Government & renamed *Suus*, 1947.

1959 sold to Indonesian Government & renamed *Laut Sawu*, 1961.

1964 sold to Sorabaya Port Authority.

*Empire Betsy*　　　　　1944–1947
Official No. 180248　　Call Sign MNNX
Gross Tons 274　　　　Built 1944
by Cochrane & Sons Ltd., Selby.
105.2′ × 26.5′ × 12.2′

850 i.h.p. 3 cylinder triple expansion engine by Amos & Smith Ltd., Hull.

1947 sold to N.V. de Bataafsche Petroleum Maats, Holland, & renamed *Soegio*.

12-2-1948 sunk by mine off Borneo in position 02° 36′S. 116° 33′E.

*Empire Wold*　　　　　1942–1944
Official No. 169021　　Call Sign BDQL
Gross Tons 269　　　　Built 1942
by J. Crown & Sons Ltd., Sunderland.
107.8′ × 26.2′ × 12.5′

3 cylinder triple expansion engine by Swan Hunter & Wigham Richardson Ltd., Newcastle.

10-11-1944 lost off Iceland with all hands.

*Empire Stella* 1945–1946
Official No. 180448    Call Sign GBKK
Gross Tons 325    Built 1945
by Cochrane & Sons Ltd., Selby.
116′ × 27′6″ × 12′7″

750 i.h.p. 3 cylinder triple expansion engine by Franklin Machine & Foundry Corp., Providence, Rhode Island, U.S.A.

1-1-1946 had a boiler explosion in Thames Estuary.

Sold to United Towing Co., Hull, in damaged condition.

Re-engined & renamed *Serviceman*.

1961 re-engined with a British Polar 6 cylinder diesel engine.

1969 sold to Rimorchiatori Sardi S.P.A., Cagliari, Sardinia & renamed *Poetto*.

*Assiduous* 1943–1945
Official No. 169321
Gross Tons 597    Built 1943
by Cochrane & Sons Ltd., Selby.
156′8″ × 33′2″ × 14′9″

1,350 i.h.p. 3 cylinder triple expansion engine by C. D. Holmes & Co., Ltd., Hull.

Wartime pennant No. W142.

1946 dockyard tug.

1958 sold to J. D. Irvine Ltd., St. John N.B., Canada.

1961 renamed *Irvine Tamarack*.

1969 sold to Canadian Shipbreakers.

*Foremost 22*           194?–1945
Official No. 147740     Call Sign GFJM
Gross Tons 195        Built 9-1924
by J. Meyers Shipbuilding Co., Zalt-Bommel, Holland
100.4′ × 27.2′ × 12.2′

110 n.h.p. 900 i.h.p. 3 cylinder triple expansion engine, by H. Beardmore & Co. Ltd., Coatbridge for James Dredging, Towage & Transport Co. Ltd., Southampton.

1924 sold to Newhaven Harbour Co., Newhaven.

1926 sold to Southern Railway Co. & stationed at Newhaven.

1948 to British Transport Commission.

1961 sold to Cantier Nav. Santa Maria S.P.A., La Spezia, Italy, & renamed *Terranova*.

1978 sold for scrap.

*Lynch*             194?–1945
Official No. 148512     Call Sign MNQY
Gross Tons 211        Built 10-1924
by J. Meyers Shipbuilding Co., Zalt-Bommel, Holland.
100.4′ × 27.2′ × 12.2′

650 i.h.p. 3 cylinder triple expansion engine by H. Beardmore & Co. Ltd., Coatbridge, as *Foremost 23* for James Dredging, Towage & Transport Co. Ltd., Southampton.

1925 sold to Falmouth Docks & Engineering Co. Falmouth, & renamed *Lynch*.

1931 sold to Falmouth Towage Co. Ltd.

1968 sold to Haulbowline Industries Ltd., Cobh, Ireland.

Demolition commenced November 1968.

*Fairplay One*        1940–1945
Official No. 166573    Call Sign MSRD
Gross Tons 162       Built 1911
by Schiffsw A. G. Hamburg.
103.4′ × 22.6′

3 cylinder triple expansion engine by the shipbuilder for Fairplay Schlepp-Dampfsch Reed., Hamburg, as *Fairplay X*.

1938 transferred to Fairplay Towing & Shipping Co. Ltd., London.

Renamed *Fairplay One*, & worked at Avonmouth.

1950 returned to Fairplay, Hamburg, & renamed *Fairplay XX*.

1951 rebuilt & fitted with a 970 b.h.p. Deutz engine & renamed *Fairplay I*.

6-9-1954 sank after colliding with *Italia* 16,777/28.

2-2-1959 sank assisting *Solfonn* 19,810/56.

1964 sold to Augustea Impresa Maritime Spa, Palermo, Sicily & renamed *Duro*.

1986 sold to Italian shipbreakers at La Spezia.

# Gamecock Steam Towing Company Ocean Towage & Salvage Co.Ltd.
## Fleet List 1933–1950

*Falcon*                        1892–1933
Official No. 99090       Call Sign MPWN
Gross Tons 124            Built 1892
by G. Rennie & Co., London.
91.5′ × 19.1′ × 10.9′

450 i.h.p. 2 cylinder compound engine by J. Steward & Son Ltd. London.

1933 sold to S. C. Roberts, Bristol. (Commonwealth Steam Tug Co.)

1939 company acquired by Fairplay Towage & Shipping Co. Ltd.

1949 scrapped at Penarth by Marine Metals Ltd. & demolition commenced 2-3-1949.

*Spread Eagle*              1911–1938
Official No. 129184     Call Sign MGKX
Gross Tons 143            Built 1911
by Robertson & Co., London.
96′ × 21.1′ × 11′

500 i.h.p. 2 cylinder compound engine by Aitchison, Blair & Co. Ltd., Glasgow.

1938 sold to Newport Screw Towing Co., & renamed *Dunson*.

1961 sold for scrap to John Cashmore Ltd., Newport & demolition commenced 11-4-1961.

*Watercock*                1925–1966

Official No. 147079        Call Sign KNVF
                           later MLKN

Gross Tons 200             Built 1923

by Cochrane & Sons Ltd., Selby.

96.6′ × 24.5′ × 11.8′

750 i.h.p. 3 cylinder triple expansion engine by Earles Shipbuilding & Engineering Co. Ltd., Hull, for United Towing Co. Hull, as *Masterman*.

1925 acquired by Gamecock Steam Towing Co. & renamed *Watercock*.

1-2-1950 to Ship Towage (London) Ltd.

4-7-1966 towed Antwerp for scrap by Scrappingco S.A & demolition commenced at Willebroek 7-1966.

*New Stormcock*            1922–1949

Official No. 146556

Gross Tons 197             Built 1921

by Danziger Werf, Danzig, Germany.

104.2′ × 21′ × 10.1′

600 i.h.p. 3 cylinder triple expansion engine by the shipbuilder.

April 1922 acquired by Gamecock Steam Towing Co.

1948 sold to W. Crosthwaite, Middlesborough & renamed *Kings Cross*.

1957 scrapped by C. W. Dorking & Co., Gateshead.

*Crested Cock* (i)      1930–1934
Official No. 161393
Gross Tons 214      Built 1930
by Alexander Hall & Co. Ltd., Aberdeen.
100′ × 26.1′ × 12.3′

139 n.h.p. 1,150 i.h.p. i.h.p. 3 cylinder triple expansion engine by the shipbuilder.

1934 sold to Russia, & renamed *Shuga*.

1960 deleted from register due to lack of information.

*New Gamecock*      1930–1933
Official No. 161394
Gross Tons 214      Built 1930
by Alexander Hall & Co. Ltd., Aberdeen.
100′ × 26.1′ × 12.3′

139 n.h.p. 1,150 i.h.p. 3 cylinder triple expansion engine by the shipbuilder.

1933 sold to Government of Palestine, & renamed *Steady*.

1948 Transferred to Government of Israel, & renamed *Eytanah*.

1966 sold to Tsavliris (Salvage & Towage) Ltd., Piraeus & renamed *Nisos Hydra*.

1975 sold to Maritime Commercial Enterprises Ltd., Piraeus & renamed *Achilleus*.

*Ocean Cock*        1932–1969
Official No. 162695     Call Sign MBBN
Gross Tons 184       Built 1932
by Alexander Hall & Co., Ltd., Aberdeen.
96′ × 25.1′ × 11.8′

1,000 i.h.p. 3 cylinder triple expansion engine by the shipbuilder.

9-6-1938 sank in Gravesend Reach after collision with *Port Nicolson.*

1-2-1950 to Ship Towage (London) Ltd.

1966-Sept. 1968 transferred to Gaselee (Felixstowe) Ltd.

27-1-1969 to London Tugs Ltd.

25-2-1969 towed Antwerp for scrap by *Moorcock.* Demolition carried out by Scrappingco S.A.

*Atlantic Cock*      1932–1970
Official No. 162687     Call Sign MBBM
Gross Tons 182       Built 1932
by Alexander Hall & Co. Ltd., Aberdeen.
96′ × 25.1′ × 11.8′

1,000 i.h.p. 3 cylinder triple expansion engine by the shipbuilder.

1-2-1950 to Ship Towage (London) Ltd.

27-1-1969 to London Tugs Ltd.

February 1970 towed Antwerp for scrap by Scrappingco S.A.

*Crested Cock* (ii)     1935–1970
Official No. 164441     Call Sign MBKX
Gross Tons 177     Built 1935
by Alexander Hall & Co. Ltd., Aberdeen.
96′ × 25.1′ × 11.8′

1,000 i.h.p. 3 cylinder triple expansion engine by the shipbuilder.

1-2-1950 to Ship Towage (London) Ltd.

27-1-1969 to London Tugs Ltd.

February 1970 towed Antwerp for scrap.

*King Lear* (salvage     19??–1949
ship)
Official No. 123234     Call Sign HFTM,
later GDPR
Gross Tons 290     Built 1906
by Earles Co. Ltd., Hull.
148.4′ × 23′ × 11.2′

96 n.h.p. 3 cylinder triple expansion engine by Amos & Smith, Hull.

1949 sold to Loucas Matsas & Sons, Piraeus & renamed *Marigo Matsas*.

1958 sold to K. Syrmalakis, Piraeus & renamed *Manos S*.

1976 deleted from register.

# Elliott Steam Tug Co. Ltd.
# Fleet List 1933–1950

*Champion*                                      1892–1936
Official No. 101948        Call Sign MQJV
Gross Tons 116                Built 1892
by A. W. Robertson & Co., Canning Town.
89.1′ × 19′ × 11.1′

2 cylinder compound engine by the shipbuilder.

1936 sold to T. W. Ward & Son, Grays, Essex for scrap.

*Vanquisher* (i)                           1909–1939
Official No. 129025        Call Sign MDBT
Gross Tons 179                Built 1899
by J. P. Rennoldson & Sons, South Shields.
for Abeille Towage & Salvage Co. Ltd., Le
Havre as *Abeille No. 10*.
106.8′ × 21.1′ × 11.2′

3 cylinder triple expansion engine by the shipbuilder.

1909 acquired by Elliott Steam Tug Co. Ltd., & renamed *Vanquisher*.

7-1914–1919 requisitioned by the Royal Navy, & renamed H.M.S. *Ceylon* & H.M.S. *Daunter*.

9-1941 sold for scrap to T. W. Ward, Grays, Essex.

Revenger                    1922–1934
Official No. 146125
Gross Tons 187            Built 1880
by D. Dekker & Co., Antwerp, for
Remorquage A'Helice, Antwerp as *John Bull*.
108′ × 21.1′ × 11.8′

2 cylinder compound engine by J. Geneffe & Co., Liege.

1902 re-engined with a 75 n.h.p. 3 cylinder triple expansion engine by G. T. Grey & Co., South Shields.

1922 acquired by Elliott Steam Tug Co. Ltd., & renamed *Revenger*.

10-5-1934 sold for scrap to T. W. Ward, Grays, Essex.

Crusader                    1922–1935
Official No. 146124
Gross Tons 183            Built 1881
by De Dekker & Co., Antwerp, for
Remorquage A'Helice, Antwerp as *Washington*.
108′ × 21.1′ × 11.8′

2 cylinder compound engine, by J. Geneffe & Co., Liege.

1902 re-engined with a 75 n.h.p. i.h.p. 3 cylinder triple expansion engine by G. T. Grey & Co., South Shields.

1922 acquired by Elliott Steam Tug Co., & renamed *Crusade*.

1935 sold for scrap to T. W. Ward & Son, Grays, Essex.

Security                    1927–1946
Official No. 118084         Call Sign MNTC
Gross Tons 188              Built 1904
by J. P. Rennoldson & Sons, South Shields, for Liverpool Steam Tug Co. Ltd. as *Kingfisher*.
102′ × 23.1′ × 12′

3 cylinder triple expansion engine by the shipbuilder.

22-3-1906 sold to the Royal Navy & renamed *Diligence*.

1914 renamed *Security*.

8-2-1927 sold to Elliott Steam Tug Co.

8-1939 requisitioned by Royal Navy.

1942-8-1944 renamed H.M.S. *Stoke*.

8-12-1946 foundered 12 miles from Anvil Point while towing *Kelletia* with *Contest* & *Watercock*, 4 crew members lost.

Venturous                   1927–1945
Official No. 117517
Gross Tons 179              Built 1904
by Dublin Dockyard Co., Dublin.
106′ × 22.1′ × 10.5′

3 cylinder triple expansion engine, by Lees, Anderson & Co., Glasgow, for Dublin Docks Board as *Anna Liffey*.

1927 acquired by Elliott Steam Tug Co. Ltd., & renamed *Venturous*.

1945 scrapped by T. Ward at Grays, Essex.

*Challenge*                    1931–1973
Official No. 162549      Call Sign MPZB
Gross Tons 212              Built 1931
by Alexander Hall & Co. Ltd., Aberdeen.
100′ × 26.1′ × 12.3′

1,150 i.h.p. 3 cylinder triple expansion engine by the shipbuilder.

1-2-1950 to Ship Towage (London) Ltd.

27-1-1969 to London Tugs Ltd.

29-10-1973 sold to Taylor Woodrow Ltd., London for preservation in St Katherines Dock, London.

*Contest* (iii)                1933–1972
Official No. 163323      Call Sign MBCR
Gross Tons 213              Built 1933
by Alexander Hall & Co. Ltd., Aberdeen.
100′ × 26.1′ × 12.3′

1,150 i.h.p. 3 cylinder triple expansion engine by the shipbuilder.

1-2-1950 to Ship Towage (London) Ltd.

27-1-1969 to London Tugs Ltd.

7-4-1972 scrapped by T. Ward at Grays, Essex.

# Gravesend United Steam Tug Co.
## Fleet List 1933–1937

*Florida*             1902–1933
Official No. 115929    Call Sign MFTM
Gross Tons 114       Built 1902
by Hepple & Co. Ltd., South Shields.
90.5′ × 19.6′ × 10.8′

2 cylinder compound engine by the shipbuilder.

January 1933 sold to J. H. Lamey Ltd., Liverpool, without change of name.

1956 scrapped by T. W. Ward Ltd., & delivered at Barrow 19-10-1956.

*Doralia*            1914–1937
Official No. 136661    Call Sign MFDC
Gross Tons 155       Built 1914
by J. P. Rennoldson & Sons, South Shields.
90.3′ × 22.1′ × 10.7′

550 i.h.p. 2 cylinder compound engine by the shipbuilder.

June 1937 company acquired by William Watkins Ltd.

June 1938 renamed *Napia*.

17-12-1939 sunk by mine off Ramsgate, with the loss of all hands.

*Tamesa*                1925–1937
Official No. 148586
Gross Tons 157.05     Built 1925
by J. P. Rennoldson & Sons, South Shields.
90′ × 22′ × 10.6′

550 i.h.p. 2 cylinder compound engine by the shipbuilder.

June 1937 company acquired by William Watkins Ltd.

June 1938 renamed *Cervia*.

1942–1945 requisitioned by Royal Navy and served at Methil & Londonderry.

24-5-1946 sold to Ridley Tugs, Newcastle & renamed *Monty*.

1954 sold to J. H. Pigott, Grimsby & renamed *Lady Elsie*.

1962 renamed *Lady Hazel*.

1963 sold for scrap to Arie Rijsdijk Boss & Zooms, & demolished at Hendrik Ido Ambacht.

*Dilwara*            1930–1937
Official No. 162492    Call Sign MDLX
Gross Tons 163       Built 1930
by Cochrane & Sons Ltd., Selby.
95′ × 24.1′ × 11.2′

900 i.h.p. 3 cylinder triple expansion engine by Earles Shipbuilding & Engineering Co. Ltd., Hull.

1935 renamed *Denderra*.

June 1937 company acquired by William Watkins Ltd.

June 1938 renamed *Racia*.

1-2-1950 to Ship Towage (London) Ltd.

31-7-1967 scrapped Antwerp by Van den Bossche & Co., work commenced 2-8-1967 at Boom.

*Dongarra* 1932–1937

Official No. 162684 Call Sign MLNF

Gross Tons 165 Built 1932

by Cochrane & Sons Ltd., Selby.

95′ × 24.1′ × 11.2′

900 i.h.p. 3 cylinder triple expansion engine by Earles Shipbuilding & Engineering Co. Ltd., Hull.

June 1937 company acquired by William Watkins Ltd.

June 1938 renamed *Persia*.

9-4-1941 burnt out and a C.T.L. when tanker *Lunula* mined at Thames Haven.

1943 returned to service after being rebuilt at Ramsgate.

1946 renamed *Muria*.

1-2-1950 to Ship Towage (London) Ltd.

11-4-1967 towed to Antwerp for scrap by *Ionia* by Scrappingco S.A., Belgium.

# W. H. J. Alexander Ltd. (Sun Tugs)
## Fleet List 1933–1969

*Sunlit*          1890–1938

Official No. 98041

Gross Tons 47.26     Built 1890

67.5′ × 15.1′ 7.8′

45 n.h.p. 2 cylinder compound engine, as *Stockwell*, renamed *Sunlit*, 1899, when all tugs given Sun names.

3-10-1938 sold to Silvertown Services for £1,000 & renamed *Silverlit*.

1942 sold to British Government, fate unknown.

*Sunclad*        1892–1938

Official No. 101971

Gross Tons 54.38     Built 1892

by Summers & Scott, Gloucester.

67.6′ × 16.2′ × 7.95′

50 n.h.p. 2 cylinder compound engine, as *Star of the East*, renamed *Sunclad*, 1899, when all tugs given Sun names.

3-10-1938 sold to Silvertown Services for £1,000 & renamed *Silverclad*.

1950 scrapped by T. Ward, Grays, Essex.

*Sunrise* (i)                1899–1947

Official No. 112648          Call Sign SMND
                             later MFFR

Gross Tons 103               Built 1899

by J. G. Fay & Co. Ltd., Southampton.
80.3′ × 19′ × 9.9′

63 n.h.p. 450 i.h.p. 2 cylinder compound engine by the shipbuilder.

1947 scrapped T. Ward, Grays.

*Sunshine*                   1899–1960

Official No. 112637          Call Sign SMNC
                             later MFFQ

Gross Tons 103               Built 1899

by J. G. Fay & Co. Ltd., Southampton.
80.3′ × 19′ × 9.9′

63 n.h.p. 450 i.h.p. 2 cylinder compound engine by the shipbuilder.

13-2-1960 scrapped T. Ward, Grays.

*Sundial*           1916–1938
Official No. 110060
Gross Tons 54.81     Built 1899
as *Prince* for Samual Williams Ltd. 1916 sold to W.H.J. Alexander Ltd. & renamed *Sundial*.
69' × 16.4' × 9.2'

60 n.h.p. 2 cylinder compound engine.

3-10-1938 sold to Silvertown Services for £1,500 & renamed *Silverdial*.

4-7-1940 bombed & sunk in Portland Harbour.

*Sunbeam*           1901–1938
Official No. 114804
Gross Tons 60.21     Built 1901
in Holland at Papendrect.
72' × 17' × 8.65'

70 n.p.h. 2 cylinder compound engine.

December 1914 sunk by ship while attending pontoon bridge between Gravesend and Tilbury.

3-10-1938 sold to Silvertown Services for £1,500 & renamed *Silverbeam*.

2-1940-1947 hired by Royal Navy as Dockyard tug.

1948 sold to Milford Docks Co., Milford Haven & renamed *St. Govans*.

1965 sold to C. Purdy (local shipbreakers) & scrapped.

*Sun* 1906–1964

Official No. 120665    Call Sign HGFC
                       later MCLE

Gross Tons 130         Built 1906

by R. Cox & Sons, Appledore.

87.3′ × 22.3′ × 10.5′

550 i.h.p. 3 cylinder triple expansion engine by J. Stewart & Son Ltd. Blackwall. 15-4-1964 scrapped T. Ward, Grays, Sussex.

*Sunbird* 1907–1961

Official No. 125638

Gross Tons 64          Built 1907

by Jonker & Stans Hedrikido, Ambacht.

72.1′ × 18.5′ × 8.8′

350 i.h.p. 2 cylinder compound engine by J. Stewart & Son, Ltd., London.

24-11-1947 sank in Limehouse Reach while making fast to *Angelo* 2199/40.

17-3-1961 sold for scrap to T. Ward, Grays, Essex.

*Sunfish*                     1907–1962
Official No. 125610
Gross Tons 70          Built 1907
by Jonker & Stans Hendrikido, Ambacht.
72′ × 18.5′ × 9.2′

350 i.h.p. 2 cylinder compound engine by J. Stewart & Son Ltd., London.

4-3-1960 sank dragging through Tower Bridge.

28-6-1962 scrapped T. Ward, Grays.

*Sun II* (i)                  1909–1956
Official No. 129010    Call Sign HPDV
                              later MCZB
Gross Tons 197         Built 1909
by Earles Co. Ltd., Hull.
100′ × 25.6′ × 11.3′

750 i.h.p. 3 cylinder triple expansion engine by the shipbuilder.

20-3-1956 sold to J. H. Pigott, Grimsby & renamed *Lady Thelma*.

1966 sold for scrap to P. & W. Maclellan Ltd., & arrived Bo'ness 27-4-1966.

*Sun III* (i)                  1909–1956

Official No. 129020     Call Sign HPGW
                                    later MCZK

Gross Tons 197         Built 1909

by Earles Co. Ltd., Hull.

100′ × 25.6′ × 11.3′

750 i.h.p. 3 cylinder triple expansion engine by the shipbuilder.

31-5-1956 sold to J. H Pigott, Grimsby, & renamed *Lady Sarah*.

1967 sold for scrap to Hughes Bolchow & Co. Ltd., & arrived Blyth 23-6-1967.

*Sunfly*                     1910–1938

Official No. 87459

Gross Tons 59          Built 1882

by Finch & Co. Ltd., Chepstow, for Young & Christies, Cardiff.

70.5′ × 15′ × 9.1′

1885 sold to Thames Conservency Board, & renamed *Lizard*.

1910 sold to W. H. J. Alexander Ltd., & renamed *Sunfly*.

1938 scrapped.

*Sun IV*                                    1915–1966

Official No. 139075          Call Sign JLQT
                                             later MFXR

Gross Tons 200                Built 1915
by Earles Co. Ltd., Hull.
105′ × 25.5′ × 12.4′

750 i.h.p. 3 cylinder triple expansion engine by the shipbuilder.

1966 sold to Societa Rimorchiatori Napoletani, Naples & renamed *San Benigno*.

1979 scrapped at Naples.

*Sun V*                                     1915–1966

Official No. 139071          Call Sign JLQB
                                             later MFXN

Gross Tons 200                Built 1915
by Earles Co. Ltd., Hull.
105′ × 25.5′ × 12.4′

750 i.h.p. 3 cylinder triple expansion engine by the shipbuilder.

1966 sold to Societa Rimorchiatori Napoletani, Naples & renamed *Punta Alice*.

1979 scrapped at Naples.

*Sunny*                                      1915/6–1936
Official No. 108391
Gross Tons 25                  Built 1898
by Lobnitz & Co. Ltd., Renfrew.
50.3′ × 12.1′ × 6′

2 cylinder compound engine for S. Pearson & Co. Ltd. London, the contractors building Dover Harbour as the *Clive*.

1915/6 sold to W.H.J. Alexander Ltd. & renamed *Sunny*.

1936 sold for scrap.

*Sun VI*                                     1915–1960
Official No. 93654          Call Sign TWPK
                                             later MDSC
Gross Tons 139               Built 1902
by Allsup & Co. Ltd., Preston.
90′ × 19.6′ × 10.1′

550 i.h.p. 2 cylinder compound engine by the shipbuilder for Kings Lynn Conservancy Board as the *Conservator*.

1915 sold to W. H. J. Alexander Ltd., & renamed *Sun VI*.

20-12-1960 scrapped by T. Ward, Grays.

*Sun VII*                              1917–1941
Official No. 142325          Call Sign JSPL later
                                       MJBG
Gross Tons 202               Built 1917
by Rennie Forrest S.B. Co. Ltd., Wivenhoe.
105.2′ × 25.5′ × 12.2′

750 i.h.p. 3 cylinder triple expansion engine by Earles Shipbuilding & Engineering Co. Ltd., Hull.

6-3-1941 sunk by mine off North Knob buoy, Thames Estuary.

*Sun VIII*                             1919–1969
Official No. 143951          Call Sign MJTL
Gross Tons 196               Built 1919
by Cochrane & Sons Ltd., Selby.
100.3′ × 25.6′ × 11.8′

750 i.h.p. 3 cylinder triple expansion engine by Earles Shipbuilding & Engineering Co. Ltd., Hull.

February 1969 scrapped Antwerp by Scrappingco S.A., Belgium.

*Sun IX*                          1920–1940

Official No. 144405          Call Sign KDVW
                                          later MJWN

Gross Tons 196               Built 1920

by Cochrane & Sons Ltd., Selby.

100.3′ × 25.6′ × 11.8′

750 i.h.p. 3 cylinder triple expansion engine by Earles Shipbuilding & Engineering Co. Ltd., Hull.

21-12-1940 sunk by mine in Sea Reach, Thames Estuary.

Salvaged, but beyond repair & scrapped.

*Sun X*                           1920–1969

Official No. 144657          Call Sign KGJP
                                          later MKCS

Gross Tons 196               Built 1920

by Cochrane & Sons Ltd., Selby.

100.3′ × 25.6′ × 11.8′

750 i.h.p. 3 cylinder triple expansion engine by Earles Shipbuilding & Engineering Co. Ltd., Hull.

27-1-1969 to London Tugs Ltd.

February 1969 towed Antwerp for scrap by Scrappingco S. A., Belgium.

*Sun XI*                                    1925–1964

Official No. 148618          Call Sign KSRG
                                              later MNGS

Gross Tons 183               Built 1925
by Earles Co. Ltd., Hull.
100′ × 25.6′ × 12′

750 i.h.p. 3 cylinder triple expansion engine by Earles Shipbuilding & Engineering Co. Ltd., Hull.

1964 sold to Schelde Sleepvaartbedrijf N.V., Antwerp & renamed *Schelde X.*

1965 sold to Rimorchiatori Sardi S.M.A. Cagliari, Sardinia & renamed *Andrea.*

1985 scrapped by Co. Femer, Gagliari & broken up at Porto Torres.

*Sun XII*                                   1925–1969

Official No. 148637          Call Sign KSTV
                                              later MNJB

Gross Tons 183               Built 1925
by Earles Co. Ltd., Hull.
100′ × 25.6′ × 12′

750 i.h.p. 3 cylinder triple expansion engine by the shipbuilder.

27-1-1969 to London Tugs Ltd.

May 1969 towed Antwerp for scrap by Scrappingco S. A., Belgium.

*Sun XV*                                    1925–1969

Official No. 148696          Call Sign KTHS
                             later MNLB

Gross Tons 183               Built 1925

by Earles Co. Ltd., Hull.

$100' \times 25.6' \times 12'$

750 i.h.p. 3 cylinder triple expansion engine by the shipbuilder. Licenced to carry passengers.

To London Tugs Ltd., 27-1-1969.

May 1969 towed Antwerp for scrap by Scrappingco S.A., Belgium.

*Sun XVI*                                   1946–1962

Official No. 180964          Call Sign GQYD

Gross Tons 233               Built 1946

by Alexander Hall & Co. Ltd., Aberdeen.

$105.2' \times 27.1' \times 11.7'$

1,030 i.h.p. 3 cylinder triple expansion engine by the shipbuilder, for Ministry of Shipping & allocated the name *Empire Leonard*.

Acquired by W.H.J. Alexander Ltd. before completion as a war loss replacement & renamed *SUN XVI*.

1962 sold to Societa Rimorchiatori Napoletani, Naples & renamed *San Cataldo*.

Name later shortened to *S'Cataldo*.

1985 sold to Palermo Salvatore E. Cia & scrapped at Naples.

*Sun XVII*              1946–1968
Official No. 181517    Call Sign GQYG
Gross Tons 233        Built 1946
by Alexander Hall & Co. Ltd., Aberdeen.
105.2′ × 27.1′ × 11.7′

1,030 i.h.p. 3 cylinder triple expansion engine by the shipbuilder, for Ministry of Shipping & allocated the name *Empire Margaret*.

Acquired by W. H. J. Alexander Ltd. before completion as a war loss replacement & renamed *Sun XVII*.

1968 sold to Societa Rimorchiatori Napoletani, Naples & renamed *Rania G*. 1983 scrapped at Palermo.

*Sunrise* (ii)          1949–1966
Official No. 160624    Call Sign MFFR
Gross Tons 102        Built 1928
by Alexander Hall & Co., Aberdeen.
83′6″ × 20′7″ × 11′5″

550 i.h.p. 3 cylinder triple expansion engine by the shipbuilder, for W. R. Cunis Ltd., London as *William Ryan*.

1949 acquired by W. H. J. Alexander Ltd., & renamed *Sunrise*.

May 1966 towed Antwerp for scrap by *Sun II*, demolition carried out by Scrappingco S.A.

*Sun XVIII*            1951–1975
Official No. 184360    Call Sign GMDL
Gross Tons 105       Built 1951
by Philip & Son Ltd., Dartmouth.
88'2" × 22'1" × 9'11"

750 i.h.p. 7 cylinder Ruston & Hornsby diesel engine.

27-1-1969 to London Tugs Ltd.

1972-September 1974 transferred to Gaselee & Son (Felixstowe) Ltd.

1-1-1975 to The Alexandra Towing Co. (London) Ltd.

January 1975 sold to A. & N. Vogul & renamed *Ecclesbourne*.

1977 sold to Petros & Spyridon Rarakos Sea Towage Ltd., Kerkyra, Greece, renamed *Alexandros*.

*Sun XIX*            1956–1979
Official No. 187480    Call Sign GVVJ
Gross Tons 192       Built 1956
by Philip & Son Ltd., Dartmouth.
107'2" × 25'11" × 11'9"

1,210 b.h.p 6 cylinder Ruston & Hornsby diesel engine.

27-1-1969 to London Tugs Ltd.

1-1-1975 to The Alexandra Towing Co. (London) Ltd.

April 1979 sold to Societa Rimorchiatori Napoletani, Naples & renamed *Sole Primo*.

*Sun XX*                   1957–1979
Official No. 187573    Call Sign GWFC
Gross Tons 192         Built 1957
by Philip & Son Ltd., Dartmouth.
107′2″ × 25′11″ × 11′9″

1,210 b.h.p. 6 cylinder Ruston & Hornsby diesel engine. Licensed to carry passengers.
27-1-1969 to London Tugs Ltd.
1-1-1975 to The Alexandra Towing Co. (London) Ltd.
5-1979 sold to Societa Rimorchiatori, Naples & renamed *Sole Secondo*.

*Sun XXI*                  1959–1979 & 1981–
                           1982
Official No. 301002    Call Sign GFHQ
Gross Tons 183         Built 1959
by Philip & Son Ltd., Dartmouth.
107′2″ × 25′11″ × 11′8″

1,316 b.h.p. 6 cylinder Mirrless diesel engine.
27-1-1969 to London Tugs Ltd.
1-1-1975 to The Alexandra Towing Co. (London) Ltd.
6-1979 till 4-1981 transferred to The Alexandra Towing Co. Ltd., Southampton.
3-1982 transferred to The Alexandra Towing Co. Ltd., Gibraltar.

*Sun XXII*           1960–1975
Official No. 301082    Call Sign GFYH
Gross Tons 183       Built 1960
by Philip & Son Ltd., Dartmouth.
107′2″ × 25′11″ × 11′8″

1,316 b.h.p. 6 cylinder Mirrless diesel engine.

27-1-1969 to London Tugs Ltd.

1-1-1975 to The Alexandra Towing Co. (London) Ltd.

5-1975 transferred to The Alexandra Towing Co., Felixstowe, & renamed *Deban* 1976.

1978–9? transferred to The Alexandra Towing Co., Gibraltar.

1986 sold to Atlantic Shipping, Amsterdam.

June 1986 wrecked on rocks off South Morocco. One crew member lost.

*Sun XXIII*          1960–1984
Official No. 302598    Call Sign MECR
Gross Tons 143       Built 1961
by Philip & Son Ltd., Dartmouth.
93′9″ × 24′5″ × 11′1″

1,400 i.h.p. 6 cylinder Mirrless diesel engine.

27-1-1969 to London Tugs Ltd.

1-1-1979 to The Alexandra Towing Co. (London) Ltd.

4-1984 sold to Havelet International Ltd. Guernsey, & renamed *Sunwind*.

1985 sold to S. & H. Towing, Gravesend & renamed *Suncrest*.

5-1990 sold to Land & Marine Ltd., London.

*Sun XXIV*                          1962–1979
Official No. 302876        Call Sign GHYU
Gross Tons 113              Built 1962
by James Pollock & Sons Co. Ltd.,
Faversham.
88′3″ × 22′11″ × 9′10″

750 b.h.p. 6 cylinder Mirrless diesel engine.

27-1-1969 to London Tugs Ltd.

1-1-1975 to The Alexandra Towing Co. (London) Ltd.

4-1979 transferred to The Alexandra Towing Co., Southampton.

4-1990 sold to Mr Miller of Subsearch Marine Services Ltd., Newhaven, renamed *Kingston*.

*Sun XXV*                          1963–
Official No. 304463        Call Sign MGAE
Gross Tons 230              Built 1963
by Philip & Son Ltd., Dartmouth.
116′1″ × 28′5″ × 11′10″

2,000 b.h.p. 6 cylinder Mirrless National diesel.

27-1-1969 to London Tugs Ltd.

1-1-1975 to The Alexandra Towing Co. (London) Ltd.

1978 fitted with a Kort nozzle.

1980 issued with a passenger licence. Present fleet.

*Sun XXVI*                    1965–
Official No. 306300          Call Sign GPWE
Gross Tons 230               Built 1965
by Charles D. Holmes & Co. Ltd., Beverly.
116′1″ × 28′5″ × 11′10″

2,000 b.h.p. 6 cylinder Mirrless National diesel.

1979 Kort nozzle fitted & passenger licence issued.

27-1-1969 to London Tugs Ltd.

1-1-1975 to The Alexandra Towing Co. (London) Ltd. Present fleet.

*Sun II (ii)*                 1965–1992
Official No. 307890          Call Sign GRRA
Gross Tons 150               Built 1965
by Charles D. Holmes & Co. Ltd., Beverly.
28.58 × 7.45 × 3.74 m.

1,400 b.h.p. 6 cylinder Mirrless National diesel.

27-1-1969 to London Tugs Ltd.

1-1-1975 to The Alexandra Towing Co. (London) Ltd.

9-1992 sold to Greece.

*Sun III (ii)*         1966–1983
Official No. 308108     Call Sign GRQU
Gross Tons 150       Built 1966
by J. Pollock & Sons Co. Ltd., Faversham.
28.58 × 7.45 × 3.74 m.

1,400 b.h.p. 6 cylinder Mirrless National diesel.

27-1-1969 to London Tugs Ltd.

1-1-1975 to The Alexandra Towing Co. (London) Ltd.

23-6-1983 transferred to The Alexandra Towing Co. Swansea.

1984 renamed *Fabians Bay*.

9-1992 sold to Greece.

*Sun XXVII*          1968–
Official No. 336987     Call Sign GYYQ
Gross Tons 226       Built 1968
by J. Pollock & Sons Co. Ltd., Faversham.
35.44 × 8.69 × 4.04 m.

2,000 b.h.p. 6 cylinder Mirrless National diesel.

27-1-1969 to London Tugs Ltd.

1-1-1975 to The Alexandra Towing Co. (London) Ltd.

January–March 1990 Kort nozzle & Becker rudder fitted. Present fleet.

# Gaselee & Son Ltd.
# Fleet List 1933–1965

*Hornet*                          1880?–1937
Official No. 95433
Gross Tons 30
61.5′ × 14.2′ × 7′

17-12-1937 sold for scrap to T. Ward, Grays, Essex.

*Bee*                          1892–1932?
Official No. 101946
Gross Tons 55          Built 1892
by Summers & Scott, Gloucester.
67.6′ × 16.2′ × 7.9′

1932 Believed sold by Gaselee & Son Ltd.
27-6-1939 sold for scrap to T. Ward, Grays, Essex.

*Gnat* (i)                    1898–1934
Official No. 109964
Gross Tons 79          Built 8-1898
by Dundee Shipbuilders Co. Ltd., Dundee.
72.5′ × 18.4′ × 9.5′

2 cylinder compound engine, by White & Mair, Dundee. for Gaselee & Gush.
1902 transferred to Gaselee & Son, Ltd.
25-1-1934 sank in collision with *August Cords* in Northfleet Hope. Raised & scrapped.

*Adder*                      1907–1946
Official No. 123771
Gross Tons 54
69.2′ × 16.4′ × 8.3′

Dutch built.
1946 sold.

*Viper*            1907 – 1946
Official No. 123772
Gross Tons 54
69.2′ × 16.4′ × 8.3′

Dutch built.
1946 sold.

*Vespa* (i)         1921–1946
Official No. 146131
Gross Tons 92      Built 1921
by Cochrane & Sons Ltd., Selby.
75′ × 21.1′ × 9.5′

3 cylinder triple expansion engine by Earles Shipbuilding & Engineering Co. Ltd., Hull.

1946 sold to Harrison (London) Ltd. & renamed *Markrock*.

No further details known.

*Musca*                      1922–1960
Official No. 146648
Gross Tons 75          Built 1922
by Cochrane & Sons Ltd., Selby.
72.5′ × 18.6′ × 9.1′

3 cylinder triple expansion engine by Earles Shipbuilding & Engineering Co. Ltd., Hull.

22-12-1960 scrapped at T. Ward, Grays, Essex.

*Naja* (i)             1924–1944
Official No. 148526
Gross Tons 72          Built 1924
by Alexander Hall & Co. Ltd., Aberdeen.
73.2′ × 18.1′ × 8.5′

3 cylinder triple expansion engine, by the shipbuilder.

12-7-1944 sunk in Upper Pool of London by a V-1 flying bomb (Doodlebug).

*Culex* (i)                    1924–1957
Official No. 147721
Gross Tons 105          Built 1924
by Alexander Hall & Co. Ltd., Aberdeen.
80′ × 21.6′ × 10′

3 cylinder triple expansion engine by the shipbuilder.

17-1-1957 arrived at T. Ward, Grays, Essex for scrap.

*Tayra*                    1926–1968
Official No. 149704
Gross Tons 106          Built 1926
by Alexander Hall & Co. Ltd., Aberdeen.
80′ × 21.6′ × 8.4′

3 cylinder triple expansion engine, by the shipbuilder.

1946 converted to diesel at Lowestoft & fitted with a 5 cylinder 700 b.h.p. British Polar 2 stroke diesel.

1968 sold for scrap in Belgium.

*Fossa* (i)                1929–1940
Official No. 161295
Gross Tons 105          Built 1929
by Alexander Hall & Co. Ltd., Aberdeen.
80′ × 21.6′ 2 10′

69 n.h.p. 3 cylinder triple expansion engine, by the shipbuilder.

2-6-1940 grounded and abandoned during evacuation from Dunkirk.

Believed salved by the Germans.

*Betty*                    1927–1946
Official No. 125582
Gross Tons 119          Built 1907
by J. Cran & Co., Leith.
82′ × 22.2′ × 10.9′

75 n.h.p. 3 cylinder triple expansion engine by the shipbuilder, for A. J. Humphrey, London.

1914 owners trading as Arthur J. Humphrey & Henry Grey, London.

1926 transferred to Humphrey & Grey (Lighterage) Ltd.

1927 sold to Gaselee & Son.

1946 sold to Heyglien Freres & scrapped at Ghent.

*Aboma*            1933–1968
Official No. 163375
Gross Tons 66       Built 1933
by Cochrane & Sons Ltd., Selby.
70.5′ × 17.1′ × 7.2′

390 b.h.p. 6 cylinder British Polar diesel.

1967 to Gaselee & Knight Ltd.

1968 sold to Belgium shipbreakers.

*Gnat* (ii)         1934–1970
Official No. 163529
Gross Tons 66       Built 1934
by Cochrane & Sons Ltd., Selby.
70.6′ × 17.1′ × 7.2′

390 b.h.p. 6 cylinder British Polar diesel.

1967 to Gaselee & Knight Ltd.

1970 sold to Henry & Co. Waterford, Ireland.

*Mamba*            1934–1973
Official No. 164545
Gross Tons 67       Built 1934
by Cochrane & Sons Ltd., Selby.
70.5′ × 17.1′ × 7.2′

390 b.h.p 6 cylinder British Polar diesel.

1967 to Gaselee & Knight Ltd.

19-3-1973 sold to T. Ward, Grays, Essex for scrap.

*Agama*            1937–1970
Official No. 165431
Gross Tons 84       Built 1937
by Alexander Hall & Co., Aberdeen.
78.1′ × 21.1′ × 8.3′

500 b.h.p. 4 cylinder British Polar diesel.

1963-July 1965 transferred to Gaselee & Son (Felixstowe) Ltd.

1967 to Gaselee & Knight Ltd.

1970 sold & scrapped at Bloors Wharf, Rainham, Kent.

*Sauria*                    1937–1962?

Official No. 165613

Gross Tons 66          Built 1937

by Cochrane & Sons Ltd., Selby.

70.5′ × 17.1′ × 7.2′

450 b.h.p 6 cylinder British Polar diesel.

Sold early sixties to Wimpy (Marine) Ltd. & renamed *GW 66*.

1969 sold for scrap.

*Wasp*                     1939–1962?

Official No. 167263

Gross Tons 66          Built 1939

by Cochrane & Sons Ltd., Selby.

70.5′ × 17.1′ × 7.2′

450 b.h.p. 6 cylinder British Polar diesel.

Sold early sixties to Wimpy (Marine) Ltd. & renamed *GW 67*.

1969 sold for scrap & demolished in South Wales.

*Fossa* (ii)　　　　　1946–1961
Official No.
Gross Tons 66　　　　Built 1946
by Cochrane & Sons Ltd., Selby.
70.5′ × 17.1′ × 7.2′

450 b.h.p. 6 cylinder British Polar diesel.

1961 Sold to Humphrey & Grey (Lighterage) Ltd., & renamed *Owen Smith*.

1983 sold to Mr. W. F. Mayhew, Queenborough, & renamed *Fossa*.

1988 sold to General Marine.

*Vespa* (ii)　　　　　1946–1965
Official No. 163552
Gross Tons 72　　　　Built 1934
by Alexander Hall & Co., Aberdeen.
75′6″ × 18′1″ × 9′6″

8 cylinder Mirrlees, Bickerton & Day Ltd. diesel for Frederick Leyland & Co. Ltd., Liverpool as the *Brodstone*. Later to Blackfriars Lighterage, London as the *Evelyn Brodstone*.

1946 sold to Gaselee & Son Ltd. & renamed *Vespa*.

1953 re-engined with a 525 b.h.p. 7 cylinder British Polar diesel.

1-5-1965 sold to Ship Towage (London) Ltd.

27-1-1969 to London Tugs Ltd.

7-1970 sold to Harry Rose (Towage) Ltd., Poole & renamed *Wendy Ann*.

1981 the company ceased trading & *Wendy Ann* taken over by Poole Harbour Commissioners.

*Naja* (ii)                    1946–1973
Official No. 183133
Gross Tons 56          Built 1936
in Holland for Phillips Mills as *Servis*.
72.5′ × 18′ × 7.9′

390 b.h.p. 4 cylinder Bolinder diesel.

1946 sold to Gaselee & Son Ltd., & renamed *Naja*.

1951 re-engined with a 4 cylinder Crossley diesel.

1967 to Gaselee & Knight Ltd.

20-2-1973 sold for scrap to T. Ward, Grays, Essex.

*Rana*                         1951–1965
Official No. 184541
Gross Tons 98          Built 1951
by Cochrane & Sons Ltd., Selby.
80′3″ × 21′6″ × 8′6″

750 b.h.p. 5 cylinder British Polar diesel.

1-5-1965 sold to Ship Towage (London) Ltd.

27-1-1969 to London Tugs Ltd.

1-1-1975 to The Alexandra Towing Co. (London) Ltd.

3-1975 transferred to The Alexandra Towing Co. Ltd., Swansea.

8-1979 sold to Humphrey & Grey (Lighterage) Ltd., & renamed *Redriff*.

1984 sold to Bennet Bros., & renamed *Rana*.

1990 company now known as Medway Lighterage Ltd.

*Culex* (ii)                    1958–1965
Official No. 187697
Gross Tons 97            Built 1958
by F. Schichou, Bremerhavn.
80′4″ × 21′6″ × 10′

660 b.h.p. 8 cylinder Deutz diesel.

1-5-1965 sold to Ship Towage (London) Ltd.

27-1-1969 to London Tugs Ltd.

12-1971 sold to J.G. Efthimiou, Piraeus, & renamed *Atromitos*.

*Fossa* (iii)                   1961–1965
Official No. 302599
Gross Tons 98            Built 1961
by Henry Scarr Ltd., Hessle.
85′9″ × 21′6″ × 10′9″

1,000 b.h.p. 8 cylinder Deutz diesel.

1-5-1965 sold to Ship Towage (London) Ltd.

27-1-1969 to London Tugs Ltd.

1-1-1975 The Alexandra Towing Co. (London) Ltd.

7-1977 sold to Darling Bros., London & renamed *Kilda*.

1987 sold to Bennet Bros., & renamed *Mamba*.

1990 company now known as Medway Lighterage Ltd.

## Small launce tugs operated by Gaselee & Son.

*Dancha*

*Effgee*      Formally F. G. Towage.

*Battler*

*Boa*         Built 1959, 180 b.h.p., now owned by Tyne Towage.

*Asp*         Built 1958, 110 b.h.p., now owned by Tyne Towage.

# Port of London Authority
# Ship Towing Tugs 1933–1991

| | |
|---|---|
| *Sirdar* | 1908–1950 |
| Official No. 15907 | Call Sign |
| Gross Tons 143 | Built 1899 |
| by R. H. Green Ltd., Blackwall. | |
| 90.3′ × 21.1′ × 11.6′ | |

1,000 i.h.p. 2 × 2 cylinder 500 i.h.p. compounds engines by T. A. Young & Son, Blackwall, for London & India Docks Joint Committee.

1908 transferred to Port of London Authority when formed.

1-2-1950 scrapped by T. Ward, Grays.

| | |
|---|---|
| *Deanbrook* | 1908–1940 |
| Official No. 148740 | Call Sign |
| Gross Tons 148.9 | Built 1908 |
| by J. P. Rennoldson & Sons, South Shields. | |
| 86′ × 21.1′ × 11.5′ | |

1,000 i.h.p. 2 × 2 cylinder 500 i.h.p. compound engines by the shipbuilder, for London & India Docks Joint Committee as *Power*.

1908 transferred to Port of London Authority when formed.

1926 renamed *Deanbrook*.

8-11-1940 sunk by mine in Tilbury Dock.

27-11-1940 raised in two parts, beached & later broken up.

*Beam*                          1910–1966
Official No. 129134
Gross Tons 168          Built 1910
by Ferguson Bros., Port Glasgow
86′ × 22.6′ × 10.8′

1,000 i.h.p. 2 × 2 cylinder 500 i.h.p. compound engines by the shipbuilder.

1966 sold for scrap to Northern Slipway Ltd., Dublin, who removed pumps and machinery in the Surrey Docks, the hull being broken up at Queenborough.

*Darent*                        1908–1949
Official No. 125673
Gross Tons 172          Built 1908
by Ferguson Bros., Port Glasgow.
96′ × 23.1′ × 10.3′

700 i.h.p. 3 cylinder triple expansion engine by the shipbuilder. Built for the dredging dept. but was occasionally used for ship towing.

1949 sold to J. H. Lamey Ltd., Liverpool & renamed *Alfred Lamey*.

1957 scrapped October at Barrow.

*Beverley*                      1910–1965
Official No. 129127
Gross Tons 168          Built 1910
by Ferguson Bros., Port Glasgow.
86′ × 22.6′ × 10.8′

1,000 i.h.p. 2 × 2 cylinder 500 i.h.p. compound engines by the shipbuilder.
19-2-1965 sold for scrap to T. Ward, Grays, Essex.

*Walbrook*                      1910–1964
Official No. 129141
Gross Tons 168          Built 1910
by Ferguson Bros., Port Glasgow.
86′ × 22.6′ × 10.8′

1,000 i.h.p. 2 × 2 cylinder 500 i.h.p. compound engines by the shipbuilder.
21-3-1960 sank Tilbury Dock assisting *Langkoeas*.
March 1964 sold to Meeching Engineering (Marine) Ltd., Newhaven.
Resold to Lacmots Ltd., demolition completed July 1964 at Queenborough.

*Lea*                    1912–1940
Official No. 135164
Gross Tons 168          Built 1912
by Ferguson Bros., Port Glasgow.
86′ × 22.6′ × 11.1′

1,000 i.h.p. 2 × 2 cylinder 500 i.h.p. compound engines by the shipbuilder.

8-11-1940 sunk by mine in Tilbury Dock. 21-11-1940 refloated & beached.

29-1-1942 refloated again but too badly damaged to repair.

Scrapped Woolwich 7-1942.

*Thorney*                1947–1968
Official No. 169091    Call Sign MLSX
Gross Tons 138          Built 1943
by Richard Dunston Ltd., Thorne for the Ministry of War Transport as *Empire Percy* & placed under the management of Steel & Bennie Ltd., Glasgow.
94.1′ × 21.3′ × 9.7′

525 i.h.p. 3 cylinder triple expansion engine by McKie & Baxter Ltd., Paisley.

1947 sold to P.L.A. & renamed *Thorny*, 1948.

1968 sold for scrap to Scrappingco SA., Belgium.

*Plagal*                    1951–1986
Official No. 184520
Gross Tons 159        Built 1951
by Henry Scarr Ltd., Hessle.
92'10" × 24'2"

1,200 b.h.p. 2 × 4 cylinder Crossley diesels, re-engined 1970 with 2 × 6 cylinder Lister diesels.

1986 scrapped Barking Creek by G. & T. Services.

*Plangent*                  1951–1986
Official No. 184548
Gross Tons 159        Built 1951
by Henry Scarr Ltd., Hessle.
92'10" × 24'2"

1,200 b.h.p. 2 × 4 cylinder 600 b.h.p. Crossley diesels 1970 re-engined with 2 × 6 cylinder Lister diesels.

December 1986 sold to Hellenic Tugs, Greece & renamed *Cerberus*.

*Platina*                    1952–1973
Official No. 184578
Gross Tons 159        Built 1952
by Henry Scarr Ltd., Hessle.
92′10″ × 24′2″

1,200 b.h.p. 2 × 4 cylinder 600 b.h.p. Crossley diesels.

April 1973 sold to Holyhead Towing Co., Holyhead & renamed *Afon Goch*.

March 1976 renamed *Afon Caradoc*.

August 1979 sold and scrapped Hendrik Ido Ambacht, Holland.

*Plateau*                    1952–1973
Official No. 184731    Call Sign GSAR
Gross Tons 159        Built 1952
by Henry Scarr Ltd., Hessle.
92′10″ × 24′2″

1,200 b.h.p. 2 × 4 cylinder 600 b.h.p. Crossley diesels. Fitted with Kort nozzles.

1973 sold to Holyhead Towing Co., Holyhead & renamed *Afon Las*.

1988 sold to Mr Thorogood for use as a yacht & renamed *Alys Ann*.

1991 sold to Western Ocean Towage & renamed *Towingman*.

*Plastron*  1953–197?
Official No. 185888
Gross Tons 80  Built 1953
by Richard Dunston Ltd., Thorne
75'10" × 20'10"

440 b.h.p. 6 cylinder Crossley diesel.

Sold seventies to civil engineering contractors & later sank off north Cornish coast, 1973.

*Lord Devonport*.  1959–1992
Official No. 300921
Gross Tons 109  Built 1959
by James Pollock & Sons Co. Ltd., Faversham.
84'5" × 22'2" × 10'

950 b.h.p. 5 cylinder British Polar diesel. Built for the dredging department but used for at time as a ship towing tug.

1-1992 sold to Port of Tilbury London Ltd.

*Platoon*                    1965–1991
Official No. 306215    Call Sign GXAQ
Gross Tons 167.28      Built 1965
by Richard Dunston Ltd., Hessle.
87'7" × 26' × 9'

1,600 b.h.p. 16 cylinder Lister Blackstone diesel, driving a single Voith Schneider unit.
January 1991 sold to The Alexandra Towing Co. (London) Ltd., & renamed *Dhulia*.

*Plasma*                    1965–1991
Official No. 306353    Call Sign GXAR
Gross Tons 167.28      Built 1965
by Richard Dunston Ltd., Hessle.
87'7" × 26' × 9'

1,600 b.h.p. 16 cylinder Lister Blackstone diesel, driving a single Voith Schneider unit.
January 1991 sold to The Alexandra Towing Co. (London) Ltd., & renamed *Burma*.

*Plankton*                    1965–1991
Official No. 307825
Gross Tons 160          Built 1965
by Richard Dunston Ltd., Hessle.
87'7" × 26' × 9'

1,600 b.h.p. 16 cylinder Lister Blackstone diesel driving a single Voith Schneider unit.
1991 sold to Port of Tilbury London Ltd., & renamed *Linford*, 7-9-1991.

*Placard*                     1965–1991
Official No. 308049
Gross Tons 160          Built 1965
by Richard Dunston Ltd., Hessle.
87'7" × 26' × 9'

1,600 b.h.p. 16 cylinder Lister Blackstone diesel driving a single Voith Schneider unit.
1991 Sold to Port of Tilbury London Ltd., & renamed *Orsett* 7-9-1991.

# Ship Towage (London) Ltd.
# Fleet List 1950–1969

*Vanquisher*                1955–1982
Official No. 186203        Call Sign MVWF
Gross Tons 294             Built 1955
by Henry Scarr Ltd., Hessle.
113′3″ × 28′9″ × 12′7″

1,280 b.h.p. 8 cylinder British Polar diesel.

8-1-1976 sank undocking *Jervis Bay* from Tilbury Dock.

27-1-1969 to London Tugs Ltd.

1-1-1975 to The Alexandra Towing Co. (London) Ltd.

June 1982 scrapped at Bloors Wharf, Rainham, Kent.

*Dhulia*                     1959–1980
Official No. 300982        Call Sign GFJA
Gross Tons 272             Built 1959
by Henry Scarr Ltd., Hessle.
113′7″ × 28′9″ × 12′6¹/₂″

1,280 b.h.p. 8 cylinder British Polar diesel.

27-1-1969 to London Tugs Ltd.

1-1-1975 to The Alexandra Towing Co. (London) Ltd.

16-6-1980 transferred to Alexandra Towing Co., Great Yarmouth.

April 1983 sold.

Resold soon after to General Maritime Enterprises (Antwerp) Ltd., & renamed *Dhulia S*. (Panamanian flag).

*Moorcock* 1959–1981
Official No. 301004    Call Sign GFJH
Gross Tons 272    Built 1959
by Henry Scarr Ltd., Hessle.
113′6″ × 28′8″ × 12′6½″

1,280 b.h.p. 8 cylinder British Polar diesel.

27-1-1969 to London Tugs Ltd.

1-1-1975 to The Alexandra Towing Co. (London) Ltd.

December 1981 scrapped at Queenborough, Kent.

*Ionia* 1960–1987
Official No. 301193    Call Sign GHGX
Gross Tons 187    Built 1960
by Henry Scarr Ltd., Hessle.
99′9″ × 26′2″ × 11′7″

900 b.h.p. 6 cylinder British Polar diesel.

To London Tugs Ltd., 27-1-1969.

1973 Kort nozzle fitted.

1-1-1975 to The Alexandra Towing Co. (London) Ltd.

1987 sold to Falmouth Towing Co., Falmouth & sailed from Gravesend 24-11-1987.

1988 renamed *St Mawes*.

*Avenger* 1962–1985
Official No. 304381     Call Sign GKSU
Gross Tons 293     Built 1962
by Cochrane & Sons Ltd., Selby.
118'5" × 30'5" × 12'11½"

1,800 b.h.p. 9 cylinder British Polar engine.

27-1-1969 to London Tugs Ltd.

1974-5 fitted with Kort nozzle & C.P. propeller.

1-1-1975 to The Alexandra Towing Co. (London) Ltd. 1985 sold to Purvise Marine, Canada & renamed *Avenger IV*.

31-10-1985 sailed Gravesend bound, Great Lakes.

*Hibernia* 1962–1987
Official No. 304415     Call Sign GKTA
Gross Tons 293     Built 1962
by Cochrane & Sons Ltd., Selby.
118'2" × 30'1" × 12'

1,800 b.h.p. 9 cylinder British Polar diesel.

27-1-1969 to London Tugs Ltd.

1-1-1975 to The Alexandra Towing Co. (London) Ltd.

1975 Kort nozzle & C.P. propeller fitted.

September 1987 sold to Ahilleus II Shipping Co., Thessaloniki & renamed *Atrotos*.

1992 sold to Karapiperis, Piraeus & renamed *Karapiperis X*.

*Vespa*                          1965–1970
Official No. 163552
Gross Tons 72          Built 1934
by Alexander Hall & Co., Aberdeen.
75′6″ × 18′1″ × 9′6′'

6 cylinder Mirrless diesel.

Re-engined 1953 with a 525 b.h.p. 7 cylinder British Polar diesel for Frederick Leyland & Co. Ltd. as the *Broadstone* later to Blackfriars Lighterage, as the *Evelyn Brodstone*.

1946 sold to Gaselee & Son Ltd., & renamed *Vespa*.

1-5-1965 sold to Ship Towage (London) Ltd.

27-1-1969 to London Tugs Ltd.

July 1970 sold to Harry Rose (Towage) Ltd., Poole & renamed *Wendy Ann*.

1981 the company ceased trading & taken over by Poole Harbour Commissioners.

*Rana*                          1965–1975
Gross Tons 98
by Cochrane & Sons Ltd., Selby.
80′3″ × 21′6″ × 8′6″

750 b.h.p. 5 cylinder British Polar diesel for Gaselee & Son Ltd.

1-5-1965 sold to Ship Towage (London) Ltd.

27-1-1969 to London Tugs Ltd.

1-1-1975 to The Alexandra Towing Co. (London) Ltd.

March 1975 transferred to The Alexandra Towing Co., Swansea.

August 1979 sold to Humphrey & Grey (Lighterage) Ltd., & renamed *Redriff*.

1984 sold to Bennet Bros., & renamed *Rana*.

1990 company name changed to Medway Lighterage Co. Ltd.

281

*Culex* 1965–1971
Official No. 187697
Gross Tons 97 Built 1958
by Schichou, Bremerhavn, Germany.
80′4″ × 21′6″ × 10′

660 b.h.p. 8 cylinder Deutz diesel for Gaselee & Son Ltd.

1-5-1965 sold to Ship Towage (London) Ltd.

27-1-1969 to London Tugs Ltd.

December 1971 sold to J. G. Efthimou, Piraeus & renamed *Atromitos*.

*Fossa* 1965–1977
Official No. 302599
Gross Tons 98 Built 1961
by Henry Scarr Ltd., Hessle.
85′9″ × 21′6″ × 10′9″

1,000 b.h.p. 8 cylinder Deutz diesel for Gaselee & Son Ltd.

1-5-1965 sold to Ship Towage (London) Ltd.

27-1-1969 to London Tugs Ltd.

1-1-1975 to The Alexandra Towing Co. (London) Ltd.

July 1977 sold to Darling Bros., London & renamed *Kilda*.

1987 sold to Bennet Bros., & renamed *Mamba*.

1990 company renamed Medway Lighterage Co. Ltd.

*Burma*                              1966–1989
Official No. 309861        Call Sign GWJA
Gross Tons 166              Built 1966
by Richard Dunston Ltd., Hessle.
30.7 × 7.83 × 3.81m.

1,050 b.h.p. 8 cylinder Ruston & Hornsby diesel.

27-1-1969 to London Tugs Ltd.

1-1-1975 to The Alexandra Towing Co. (London) Ltd.

1989 sold for scrap to The Medway Drydock Co., & towed to Sheerness by the *Sun London*, 19-11-1989.

*Watercock*                       1967–1989
Official No. 334530        Call Sign GXKH
Gross Tons 161              Built 1967
by Richard Dunston Ltd., Hessle.
30.71 × 7.83 × 3.81m.

1,050 b.h.p. 8 cylinder Ruston & Hornsby diesel.

27-1-1969 to London Tugs Ltd.

1-1-1975 to The Alexandra Towing Co. (London) Ltd.

1989 sold for scrap by The Medway Drydock Co., & towed to Sheerness by the *Sun London*, 19-11-1989.

# London Tugs Ltd. 1969–1975
# No new additions while this company was in existence.

# Alexandra Towing Co. (London) Ltd.
## Fleet List 1975–1992

Sun Essex          1977–1990
Official No. 377347     Call Sign GXHS
Gross Tons 272        Built 1977
by Richard Dunston (Hessle) Ltd., Hessle.
32.92 × 9.61 × 4.91m.

2070 b.h.p. 12 cylinder Ruston Paxman V engine, driving a C.P. propeller in a Kort rudder. Fire-fighting tug.

1-1990 transferred to Alexandra Towing Co. Southampton.

*Sun Kent*          1977–
Official No. 377400     Call Sign GXIE
Gross Tons 272        Built 1977
by Richard Dunston (Hessle) Ltd., Hessle.
32.92 × 9.61 × 4.91m.

2070 b.h.p. 12 cylinder Ruston Paxman V engine, driving a C.P. propeller in a Kort rudder. Fire-fighting tug.

*Sun London*    1977–1992
Official No. 377447  Call Sign GXUW
Gross Tons 265    Built 1977
by Richard Dunston (Hessle) Ltd., Hessle.
32.92 × 9.61 × 4.91m.

2640 b.h.p. 12 cylinder Ruston Paxman V engine, driving a C.P. propeller in a Kort rudder.

4-1981 transferred to Alexandra Towing Co., Felixstowe.

6-1982 returned to The Alexandra Towing Co. (London) Ltd., Gravesend.

25-7-1992 transferred to The Alexandra Towing Co. Ltd., Felixstowe.

*Formidable*    1979–
Official No. 378077  Call Sign GYAK
Gross Tons 406    Built 1979
by Richard Dunston (Hessle) Ltd., Hessle.
35 × 10.26 × 4.9m.

2 × 8 cylinder Ruston Paxman V engines, total 3,500 b.h.p. driving twin C.P. propellers in Kort rudders.

*Waterloo* 1979–1983
Official No. 364450    Call Sign GWAV
Gross Tons 315    Built 1977
by Richard Dunston (Hessle) Ltd., Hessle
for The Alexandra Towing Co. Ltd.,
Swansea.
$33.86 \times 9.61 \times 4.81$m.

2 × 8 cylinder Ruston Paxman V engines, total 3,500 b.h.p. driving a C.P. propeller in Kort rudder.

6-1979 transferred to The Alexandra Towing Co. (London) Ltd., Gravesend.

5-1983 sold to Government of the Islamic Republic of Iran (Port & Shipping Organization).

1984 renamed *Ghorban*. Fire-fighting tug.

*Sun Swale* 1981–1990
Official No. 398886    Call Sign GCCW
Gross Tons 192    Built 1968
by Ziegler Freres, Dunkirk for Soc.
Dunkerquoise De Remorquage et De
Sauvetage, Dunkirk as *Clairvoyant*.
$27.01 \times 8.01 \times 6.3$m.

1500 b.h.p. 8 cylinder Soc. Crepelle diesel driving a single Voith Schneider unit.

Fire-fighting tug.

9-1981 Acquired by The Alexandra Towing Co. (London) Ltd., renamed *Sun Swale*.

5-1990 transferred to The Alexandra Towing Co., Gibraltar.

*Sun Thames* 1982–
Official No. 399124  Call Sign GCLE
Gross Tons 369  Built 1982
by McTay Marine Ltd., Bromborough.
31.02 × 9.52 × 3.81m.

2 × 6 cylinder Ruston Paxman engines total 2,640 b.h.p. driving twin Voith Schneider units.

Fire-fighting tug.

*Implacable* 1983–1984
Official No. 363673  Call Sign GURQ
Gross Tons 300.36  Built 1975
by Tito Shipyard, Yugoslavia.
39.62 × 9.9 × 5.31m.

Twin screw 2 × 16 cylinder Burmeister & Wain Alpha Diesels, total 4,960 b.h.p. 200 b.h.p. bow thrust. Kort rudders & C.P. propellers, for Bugge Supplyships A/B., Norway as *Sea Setter*.

1980 sold to Compagnie Champon, Marseilles, & renamed *Chambon Sirocco*.

1983 sold to Alexandra Marine Transportation Ltd., London & renamed *Implacable*, & manned by a Gravesend crew.

24-12-1984 sank 27 miles south of the Isle of Wight with the loss of one man, while bound to the Falkland Islands.

*Hendon*                                      1985–
Official No. 363073          Call Sign GWOT
Gross Tons 266                Built 1975
by Richard Dunston Ltd., Hessle for France,
Fenwick, Tyne & Wear Ltd., Newcastle.
29 × 915 × 4.9m.

6 cylinder Mirrless Blackstone diesel 3,180 b.h.p. Never accepted from builders and laid up in Hull Docks and put up for sale.

5-5-1978 acquired by The Alexandra Towing Co. Ltd., and stationed at Swansea.

1984 transferred to The Alexandra Towing Co. Ltd., Southampton.

30-6-1985 transferred to The Alexandra Towing Co. (London) Ltd., Gravesend.

*Sun Anglia*                                  1985–
Official No. 709715          Call Sign GFQN
Gross Tons 339                Built 1985
by McTay Marine Ltd. Bromborough.
31 × 9.50 × 3.80m.

2 × 6 cylinder Ruston RK270 diesel engines.

3,444 b.h.p. total, driving twin Voith Schneider units.

23-11-1985 arrived Gravesend from builders.

*Egerton* 1986–1986
Official No. 306510    Call Sign GRBH
Gross Tons 172    Built 1965
by W. J. Yarwood & Sons, Northwich.
93′ × 25′6″ × 12′6″

8 cylinder Crossley diesel 1,200 b.h.p.

Stationed at Liverpool for The Alexandra Towing Co. Ltd. Liverpool.

1973 transferred to The Alexandra Towing Co., Swansea.

1975 transferred to The Alexandra Towing Co. Ltd., Felixstowe.

4-1986 transferred to The Alexandra towing Co. (London) Ltd., Gravesend.

21-4-1986 returned to Felixstowe.

7-1990 sold to Oil transport Co. S/A Santa Domingo, renamed *Caribe 1*.

*Avenger* 1986–
Official No. 363657    Call Sign GURP
Gross Tons 299    Built 1975
by Brodogradiliste ''Tito'' Mitrovica,
Yugoslavia.
39.88 × 10.11 × 4.61m.

2 × 16 cylinder V Alpha V diesels 4,960 b.h.p.

200 b.h.p. bow thrust.

For Bugge Supply Ships, London as *Sea Diamond*.

1980 sold to Compagnie Chambon, Marseilles & renamed *Chambon Bora*.

1984 sold to The Alexandra Towing Co. Ltd. renamed *Indefatigable* and stationed at Swansea.

8-1986 transferred to The Alexandra Towing Co. (London) Ltd. Gravesend & renamed *Avenger* 2-9-1986.

*Adept*          1988–
Official No. 378063    Call Sign 2SFK
Gross Tons 48.59      Built 1971
by Ateliers Et Chantiers Ziegler Freres,
Dunkirk, France.
55.35′ × 19.8′ × 5.9′

Powered by a 12 cylinder 580 b.h.p. engine by Soc. Surgerienne De Construct Mechaniques, driving a Voith Schneider Propeller. Built for Soc Boulonnaise De Remorquage, Bologne, as *Alerte*.

Acquired by The Alexandra Towing Co., Liverpool, 1978 and placed under their lighterage subsidiary, Bulk Cargo Handling Services Ltd.

Renamed *Adept* 17-5-1978. Transferred to The Alexandra Towing Co. (London) Ltd., 1988.

Arrived Gravesend 19-9-1988 in tow of *Victoria*.

*Agile*           1988–
Official No. 378062    Call Sign 2SFJ
Gross Tons 48.59      Built 1971
by Ateliers Et Chantiers Ziegler Freres,
Dunkirk, France.
55.35′ × 19.8′ × 5.9′

Powered by a 12 cylinder Soc. Surgerienne De Construct Mechaniques engine of 580 b.h.p. driving a Voith Schneider propeller.

Built for Soc Boulonnaise De Remorquage, Boulogne.

Acquired by The Alexandra Towing Co. Ltd., Liverpool 1978 & placed under their lighterage subsidiary Bulk Cargo Handling Services Ltd.

Transferred to The Alexandra Towing Co. (London) Ltd., 1988.

Arrived Gravesend in tow of *Victoria*, 19-9-1988.

*Waterloo*                        1990–1992
Official No. 704492      Call Sign GJJB
Gross Tons 301           Built 1987
by Mctay Marine Ltd., Bromborough.
31.15 × 9.76 × 4.582m

2 × 6 cylinder Ruston diesels 3,444 b.h.p.

Built for The Alexandra Towing Co., Liverpool.

Transferred to The Alexandra Towing Co. (London) Ltd. & arrived Gravesend 6-1-1990.

24-4-1992 transferred back to Liverpool and arrived Liverpool 26- 4-1992.

*Sun Mercia*                   1990–
Official No. 718767      Call Sign MMJY5
Gross Tons 449           Net Tons 134
Built by Mctay Marine., Bromborough,
Yard No. 89.
31 × 10 × 4m.                Draft 5.3m.

2 × 6 cylinder Ruston diesels, total 3,860 b.h.p. Driving twin Voith Schneider propellers.

Keel laid December 1989.

Arrived Gravesend from builders, 20-8-1990.

*Burma*                                    1991–
Official No. 306353        Call Sign GXAR
Gross Tons 160               Built 1965
by Richard Dunston Ltd., Hessle.
87′7″ × 26′ × 9′

1600 b.h.p. 16 cylinder Lister Blackstone diesel driving a single Voith Schneider propeller.

Built for the Port of London Authority as *Plasma* for use in the enclosed docks.

Acquired by The Alexandra Towing Co. (London) Ltd., January 1991.

Renamed *Burma*.

*Dhulia*                                   1991–
Official No. 306215        Call Sign GXAQ
Gross Tons 160               Built 1965
by Richard Dunston Ltd., Hessle.
87′7″ × 26′ × 9′

1600 b.h.p. 16 cylinder Lister Blackstone diesel driving a single Voith Schneider propeller.

Built for the Port of London Authority as *Platoon* for use in the enclosed docks.

Acquired by The Alexandra Towing Co. (London) Ltd., January 1991.

Renamed *Dhulia*.

*Sun Surrey*                     1992–
Official No. 721990      Call Sign MPJV4
Gross Tons 378             Net Tons 113
Built by Richard Shipbuilders, Great
Yarmouth, Yard No. 587.
28.36 × 10.5 × 3.5m.    Draft 4.676m.

2 × 6 cylinder G.E.C. diesels, total 2,880 b.h.p. driving twin Voith Schneider propellers.

Arrived in River Thames, 18-3-1992 for bollard pull.

20-3-1992 handed over to owners at Gravesend.

*Egerton*                        1992–
Official No. 721937      Call Sign MPDL7
Gross Tons 193             Built 1969
by Ziegler Freres, Dunkirk for Societe De
Remorquage & Du Sauvetage Du Nord,
Dunkirk, as *Subtil*.
26.79 × 8 × 3.65m.

Powered by a 8 cylinder 1,500 b.h.p. Soc. Crepelle diesel engine driving a single Voith Schneider propeller.

1-9-1991 sold to The Alexandra Towing Co. Ltd. & stationed at Liverpool. Renamed *Egerton*.

21-5-1992 transferred to The Alexandra Towing Co. (London) Ltd. & stationed at Gravesend.

*Sun Sussex*          1992–
Official No. 722109     Call Sign MQVW2
Gross Tons 378         Built 1992
by Richards Shipbuilders, Great Yarmouth.
28.36 × 10.5 × 3.5m.

Powered by 2 × 6 cylinder 2,880 b.h.p. G.E.C. diesels driving twin Voith Schneider propellers.

20-7-1992 arrived in River Thames for bollard pull trials.

23-7-1992 handed over from builders to The Alexandra Towing Co. (London) Ltd.

# Reef (Underwater Services) Ltd.

*Barra Reef*             1981–1981
Gross Tons 90         Built 1937
for Thames Steam Tug & Lighterage Co. Ltd., as *Robertsbridge*.

515 b.h.p. diesel engine. Re-engined 1962 with a 450 b.h.p. diesel engine.

1964 Amalgamated with General Lighterage Ltd. & Co. renamed Thames & General Ltd.

1975 renamed *General VI*.

1-1980 Thames & General Ltd. acquired by Cory Lighterage Ltd.

1981 Chartered by Reef (Underwater Services) Ltd., & renamed *Barra Reef*.

10-1981 returned to Cory Lighterage Ltd., & renamed *General VI*. 1982 sold to Mr Mayhew of Queenborough. No further details known.

*Daunt Reef*           1981–1981
Gross Tons 160       Built 1958
by Jadewerft G.M.B.H., Wilhemlshaven, West Germany for Norddeutscher Lloyd, as *Centaur*.
97′ × 26′ × 10′

1,060 b.h.p. 8 cylinder Klockner, Humboldt, Deutz diesel engine.

1-2-1974 to Hapag–Lloyd Transport & Service G.M.B.H.

1981 chartered by Reef (Underwater Services) Ltd., & renamed *Daut Reef*.

10-1981 towed back to Bremerhavn & renamed *Centaur*.

1983 sold to Busumer Werft G.M.B.H., Busum & renamed *Fritz* & then *Moritz*.

1986 sold to Ems Offshore Service G.M.B.H., Leer, & renamed *Ems Tug*.

*Carrig Reef*                    1981–1981

Gross Tons 161              Built 1962

by Jadewerft G.M.B.H., Wilhelmshaven,
West Germany for Norddeutscher Lloyd, as
*Lowe*.

97′10″ × 24′9″

1,060 b.h.p. 8 cylinder Klockner, Humboldt, Deutz diesel engine.

1-2-1974 to Hapag-Lloyd Transport & Service G.M.B.H.

1981 chartered by Reef (Underwater Services) Ltd., London, & renamed *Carrig Reef.*

10-1981 returned to Hapag-Lloyd towed to Bremerhaven by tug *Gavant.*

1984 sold to Compania Portuaria Talcahuano Ltd., Talcahuano, Chile, & renamed *Pehuen.*

*West Reef*                    1981–1981

Gross Tons 95               Built 1958

by Jadewerft G.M.B.H. Willhelmshaven,
West Germany for Norddeutscher Lloyd,
Bremen, as *Luchs*.

22.8 × 6.2 × 3.2m.

450 b.h.p. 8 cylinder Deut diesel driving a Voith Schneider propeller.

1970 to Hapag-Lloyd Transport & Service G.M.B.H.

1981 chartered to Reef (Underwater Services) Ltd., London, & renamed *West Reef* but was not delivered to London before the company ceased trading.

1982 sold to Busumer Werft G.M.B.H., Busum & renamed *Max.*

1986 sold to Schleppbet ried Unterweser G.M.B.H. & Co., Bremen, & renamed *Greif.*

# Port of Tilbury London Ltd.

*Linford*                    1991–
Official No. 307825
Gross Tons 160          Built 1965
by Richard Dunston Ltd., Hessle.
87′7″ × 26′ × 9′

1,600 b.h.p. 16 cylinder Lister Blackstone diesel driving a single Voith Schneider unit for Port of London Authority as *Plankton*.

1991 sold to Port of Tilbury London Ltd., & renamed *Linford*, 7-9-1991.

*Orsett*                    1991–
Official No. 308049
Gross Tons 160          Built 1965
by Richard Dunston Ltd., Hessle.
87′7″ × 26′ × 9′

1,600 b.h.p. 16 cylinder Lister Blackstone diesel driving a single Voith Schneider unit for Port of London Authority as *Placard*.

1991 sold to Port of Tilbury London Ltd., & renamed *Orsett*, 7-9-1991.

# Report from Sun XV assisting evacuation of troops, Dunkirk.

On Thursday May 30th 1940 we were instructed to go to the Tilbury Landing Stage for de-magnetizing as we were going to Dunkirk to assist in bringing the B.E.F. to England, at midnight we were prepared to leave.

On instructions from the S.N.O Tilbury we took in tow twelve life boats and proceeded to Southend at 12.15 a.m. May 31 where we would receive further instruction. On arrival at Southend we received further instructions to proceed to Ramsgate where we arrived at 11.50 a.m.

At 2.30 p.m. received orders from the S.N.O. to proceed to Dunkirk and to take six of the boats in tow, at 7.30 p.m. When in company of various other craft and approaching Dunkirk Roads we were attacked heavily by twenty-eight German bombers who released several salvos of heavy bombs close by, but without scoring direct hits or causing casualties to any vessels or crews of same, we proceeded and arrived off Dunkirk pier-heads at 10.15 p.m. We then received orders from one of H.M. destroyers to proceed a further four miles to the eastward of Dunkirk which we did under continual harassing of German aircraft. When we arrived at the given destination the landing orders were cancelled and we were instructed to steam a further 6 miles easterly and land our boats on the beach to ferry troops off. We arrived there "La Panne" at midnight and anchored at midnight.

At 12.05 a.m. June 1st our boats left for the beach which was to rough estimation fifty yards distant and was under continual German artillery fire of all calibres, our boats crews under very bad circumstances managed to ferry between 70 and 80 soldiers aboard and during this we lost all our boats with the exception of one which eventually sank astern of the tug and was cut adrift. At 2 a.m. we hove up anchor and proceeded down the Roads at slow speed. We were continually machine-gunned all the way down, but with skilful management we made the open channel without harm to tug or crew and proceeded on our way to Ramsgate. At 4.50 a.m. in a position 3 miles westerly "RUYTENGIN" buoy we spoke to two small government vessels "X.149" and "Y.C.72" both disabled with engine trouble and loaded with troops. The lieutenant in charge asked us to tow them to Ramsgate as it was very dangerous to be laying there owing to raiding aircraft. We took them in tow and anchored off Ramsgate at 9 a.m. and disembarked troops by small motor craft from Ramsgate. On June 2nd at 9 p.m. we were boarded by a Naval Commander and instructed to proceed to the aid of the hospital ship s.s. "Paris" 52° 10′N 1′ 6′E. who had been bombed and in immediate need of help. We sighted the s.s. "Paris" at 11.11 p.m. and encircled ship which had a bad list to starboard to see if we could find any survivors but we found no one. We managed to get our wire made fast to ships starboard quarter fair lead but the wire parted and at the exact moment of the wire parting we were attacked by a german plane and heavily machine-gunned. We were then given orders by the Commander to proceed westerly as the aircraft made it dangerous to attempt salvage. We steamed around for several hours and at 3.40 a.m. we sighted the H.M.D. "Yorkshire Lass" disabled with engine trouble and loaded with troops. We took vessel in tow and at 4.37 a.m. the drifter made a signal to us that the engines had been repaired and we gave orders for the tow rope to be let go, and we proceeded to Ramsgate where we anchored at 7.45 a.m. At 11.20 a.m. we received orders to proceed into Ramsgate harbour to take sand bags aboard for protection for those on the bridge and we then left harbour and anchored outside Ramsgate at 1.20 p.m. with instructions that we were to proceed to Dunkirk at 5.00 p.m. for the final embarkation.

At 5.00 p.m. we proceeded to Dunkirk as ordered and arrived off the pier heads at Dunkirk at 10.35 p.m. having only slight delays on crossing by mines which the enemy had laid and making secure our four boats we were towing, we commenced to embark troops at 11.15 p.m. and steamed around in the vicinity of the harbour awaiting for other boats which came from the harbour. At 2 a.m. June 4th we entered the pier-heads and went alongside eastern arm, but we found practically all had embarked and at 2.30 a.m. we left the pier-heads and proceeded on our crossing to Ramsgate but at 3.20 a.m. when steaming full speed owing to the dawn coming in, we were attacked and machine-gunned by german aircraft without casualties and we carried on our course and speed. At 4.20 a.m. in a position 6 miles westerly of "W." buoy we took in tow H.M.D. "L.H.W.D." who had developed engine trouble and took her into Ramsgate and anchored at 8.15 a.m. At 10 a.m. we received orders to tow "Scoot Reiger" from Ramsgate to Tilbury Stage where we arrived at 7.50 p.m.